The 5 DREAMS of EVERY WOMAN

SHARON JAYNES

HARVEST HOUSE PUBLISHERS

EUGENE, OREGON

Cover photo © Elnur / Fotolia

Cover by Dugan Design Group, Bloomington, Minnesota

In order to provide privacy, some of the names in the personal stories of individuals have been changed.

Harvest House Publishers has made every effort to trace the ownership of all poems and quotes. In the event of a question arising from the use of a poem or quote, we regret any error made and will be pleased to make the necessary correction in future editions of this book.

Excerpts from *Anne of Green Gables* are used with the permission of L.M. Montgomery Inc. *Anne of Green Gables* and other indicia of "Anne" are trademarks and Canadian official marks of the Anne of Green Gables Licensing Authority Inc. *L.M. Montgomery* and other names and images created by L.M. Montgomery are trademarks of Heirs of L.M. Montgomery Inc.

THE 5 DREAMS OF EVERY WOMAN...AND HOW GOD WANTS TO FULFILL THEM
Copyright © 2004 and 2011 by Sharon Jaynes
Published by Harvest House Publishers
Eugene, Oregon 97402
www.harvesthousepublishers.com
Library of Congress Cataloging-in-Publication Data
    Jaynes, Sharon.
    The 5 dreams of every woman—: and how God wants to fulfill them / Sharon Jaynes.
        p. cm.
    Rev. ed. of: Dreams of a woman.
    ISBN 978-0-7369-2939-4 (pbk.)
    1. Christian women—Religious life. 2. Self-realization—Religious aspects—Christianity. I.
Jaynes, Sharon. Dreams of a woman. II. Title.
    BV4527.J385 2011
    248.8'43—dc22

                                                          2010026220

11 12 13 14 15 16 17 18 19 / LB-SK / 10 9 8 7 6 5 4 3

To my husband, Steve—the man of my dreams.
The moment I met you, I felt as though I had known you all my life,
for I had dreamed of you from my earliest remembrance.

Acknowledgments

I am deeply indebted to the many women who have shared their dreams with me: Gayle Montgomery, Anabel Gillham, Madeline Rivers, Genia Rogers, Suzi Kallam, Cynthia Price, Luanne Johnson, Patricia Dilling, Amanda Bailey, and Wendy Ellis—just to name a few. I have been blessed by your transparency and willingness to share your heart with so many others.

Special thanks to:

Judie Lawson, for sharing her gifts and talents in the words of "Wedding Feast of the Lamb."

My prayer team: Barbara Givens, Bonnie Cleveland, Bonnie Schulte, Cissy Smith, Cynthia Price, Dawn Lee, Gwen Smith, Linda Eppley, Kathy Mendietta, Linda Butler, Mary Southerland, Risa Tucker, Van Walton, and Jill Archer.

The Harvest House Publishers team: Bob Hawkins Jr., LaRae Weikert, Terry Glaspey, John Constance, and Barb Sherrill, who made the book possible; Shane White and Christianne Debysingh, who made the book visible; Katie Lane, who made the book beautiful; and Betty Fletcher, who kept us all on schedule (no small feat). My editor, Kim Moore, whose keen eye and kind heart made sure every word kept to the mission of helping women see themselves through Jesus' eyes. My tech-savvy friend, Abby Van Wormer, who helps me in the video world.

Mark Maddox, who believed in and championed for this project many years ago.

My heavenly Father, who equips me; Jesus Christ, who envelops me; and the Holy Spirit, who guides and empowers me.

My husband, Steve, who daily holds up the mirror of God's Word for me to see myself as a dearly loved, cherished child of God, and encourages me to help other women see themselves the same.

Contents

I Dreamed a Dream

I sat in the darkened opera hall and watched as Fantine, the leading lady in the musical *Les Misérables,* sang a lament about her life. She clutched her chest and spilled her heart to the invisible audience peering from the darkness.

> *I dreamed a dream in time gone by*
> *When hope was high and life worth living.*
> *I dreamed that love would never die,*
> *I dreamed that God would be forgiving.*
>
> *Then I was young and unafraid,*
> *And dreams were made and used and wasted.*
> *There was no ransom to be paid*
> *No song unsung, no wine untasted.*
>
> *But the tigers come at night*
> *With their voices soft as thunder.*
> *As they tear your hope apart,*
> *As they turn your dream to shame.*
>
> *He slept a summer by my side.*
> *He filled my days with endless wonder.*
> *He took my childhood in his stride,*
> *But he was gone when autumn came.*
>
> *And still I dreamed he'll come to me,*
> *That we would live the years together.*

But there are dreams that cannot be
And there are storms we cannot weather.

I had a dream my life would be
So different from the hell I'm living.
So different now from what it seemed.
Now life has killed the dream I dreamed.[1]

When Fantine sang her last note and the house lights went up, I noticed many people, men and women, wiping tears from their eyes. I don't believe the tears were only for Fantine. I believe they were also for the disappointments in their own lives—for misspent years, broken promises, unattained goals—for the life that killed the dreams *they* dreamed.

"I Dreamed a Dream" is not simply the song of a character in a play. It is the song of many women all around the world—women whose lives have been shattered, broken, and beaten down by life. Perhaps their dreams were not shattered in the same way as Fantine's, but many are forlorn because life simply didn't turn out the way they had hoped.

As a little girl, I remember reading the story of Cinderella time and time again. I wanted so much to be a beautiful princess and be carried away by a handsome prince. But real life usually isn't like Cinderella's. Think about it. Cinderella was doomed to scrubbing floors, received a beautiful dress, and then finally met her handsome prince. However, in real life we are more likely to meet our handsome prince, get the beautiful dress, and then spend the rest of life scrubbing floors!

Author and Bible teacher Beth Moore said it this way:

> The enemy is an expert archer with lots of practice aim-
> ing fiery darts. When women are the targets, often the
> bull's-eye is childhood dreams or expectations. We grew
> up believing in Cinderella, yet some of us feel as if our pal-
> ace turned out to be a duplex, our prince turned out to be
> a frog, and the wicked stepmother turned out to be our
> mother-in-law. Our fairy godmother apparently lost our
> addresses. Anyway, what we would like to do to her with
> that wand of hers might not be pretty.[2]

When I was a little girl, I had many dreams, but five are prominent pictures in my mind. Now that I'm older, I have come to realize that most women I meet had similar longings. I dreamed that I would have a daddy who loved me like the men I saw walking through the park hand in hand with their little girls; that one day I would be a bride in a flowing satin gown, waltzing down a long, red-carpeted church aisle; that I would be a mommy with a house full of children to adore and who would adore me; that I would be beautiful like a princess in a fairy tale; and that I would have a lifelong best friend.

I asked my friend Linda what she dreamed of being when she was a little girl. She quickly answered, "I wanted to be a princess." Then she tried to correct herself through her giggles. "No, I'm just kidding. Let me think a minute." But she wasn't kidding. It was a moment of truth that slipped out before she could catch herself.

As this idea of the dreams of women unfolded in my heart, I began to survey women across the country about their childhood dreams. The list reads like a stroll down the Barbie aisle in the toy store: gymnast, astronaut, teacher, nurse, nun, career woman, Barbara Walters, TV anchor, country club luncheon lady, veterinarian, missionary, dancer, flight attendant, singer, and so on. But when the questions left the surface and dove deep into the women's hearts, the five most common dreams were the same as mine: to have a daddy who loves me, to be a bride, to be a mommy, to be beautiful, and to have a best friend.

In our journey together, we will take a look at those five common childhood dreams and discover how God longs to fulfill them. We will meet women in the Bible and see how they handled their dreams—Sarah, who interfered with God's dream; Naomi, who forgot her dream; and Esther, who fulfilled God's dream. We will also look at shattered dreams, which are inevitable; restored dreams, which are sometimes inconceivable; and interrupted dreams, which are instrumental in our spiritual growth. Then we'll look at how to discover God's dreams for our lives and learn to dream again.

You'll also meet many women along the way who will share their dreams, their personal struggles, and their victories. Don't be surprised if you see your heart's desires, disappointments, and daring hopes for the future penned in the words of women you haven't met. Whether I spoke with a woman with a six-figure income or a woman in a homeless shelter, the dreams of women are much the same.

Life may not have turned out as you had hoped or expected, but it can be better than you ever imagined. You may even discover that God has indeed fulfilled your dreams, but you hadn't recognized that because it was not in the way you had anticipated.

Let's take a look at those forgotten dreams, discover God's dreams for our lives, and see how He longs to fulfill them. Place your hand firmly in His, take a deep breath, and begin the exciting journey to a place you thought you would never find as you dare to dream again.

Childhood Dreams

To Have a Daddy Who Loves Me

Once upon a time, not so very long ago or far away, a baby girl was born to parents who could not keep her. While neither parent was willing to release her for adoption, neither was able to care for her. So while the legal system shuffled her case back and forth, the baby girl grew into a toddler in a foster home.

Her care was adequate. Her physical needs were met, and she never went hungry. Her clothes, though not new, were never dirty. Her toys, though not her own, were always sufficient. This little girl was not mistreated or abused, and yet in her heart was a hollow space. She desperately wanted what she had never had—a mommy and a daddy of her very own.

Only a few doors down from the foster home lived a kind couple with a teenage son. The little girl needed a family, the family wanted a little girl, and the details of a trying and lengthy adoption were finally settled. And while this little girl received a wonderful mommy and an adoring big brother, it was her daddy and their relationship that was extra special.

Ashley was two years old when she entered her daddy's life. She was thin, pale, and clingy. By the time the adoption was finally complete, she was almost three. Ashley had never seen the ocean, eaten a Happy Meal, or slept in a bed in a room of her own.

A few months after the adoption, Ashley traveled to the beach for her first family reunion. She was overwhelmed with excitement and pride. She had received so much so fast, and it was hard to take it all in. Ashley asked everyone she met if they were part of her family.

"Are you my aunt?" "Are you my uncle?" "Are you my cousin?" She ran from person to person showering hugs and kisses on her newly acquired family. "I love you!" she told them. "I love you all!"

When her new daddy took her to McDonald's for the first time, Ashley couldn't join in with the other children who played busily on the playground equipment. She was too busy asking important questions. "Do you have a daddy? I have a daddy! See, that's my daddy over there," she exclaimed with excitement and wonder. "Isn't he wonderful?"

"There is a lot of hurt when I think about having a daddy who loves me. I dreamed of long walks, talks, cuddles, And strong arms that would always be there to protect me. I dreamed of daddy's tears when his little girl got married, when he held my babies as they were born, and falling asleep in my rocking chair." Laura

---

"What's your name?" she asked. "My name is Ashley Jordan AMBROSE—just like my daddy. I'm named after my daddy!"

Five years later, tanned, transformed, and confident, Ashley again returned to the annual family reunion. This time she brought a scrapbook of pictures to share with anyone who would sit still long enough to listen.

"This is my story," she would say. "See, this is where I lived before Mommy and Daddy adopted me. They picked me out special. See, this is my room now—it's all my own. And these are my toys, and my *own* clothes, and here's a picture of my kitty and one of my dog and…"

Ashley has love overflowing for just about everyone, but no one is higher on her list than her daddy. He knows how to polish toenails, drip sandcastles, tie hair ribbons, hold her in the night—and he calls her his "little Princess."[1]

My Dream

When I was a little girl, my father spent most of his waking hours working at his building supply company, observing construction sites, or socializing with his colleagues and associates. Even though his place of business was only a few blocks from our home, his heart was miles away in a place I could never find.

My father didn't drink alcohol every day, but when he did, it consumed him. Dad was filled with a rage that always seemed to be boiling just beneath the surface of his tough exterior. When he drank, that rage spewed out like hot lava onto those around him. Unfortunately, my mother was the most common target.

As a child, many nights I crawled into bed, pulled the covers tightly under my chin or even over my head, and prayed that I would quickly fall asleep to shut out the noise of my parents yelling and fighting. Crashing furniture, smashing glass, and fist upon flesh were common sounds that pierced my little girl nights. Occasionally I'd tiptoe over to my pink ballerina jewelry box, wind up the key in the back, open the lid, and try to focus on the tinkling melody that came from the music box as the dancer twirled with hands overhead. I wanted to be wherever she was...anywhere but at home.

I was afraid of my father. Even when he was sober I kept my distance. At the same time, I observed how other daddies cherished their little girls. I saw daddies snuggle their daughters in their laps, hold their hands while walking in the park, or kiss their cheeks as they dropped them off at school in the mornings. Deep in my heart, a dream was birthed. I dreamed that one day I would have a daddy who loved me like that—not because I was pretty or made good grades or could play the piano well, but just because I was his. I dreamed that one day I would be a cherished daughter and the apple of my daddy's eye.

A Common Dream

In talking to women all across the country, I have seen eyes fill with tears when I talk about the dream of having a daddy who loves me. But the tears are not for me. Those tears reveal the longing in their own hearts. "Butterfly Kisses," a popular song by Bob Carlisle, is about the tender love between a father and his daughter, starting from her birth to her wedding day. Mr. Carlisle said, "I get a lot of mail from young girls who try to get me to marry their moms. That used to be a real chuckle because it's so cute, but then I realized they didn't want romance for mom. They want the father that is in that song, and that just kills me."[2]

What did the little girls long for? They wanted a daddy to scoop them up in his strong arms. They wanted to plant butterfly kisses on his scruffy face. They wanted to see tears in his eyes when he walked them down their aisle on their wedding day. Little girls and grown women alike long for a father to protect them, help them, guide them, nurture them, and cheer them on through the struggles of life.

The Invitation

In the Old Testament, God has many names. He is Elohim, the Creator; El Elyon, God Most High; El Roi, the God who sees; El Shaddai, the All-Sufficient One; Adonai, the Lord; Jehovah, the Self-Existent One; Jehovah-Jireh, the Lord will provide; Jehovah-Rapha, the Lord who heals; Jehovah-Shalom, the Lord is peace; Jehovah-Raah, the Lord my Shepherd; and many more. His covenant name with the people of Israel was I AM.

"I dreamed I would have a daddy who spent time
with me, loved me, and defended me." Lisa

In the New Testament, Jesus introduced a new name for God: Father. In the Gospel of John alone, God is referred to as Father at least 120 times. It is the name Jesus referred to more than any other, and the name He invites us to use to address the Creator of the universe. Just stop and think about that for a moment. The God of the universe, who created the heavens and the earth, who always has been and always will be, who is all-knowing, all-powerful, and present everywhere at once—that same God invites you to call Him Abba Father. He invites you to call Him *Daddy!*

When the disciples asked Jesus to teach them how to pray, He said:

> When you pray, go into your room, close the door and pray to your *Father,* who is unseen. Then your *Father,* who sees what is done in secret, will reward you. And when you pray, do not keep on babbling like pagans, for they think they will be heard because of their many words. Do not be like them, for your *Father* knows what you need before you ask him. This, then, is how you should pray: "Our *Father* in heaven, hallowed be your name" (Matthew 6:6-9, emphasis added).

J.I. Packer wrote: "For everything that Christ taught, everything that makes the New Testament new and better than the Old, everything that is distinctly Christian as opposed to merely Jewish, is summed up in the knowledge of the fatherhood of God.[3] All other religions demand followers to worship created beings, such as Mohammad or Buddha, but God invites us to crawl up in His lap, become His child, and call Him Father. He said, "I will be a *Father* to you, and you will be my sons and daughters" (2 Corinthians 6:18, emphasis added).

The Only Perfect Parent

For many, the idea of God being their father may not be a pleasant one. We have a human tendency to project our experiences with our earthly fathers onto our perceptions of the fatherhood of God. Some never knew their earthly fathers, some had abusive fathers, and some were deserted by their fathers. Some had loving, endearing fathers, and some lost their fathers to sickness or catastrophe. Those life experiences tend be the lens through which we view God.

Even the best earthly fathers have feet of clay and will disappoint their children.

When I was a child, I never had lengthy conversations with my father. As a result, when I became a Christian, it was very difficult for me to have lengthy conversations with my heavenly Father. Prayer was difficult. I had to remove the mask of my earthly father from the face of God.

No matter what your past experience with your earthly father has been, your heavenly Father is the perfect parent. He loves you uncondionally, cares for you completely, provides for you unceasingly, trains you tenderly, and welcomes you unreservedly. He will never leave you or forsake you. You are the apple of His eye.

The Amazing Grace of Adoption

One reason Ashley's story at the beginning of this chapter is so precious to me is because she was adopted by a loving father...so much like you and me. The Bible says we have been adopted into God's family (Ephesians 1:5). We are His children (1 John 3:1-2). Let's take a look at how adoption was carried out in Jesus' day in order to get a better picture of ours.

In ancient Rome, fathers chose a child for adoption when they weren't able to have children of their own. They adopted a son in order to have someone to carry on the family name and inherit their property. It was a legally binding relationship. All ties to the child's natural family were severed. The child was placed in a new family with the same prestige and privileges as a natural child, including becoming an heir. If the child had any debt, it was immediately canceled. The adoption was a sealed process with many witnesses making it official.[4]

In modern times, when it comes to adoption, we tend to think of adopting a baby. However, in biblical times adoption usually took place after the child was older and had proved worthy to carry on the family name.[5] How incredible that our heavenly Father chose us, not because of any merit of our own, but before the beginning of time. He chose us, not because we were worthy, but in spite of the fact that we were not.

> He chose us in him before the creation of the world to be
> holy and blameless in his sight. In love he predestined us
> to be adopted as his sons through Jesus Christ, in accor-
> dance with his pleasure and will—to the praise of his glori-
> ous grace, which he has freely given us in the One he loves
> (Ephesians 1:4-6).

I love Eugene Peterson's paraphrase of that same verse found in *The Message*:

> Long before he laid down earth's foundations, he had us in mind, had settled on us as the focus of his love, to be made whole and holy by his love. Long, long ago he decided to adopt us into his family through Jesus Christ. (What pleasure he took in planning this!)

Our adoption takes place the moment we accept Jesus Christ as our Lord and Savior. Our debt because of sin is canceled (paid in full), and we are placed in God's family to carry on His name and become an heir. Paul wrote: "You also were included in Christ [in His family] when you heard the word of truth, the gospel of your salvation. Having believed, you were marked in him with a seal, the promised Holy Spirit, who is a deposit guaranteeing our inheritance until the redemption of those who are God's possession—to the praise of his glory" (Ephesians 1:13-14).

"I never knew my dad cared about me, let alone loved me. I grew up with abuse and being shipped back and forth from parent to parent. No roots, no identity, no love, no security." Debbie

---

Many verses refer to God's children as "sons." This does not mean God only has male children or that only male children inherit the kingdom of God. The Hebrew word for "son" does not necessarily mean male offspring. In the Old Testament, the Hebrew word *ben* can mean male son or children of both genders, male or female. Genesis 1 says that God created man in His own image. Then the writer goes on to say, "Male and female he created them" (Genesis 1:27). As the word "man" can mean male or female humans, the word "son" can mean the male or female offspring of a human.

In the New Testament Greek, the word *huios* is translated "son." And like the Hebrew word *ben,* it can mean a male child or it can refer to offspring, both male and female. "In calling believers His sons, God is communicating that believers find their origin in Him (as off-spring) and bear the same nature He does."[6] The apostle Paul wrote to the Galatians, "You are all sons of God through faith in Christ Jesus… There is neither Jew nor Greek, slave nor free, male nor female, for you are all one in Christ Jesus" (Galatians 3:26-28).

In J.I. Packer's words: "Adoption is a family idea, conceived in terms of love, and viewing God as father. In adoption, God takes us into His family and fellowship, and establishes us as His children and heirs. Closeness, affection, and generosity are at the heart of the relationship. To be right with God the judge is a great thing, but to be loved and cared for by God the father is greater."[7]

I grew up singing "Jesus loves me! This I know, for the Bible tells me so," but I really didn't believe it. I wasn't sure God even liked me. It wasn't until I was much older that I caught a glimpse of His uncondi-tional, unfailing, unlimited love for me.

He Loves You Unconditionally

Most of us live in a world of performance-based acceptance. We make good grades, and Mommy is proud. We look pretty, and Daddy smiles. We do a good job at work, and the boss is pleased. We serve at church, and the congregation thinks we are "good Christians."

Unfortunately, that same sense of having to perform well to be accepted by people can easily roll over into our relationship with God. We falsely believe we must perform well to be loved and accepted by Him when nothing could be further from the truth. As a result, we strive to obtain something that we already have…God's unconditional love.

Anabel Gillham was a woman who loved God, but she had trou-ble accepting that God could love her. She knew the Bible verses that talked of God's unconditional love for her, yet she knew herself and doubted a God who knew her innermost thoughts would approve of her.

The root of her problem was how she viewed God and how she believed God viewed her. She knew what kind of God He was. She read Exodus 34:6: "Then the LORD passed by in front of him [Moses] and proclaimed, 'The LORD, the LORD God, compassionate and gracious, slow to anger, and abounding in loving kindness and truth…'" (NASB), but she believed she had to earn that love. Then God used a very special person to help Anabel understand the depths of God's love for her—her second child, Mason David Gillham, who had a profound mental disability. Let's let Anabel tell you her story as she relates it in her book, *The Confident Woman*.

> Mace could sing one song with great gusto, just one: "Jesus Loves Me." He would throw his head back and hold on to the first "Yes" in the chorus just as long as he could, and then he would get tickled and almost fall out of his chair. I can still hear him giggle when I think back on those days that seem so distant and so far away. How poignant that memory is to me.
>
> I never doubted for a moment that Jesus loved that profoundly retarded little boy. It didn't matter that he would never sit with the kids in the back of the church and on a certain special night walk down the aisle, take the pastor by the hand, and invite Jesus into his heart. It was entirely irrelevant that he could not quote a single verse of Scripture, that he would never go to high school, or that he would never be a dad. I knew that Jesus loved Mason.
>
> What I could not comprehend, what I could not accept, was that Jesus could love Mason's mother, Anabel. You see, I believed that in order for a person to accept me, to love me, I had to perform for him. My standard for getting love was performance based, so I "performed" constantly, perfectly. In fact, I did not allow anyone to see me when I was not performing perfectly. I never had any close friends because I was convinced that if a person ever really got to know me, he wouldn't like me.[8]

Anabel carried that belief into her relationship with God, and she was horrified to learn that He knew her every thought, let alone everything she said or did (Psalm 139:1-4). She realized God knew her completely. He saw when she wasn't "performing perfectly." Because of her perception of performance-based acceptance, she concluded without a doubt that God could not possibly love her, that He could never like what He saw in her.

Mace could never have performed for his parents' love, or for anyone's love, but oh, how they loved him. His condition deteriorated to such a degree—and so rapidly—that they had to place him in an institution when he was very young. His parents enrolled him in the Enid State School for Mentally Handicapped Children. They regularly drove the 120 miles to see him, but they occasionally also brought him home for a visit.

"I was a daddy's girl. When I entered a room,
my daddy's eyes would sparkle and a big smile would
spread over his face. He always would take me places with
him and show me off. We were inseparable." Karen

On one particular visit, Mace had been with them since Thursday evening. On the following Saturday afternoon God painted a vivid picture of His great love for Anabel through Mason. She was standing at the kitchen sink, dreading what lay ahead. In just a few moments, she would be gathering Mace's things together and taking him back to "his house." She had done this many times before—and it was never easy—but today God had something in mind that would change her life forever.

As she was washing the dishes, Mason was sitting in his chair watching her, or at least he was looking at her. That's when it began. Her emotions were spinning. Her stomach started tumbling with the familiar sickening thoughts of packing up Mason's toys and clothes and taking him away again. She stopped washing the dishes and went down on her knees in front of Mace. Anabel took his dirty little hands in hers and tried desperately to reach him.

"Mason, I love you. I love you. If only you could understand how much I love you."

He just stared. He couldn't understand; he didn't comprehend. She stood up and started on the dishes again, but that didn't last long. This sense of urgency—almost a panic—came over her, and once more she dried her hands and knelt in front of her precious little boy.

"My dear Mason, if only you could say to me, 'I love you, Mother.' I need that, Mace."

Nothing.

"I stood up to the sink again," she continued. "More dishes, more washing, more crying—and thoughts, foreign to my way of thinking, began filtering into my conscious awareness. I believe God spoke to me that day, and this is what He said: *Anabel, you don't look at your son and turn away in disgust because he's sitting there with saliva drooling out of his mouth; you don't shake your head, repulsed because he has dinner all over his shirt or because he's sitting in a dirty, smelly diaper when he ought to be able to take care of himself. Anabel, you don't reject Mason because all of the dreams you had for him have been destroyed. You don't reject him because he doesn't perform for you. You love him, Anabel, just because he is yours. Mason doesn't willfully reject your love, but you willfully reject Mine. I love you, Anabel, not because you're neat or attractive, or because you do things well, not because you perform for Me but just because you're Mine.*[9]

And, friend, that's exactly how God feels about you. He loves you just because you are His.

The New Testament Greek word for the type of love that God has for us is *agape*. This is unconditional, unchanging, unfathomable, immeasurable love. Paul wrote, "I am convinced that neither death nor life, neither angels nor demons, neither the present nor the future nor any powers, neither height nor depth, nor anything else in all creation, will be able to separate us from the love of God that is in Christ Jesus our Lord" (Romans 8:38). Can I say that again? Nothing can separate us from the unconditional love of our Father—not even our own messiness and mistakes.

This was what I had longed for all my life—to have a daddy who loved me, not because I was pretty or made good grades or behaved like a little lady in public or could play the piano well or hit a baseball out of the park—but just because I was his.

He Cares for You Unfailingly

The year 2002 was a time of transition for me. I changed positions at the ministry where I served, my son packed up to go away to college, my thyroid went out of control and had to be purposely destroyed with radioactive iodine, my first book went out of print, the grocery store quit carrying my favorite coffee, and Revlon discontinued the eyeliner I'd been using for ten years. Like a little girl having a hissy fit, I whined, "Doesn't anything ever stay the same? Isn't there not one thing I can count on being the same tomorrow as it is today?"

Then I heard that gentle whisper I've grown to love: "'Though the mountains be shaken and the hills be removed, yet my unfailing love for you will not be shaken nor my covenant of peace be removed,' says the LORD, who has compassion on you" (Isaiah 54:10).

Yes, there is one thing that will never change: God's unfailing love and care for His children. He is the same yesterday and today and tomorrow (Hebrews 13:8), and on that we can always depend. Solomon tells us that the one thing each of us longs for is unfailing love (Proverbs 19:22). And that is exactly what we have in the love of our heavenly Father.

The word "compassion" in Isaiah 54:10 is the Hebrew word *racham*, which means "to soothe; to cherish; to love deeply like parents; to be compassionate, be tender…This verb usually refers to a strong love which is rooted in some kind of natural bond, often from a superior one to an inferior. (Now here's the best part.) Small babies evoke this feeling."[10]

When my son, Steven, came into the world, a love was birthed in my heart that I never thought possible. Elizabeth Stone said it well: "To make a decision to have a child is momentous. It is to decide to have your heart go walking around outside of your body for the rest of your life." That is how our heavenly Father feels about His children!

The beautiful Hebrew word *hesed* is translated "unfailing love" in Isaiah 54:10. It is often translated loving-kindness, steadfast love, grace, mercy, faithfulness, goodness, and devotion. This word is used 240 times and is considered one of the most important concepts in the vocabulary of the Old Testament.[11] Why? Because God's unfailing love is one of the most important themes of the entire Bible. It is who He is and what He does (1 John 4:8).

"I was never a daddy's girl in real life,
but I always dreamt I was." Loretta

How would you like to memorize half a psalm in the next 60 seconds? Want to give it a try? Turn to Psalm 136. After each sentence, there is an echo, "His love endures forever." Just say that sentence 26 times, and you have quoted half of the psalm! The psalmist begins by reminding us of how God created the universe and all it contains. Then he continues by reminiscing how God led the captive Israelites out of Egypt, across the parted Red Sea, through the arid desert, and into the lush Promised Land, conquering enemies at every turn. And through it all, one thing remained the same—"His love endures forever!"

There may be times in our lives when we cry, "Where are You, God? Don't You care about what is happening to me? I can't hear You. I can't see Your hand working in my life." But be assured of this: Even when we can't sense God's presence, He is always there. Always. And through it all, one thing remains the same—"His love endures forever!"

He Provides for You Unceasingly

Cary and Madeline Rivers read about the overcrowded orphanages in Eastern Europe, and God stirred their hearts to look into adoption. Foreign adoptions are very costly, but God had blessed the couple financially, and the cost was not prohibitive for them. They decided to adopt not one, two, or three, but four children. After eleven months and miles of red tape, the adoption process was complete, and the couple traveled across the ocean to gather their new family.

The trip home took 22 hours, so when they arrived at the Atlanta airport for a two-hour layover, the family decided to let the rambunctious boys run around the terminal to work out some of their pent-up energy. Of course, they never let their new sons out of their sight. After a short while, Madeline noticed one of the boys watching a man drinking at a water fountain. Even though the child could not speak English, he seemed to be using his hands and body language to communicate. To Madeline's horror, the man reached in his pocket and handed her new son a dollar bill.

She rushed over to the man and asked, "What are you doing?"

"Well, I could tell this boy couldn't speak English, but I could also tell that he was begging. So I gave him a dollar."

The parents looked in the boy's pocket and saw that he had ten one-dollar bills! The little boy had no idea of the riches that came with his adoption. Even though he was now part of a family with great wealth, he continued to do what he had done all his life...beg.

Oh, dear sister, do you see yourself in the little boy's eyes? Are you begging for handouts when your daddy owns the "cattle on a thousand hills" (Psalm 50:10)? Are you scavenging for crumbs when your heavenly Father provides everything you need "for life and godliness through our knowledge of him who called us by his own glory and goodness" (2 Peter 1:3)? Are you searching for acceptance and approval from others when God longs to lavish you with His? Are you begging for what is already yours?

John wrote: "How great is the love the Father has lavished on us, that we should be called children of God!" (1 John 3:1). To "lavish" is to give freely, profusely, extravagantly, and abundantly. He doesn't give us everything we want when we want it. No father wants spoiled children. Rather, He gives us everything we need to produce well-behaved children who bear His name well. He is our Provider.

He Welcomes You Unreservedly

One of my favorite people is author and speaker Patsy Clairmont. We were discussing my first book on the telephone one day and trying to set up a time to meet face-to-face when she came to speak at a Women of Faith Conference in my hometown.

"Patsy, I'd love to spend some time with you before the conference, but I don't have a backstage pass. I won't have access to the part of the convention center where you will be."

"No problem," she replied. "Just go to my book table and tell my son who you are. He'll bring you to me."

The day of the conference arrived, and I swam through a sea of women to reach Patsy's crowded book table. It wasn't hard to spot her son—a male version of Patsy herself. After proper introductions, Jason and I were off to find his mom. First we passed through heavy mahogany double doors that led to an area called the Crown Room, which was a place for the VIPs who attended professional basketball games and other events.

Then we entered an elevator that took us to an area where the speakers were tucked away. As soon as we stepped into the elevator, a stern-faced security guard rushed over, pointed his finger in my face, and said, "Where's your backstage pass? You're not supposed to be here, young lady. You're in a lot of trouble."

Then he whipped out his walkie-talkie, and he was not afraid to use it. But before I could force one word out of my dry mouth, Patsy's son stepped forward, showed the guard his credentials, and gallantly stated, "It's okay. I'm one of the speaker's sons. I have a backstage pass, and she's with me."

"That's right," I agreed after I had found my voice. "He's Patsy Clairmont's son, and I'm with him."

"Oh. Okay then," the guard said as he put the walkie-talkie back in its holster. He exited the elevator and was off to seek other dangerous Christian women like myself who were attending the conference.

I had a wonderful visit with Patsy and left the conference inspired by each one of the speakers. But perhaps the most important lesson I learned was on that elevator ride. Revelation 12:10 says that Satan stands before God accusing us day and night. He questions our credentials as he points his gnarly finger and tells us we're not good enough to pass through heaven's doors. But just when we begin to feel unworthy to approach the throne room, God's Son steps forward and says, "Leave her alone. She's with me, and I'm all the credentials she needs."

In the Old Testament, there is a sense that God was unapproachable because of His holiness and our sinfulness. In the temple a veil separated the Holy of Holies, where God resided, from the other areas of the temple, where the priests attended daily. Only the high priest entered the Holy of Holies once a year on the Day of Atonement. Before he could enter, the priest went through a rigorous ceremonial cleansing process. Bells were hemmed to the bottom of his robe, and a rope was tied around his ankle. When the priest entered the Holy of Holies, the men outside listened for the tinkling bells to make sure he was still alive. If God was not pleased, and the sound of the bells ceased, they pulled out the dead priest by the rope.

But in the New Testament all that changed. God was and is still the holy great I AM, but we can enter the Holy of Holies with the confidence of a child approaching her daddy. When Jesus died on the cross of Calvary, God tore the veil of the Holy of Holies from top to bottom, inviting all who believe in His Son as Savior and Lord to enter His presence with assurance and confidence. (Mark 15:38). The writer of Hebrews says, "Let us then approach the throne of grace *with confidence,* so that we may receive mercy and find grace to help us in our time of need" (Hebrews 4:16, emphasis added). Paul reminds us, "In him and through faith in him we may approach God with *freedom and confidence* (Ephesians 3:12, emphasis added). As a child of God, your Father welcomes you into His presence. Not only that…He longs for you to come.

He Calls You by Name

There have been several people in my life who never seem to remember my name. A few of my more popular aliases are Sarah James, Susan James, Shannon James, and Jane Jaynes. Then there are the people who just can't remember me altogether and don't even try to fish a name from their memory pool. To tell you the truth, it never has really bothered me. I'm not that good with names, either.

But names are important to God. In the Bible, a person's name revealed a unique quality of his or her character. Moses meant "Drawn out of water." Ruth meant "woman friend." Naomi meant "pleasant," and after her husband died, she changed her name to "Mara," which meant "bitter." Her two sons' names meant "puny" and "pining." Needless to say, these two fellows weren't exactly strapping young bucks, and both died at an early age. If a person had an encounter with the living God, many times He changed their name to better fit the experiences He had planned for their futures. God changed Abram's name to Abraham, Sarai to Sarah, and Saul to Paul.

"When I think about my dreams of being a bride and even my relationship with my dad, I see how much impact my dad had in my life. He allowed me to be a kid and just have fun like kids should. When I was looking for a husband, I looked for someone just like my dad." Geneva

---

Yes, names are very important. That's why when someone very dear to me forgot mine, it broke my heart.

My father accepted Jesus as his Savior when I was 21 years old. The transformation I saw in him was nothing short of miraculous. One of the benefits I received was that he learned how to love me. In my father's later years, we had a tender and dear relationship, but it was short lived.

A few years after Dad committed his life to Christ, I noticed him becoming forgetful. At first it was small matters: forgetting an order at work, misplacing his shoes or keys, not remembering what day it was, drawing a blank on a close friend's name. Then it progressed to more serious absentminded behavior: forgetting where he parked in a parking deck (and even which parking deck); coming home to take my mother to the market, forgetting he had already taken her an hour before; and becoming confused when taking measurements for cabinets, a task he had been doing for more than 40 years. In 1987 our greatest fears were confirmed. Dad had Alzheimer's disease. He was 55 years old.

My dad had been a tough cookie as a young man. From the time he was 55 to 65, I watched a strapping, quick-witted entrepreneur reduced to a man who could not remember how to speak, button his shirt, or move a spoon from his plate to his mouth. But what pained me the most was the day he forgot my name. I still remember holding his face in my hands and saying, "Daddy, it's me. Do you know who I am?" But I was only met by a childish grin and eyes that seemed to look straight through me.

Names are important. In Isaiah 43:1, God says, "Do not fear, for I have redeemed you; I have called you by name; you are Mine" (NASB). In Isaiah 49:1, the prophet announces, "Before I was born, the LORD called me; from my birth he has made mention of my name."

As God's child, He has called you by name, and the Bible promises He will never forget it. Your name is engraved on the palm of His hand (Isaiah 49:16).

On a Friday morning in May 1996, the Lord graciously came and took my father to his new home in glory. He's probably up there right now measuring for cabinets and working on all those rooms in God's mansion we have read so much about. His memory has been restored, and I look forward to the day when my earthly father and my heavenly Father welcome me with open arms and say, "Welcome, Sharon, my daughter, my child."

As I mentioned earlier, my earthly father did learn how to love me, but my dream to have a daddy who loved me came true years before that. The moment I accepted Jesus Christ as my Lord and Savior, my adoption was final, and I became a precious, chosen, dearly loved child of God. What a joy to have a Daddy who loves me. It is a dream come true.

Why Is This So Important?

Like any good father, our heavenly Father has dreams for His daughters, and we're going to talk more about that as we get deeper into our journey together. However, this is the first step to discovering God's incredible plan for your life.

Just before Jesus began His earthly ministry, He traveled to the Jordan River and was baptized by His cousin John. When Jesus came up out of the water, God said, "This is my Son, whom I love; with him I am well pleased" (Matthew 3:17). Even Jesus needed the assurance that He was God's dearly loved child before He began to fulfill God's incredible plan for His life.

I truly believe women aren't moving forward in their God-appointed destiny because they don't understand who they are, what they have, and where they are as a child of God. In order to fulfill God's dream for your life, just as Jesus fulfilled God's plan for His life, we must understand His great love for us. You are God's daughter, whom He loves. With you He is well pleased. You have a Daddy who loves you.

2

To Be a Bride

I was five years old, just a wisp of a little girl living in a dream world all my own. On this particular afternoon, I gathered my supplies and prepared for the big day. First, I wrapped a long white sheet around my slender body and draped the excess over my shoulder and down my back. Then I draped a bath-sized towel over the crown of my head. I clutched a bouquet of plastic flowers to my chest and stood at the end of our ranch-style home's long hallway. Suddenly, in my imagination, the sheet became a pearl-studded wedding gown with a satin train, and the towel became a delicately detailed lace veil. I could almost hear the trumpets sounding and the organ filling the air with the "Wedding March" as I proceeded to waltz down the hall. Yes, all eyes were on me as they stood to honor the bride.

I had seen the *Sound of Music,* and I wanted to be Julie Andrews and have a wedding in a great cathedral like Sister Maria. Oddly enough, I never did make it to the end of the hallway to see whom the groom would be. That didn't really matter. This was all about me and my dream of becoming a beautiful bride. It had nothing to do with becoming a wife.

Little girls (and big girls) love to dream about becoming a bride. And I've noticed that women reading bridal magazines are not necessarily engaged. Yes, most little girls dream of one day wearing the long, white-satin-and-pearl-studded dress with a lacy trailing veil and walking down the aisle to meet the man of her dreams.

A Little Girl's Dream

Have you ever studied the face of a bride as she glides down the aisle? I don't think a woman ever looks lovelier—she's so full of hope and promise. But for many, what occurs after the couple says "I do" is not what they expected. Studies show that 50 percent of marriages end in divorce, and of the remaining 50 percent, only a small percent reach true oneness. As the couple lights the unity candle on their wedding day and snuff out their individual candles, many couples begin the process of snuffing out each other. They remember that the pastor said, "And the two shall become one," but they just aren't sure which one.

No matter what your marital state is—married, divorced, single, or widowed—most women dream of having a magical marriage with a man who loves, cherishes, honors, and protects them.

"When I was a little girl, I dreamed about being married. I loved romance books and movies where the girl is chosen. I recently saw *The Princess Diaries* and cried as I watched the timeless story of love and beauty unfold. I turned to my friend, Mike, who is 46 and also single, And gushed, 'Wasn't that just great?' He shrugged and said, 'Yeah, I liked it all right.'" Mariana

---

Glancing through the magazine racks in the bookstores, I saw several bride magazines, but when I asked where the groom magazines were located, the store clerk just grinned. Of course, there were none. The dream of having a fairy-tale wedding is strictly a female fancy. While men long for a battle to fight and an adventure to live, women long for intimacy and romance.

I watched a movie about a young couple's wedding day. Sitting on her bed, the young bride, Sarah, still in her wedding dress, cried, "This was the most beautiful day of my life. The day I've always dreamed of—and now it's over!" (Tears and more tears.) The scene flashes back to Sarah as a little girl, pretending to be a bride. She held a bouquet of flowers to her chest as her girlfriends stood admiringly by. The scene comes back to the newlyweds, and Sarah turns to her bewildered young husband. "Did you dream of your wedding day when you were a little boy?"

His mind flashes back to pretend sword fights on the playground with his rough-and-rowdy buddies, battling foes left and right, and wearing torn jeans and a dirt covered T-shirt. "Well, sort of, I guess," he fibs.

Various cultures have differing wedding customs, and the ancient Hebrew custom of marriage paints one of the most beautiful pictures of what it truly means to be a bride. Let's take a journey back to the days of the Old Testament to discover the Hebrew marriage tradition. Instead of telling you the particulars, imagine with me for a moment. Dream a little dream with me about an imaginary family living during the time of Jesus, somewhere in the Middle East.

A Bride for Samuel

Samuel was finally approaching the age of maturity. His father knew the day was coming as he saw the boy's beard thicken and his shoulders broaden. Yes, it was time for Abram to begin searching for a bride for his firstborn son.

On a warm summer morning, Abram prepared for a journey to visit some of his friends from days gone by. He made a mental list of the ones who had daughters of marrying age and plotted his course.

"Goodbye," Abram called to his son as he worked diligently in the carpentry shop. "I'll be home in a few weeks."

"Where are you going?" Samuel asked.

"You'll find out soon enough," Abram replied. "You just take care of your mother, brothers, and sisters while I am away."

While stopping at many small villages, Abram visited the homes of friends with prospective brides for his son. He saw young girls of every shape, size, and stature, but when he saw Miriam, something stirred within him. Her form was lovely, her eyes like doves, and her silky black hair glistened in the sunlight as she played and cared for her younger brothers and sisters. *Yes, she would be a lovely wife for my son,* he mused. After a dinner of roast lamb, baked bread, and aged wine, Abram revealed the real reason for his visit to Miriam's father, Mathias.

"I have come to seek a wife for my son Samuel," he explained. "I have watched your daughter Miriam and noticed how she serves others, cares for her younger siblings, and honors the God of Abraham, Isaac, and Jacob. Would you consider giving your daughter in marriage to my son?"

"It would be an honor for our families to join by such a union," Mathias agreed. "Please, Abram, send the boy to our home, and assuming Miriam agrees, we will make the necessary arrangements."

Abram rode his donkey home as quickly as the old animal could go. "Mariah! Mariah!" he exclaimed as he burst through the door of their modest home. "I've found the perfect wife for our son!"

"Was anyone going to tell me about his?" Samuel asked as he poked his head around the corner of his room.

"Son, you know it is tradition for your father to find your bride," his mother chided. "Now that he has, you are the first to know."

"Well, actually the second," Abram corrected.

"Tell me what she is like, Father."

"Why don't you find out for yourself? I've arranged for us to return to the house of Mathias tomorrow!"

That night Samuel soaked in the washtub longer than usual, trimmed his beard, and laid out a clean tunic for the next day's journey. His mother packed gifts for Miriam's family, the gold and silver for the bride price, and a scarlet tunic she had crafted several years ago for her future daughter-in-law. Of course there was no sleep in the house of Abram that night. Tomorrow Samuel would meet his bride!

The following day father and son traveled to the house of Mathias. All the while Samuel wondered what he would find at the end of their journey. When they arrived, a servant led their horses to the stable, and then the duo made their way to the front door. With one knock the door slowly creaked open, and a set of onyx eyes like Samuel had never seen before met his gaze.

"Samuel," his father said, "I'd like for you to meet Miriam."

The two nodded a greeting. Samuel was grateful for the thickness of his tunic that hid the pounding of his heart.

After dinner Samuel followed the procedure he had practiced with his parents many times before.

"Mathias, I would like to ask permission to marry your daughter Miriam."

"And what is your *mohar*, the price you are willing to pay for my daughter?" Mathias asked.

Samuel brought forth the box of gold and silver coins he had been saving since boyhood and handed it to Mathias. "I bring twenty shekels of silver, one talent of gold, ten head of cattle, and five of our finest sheep."

"Miriam," her father asked, turning to his daughter, "are you willing to go with this man?"

"I am," she replied.

"Very well, then." Mathias poured a goblet of wine. "Now we shall drink to signify the acceptance of the marriage covenant." He first passed the wine to Miriam. Then he held the cup for Samuel, who placed his lips on the very spot where his bride's had been.

"I had many dreams that came and went through the years,
but being a wife and mother always stayed." Vickey

Looking at first one and then the other, Mathias continued with the ceremony. "This wine that you drink today signifies the acceptance of the wedding contract. As Miriam has drunk from the cup, this signifies her acceptance of your proposal. As you, Samuel, have drunk from the cup, this signifies your promise to care for her. This *ketubah*, this unbreakable covenant, is legally binding. You will not drink of a second cup until the day you take your bride to her new home and consummate your vows. As you know, the *erusin*, or time of engagement, is more important than the wedding day itself. From this time forward, you are legally married, though not living together." Then Miriam's father placed a veil over his daughter's face just below her eyes, which would not be removed until her groom lifted it on their wedding day.

A grand celebration was held that night as Rebecca invited her neighbors and friends to join in their happiness and meet their future son-in-law. During the festivities, Samuel and his father crept up onto the roof to catch a breath of fresh air and gather their thoughts about what had just happened in the past few hours. After many minutes of silence, Samuel spoke, "Father, you did well."

Both men let out a hearty laugh and then embraced and slapped each other on the back. Their laughter slowly turned to tears of joy as father and son realized the magnitude of what had just taken place. Yesterday, Samuel had been a boy—today he was a man.

Before Samuel departed for home the next day, he left gifts for Miriam to remind her of her groom until he returned. Samuel also left gifts for her family. Then he was off to build a home for the two of them.

For the next 12 months Samuel worked diligently on a home for his new bride. The *huppah*, as it was called, was a room or a bridal chamber built onto the groom's father's house.

"I dreamed of being a bride with lots of beautiful lace, roses, and a flowing gown." Yvonne

---

While Samuel was away preparing the new home for his bride, Miriam had preparations of her own. The time of separation, called *kiddushin*, was a time of sanctification or consecration. It was a time for her to be "set apart" or "holy." Before the ceremony, she took a special bath called a *mikveh* in a pool of water used for ritual purification. It was a part of a ceremonial cleansing that prepared her for the days ahead. This bath represented a separation from her old life and prepared her for the new one to come. It also represented a change in authority—coming out from the authority of her father and into the authority of her husband.

The bride and her attendants had no idea when the groom would return to whisk her away. Even Samuel did not know the day. That was in the father's hands. Samuel could not return for his bride until his father said the house was constructed to his satisfaction.

When Abram gave the signal, Samuel, along with several of his friends, ran to steal the bride away. As tradition would have it, they ran down the street in the middle of the night. With blazing torches lighting the night sky and blaring ram's horn breaking the silence, the ruckus let Miriam and her attendants know the groom and his grooms-men were on their way. Oil lamps lit up house after house as sleep-ing families stirred to see the merry band heading toward the house of Mathias. Misty-eyed women smiled. Knowing men grinned.

Mariah heard the noise. Her bags were packed. She was ready!

After Samuel kidnapped his bride, he whisked her off to the bridal chamber he had prepared to consummate their marriage. His best friend stood outside the door and waited for the traditional knock to let everyone know they were now officially man and wife.

Afterward, their family and friends joined them for a grand wed-ding party that lasted for seven days. When the marriage ceremony was over, Samuel lifted Miriam's veil and kissed his bride. It was then they drank from a second cup of wine.

A Dream Come True

What a romantic scenario! Can't you just see the oil lamps springing to life along the darkened street as the groom made his way to capture his bride in the middle of the night! Can't you imagine the excitement of the bride as she waited to be kidnapped and taken to the new home her groom had prepared for her!

Friends, this is no fairy tale. It is my story and your story as well. Whether you are married, single, divorced, or widowed, I have good news for you. Your dream of becoming a bride came true the moment you accepted Jesus Christ as your Savior. In Revelation 19:7, God refers to Christians as the bride of Christ, and He left no detail unchecked. Our Bridegroom woos, wins, and weds the bride His Father has cho-sen for Him. Let's go back and see how the Hebrew tradition was a fore-shadowing of our becoming the bride of Christ.

You Were Chosen

Just as Abram sought out and chose a bride for his son Samuel, God sought out and chose you to be the bride for His Son, Jesus. Jesus said to His disciples, "You did not choose me, but I chose you" (John 15:16). Jesus never did anything except what the Father told Him to do.

In other words, Jesus chose you because His Father told him to. God sought far and wide and decided you were a perfect match for His Son. You might say you were made for each other.

You Are Given a Choice

Even though the Father chose you, He still waits for you to accept the invitation. "God so loved the world that he gave his one and only Son, that whoever *believes* in him shall not perish but have eternal life" (John 3:16, emphasis added). Just as Miriam had a choice to accept or reject Samuel's proposal, you have a choice to believe (accept) or reject as well.

Kathy Troccoli, in her book co-authored with Dee Brestin, *Falling in Love with Jesus,* wrote of the day she said "yes" to Jesus:

> Walking out of church that day, I knew I had an escort. I felt like a beautiful bride, a princess. The perfect man had found me. Men had disappointed me so much, and all of a sudden I was face-to-face with perfect love and promises that wouldn't be broken. I knew in my spirit that His hand would never let go of mine, and that He had just been waiting for my "Yes."…Something wonderful was happening in my life. What was it? It was Jesus. My "once upon a time" had started; the book had begun; the pages were turning.[1]

Theologians have debated for years about this: Does God choose us or do we choose God? Sisters, I believe it is both. The sovereignty of God and the free will of man somehow work perfectly together in a way that our finite minds cannot fully understand. And while I may never understand all the theological ramifications of sovereignty and free will, I do understand that while the Father chooses the bride, the bride still has the choice to accept or reject the Groom.

Jesus Paid the Bride Price

Samuel paid a *mohar,* or bride price, for his bride, and Jesus has paid a bride price for you. But He gave something much more valuable than silver and gold, cattle and sheep—He gave His life. The Bible tells us: "You were *bought* at a price" (1 Corinthians 6:20; 7:23, emphasis added). "Husbands, love your wives as Christ loved the church and *gave himself up for her*" (Ephesians 5:25, emphasis added).

Jesus Offered the Cup of the Covenant

As Samuel and Miriam drank from the cup of wine to seal their marriage covenant, Jesus drank from a cup of wine to seal His marriage covenant with the church. He also said He would not drink of that same cup until He comes to take her home. In the upper room at the last supper before His crucifixion, Luke records, "He took bread, gave thanks and broke it, and gave it to them, saying, 'This is my body given for you; do this in remembrance of Me.' In the same way, after the supper he took the cup, saying, 'This cup is the new covenant in my blood, which is poured out for you'" (Luke 22:19-20). Jesus went on to say, "I will not drink of this fruit of the vine from now on until that day when I drink it anew with you in my Father's kingdom" (Matthew 26:29).

Jesus Left Gifts for the Bride

Just as Samuel left gifts for his bride, Jesus left gifts for His. One of those gifts is the Holy Spirit. Paul calls the Holy Spirit a down payment for all the riches still to come. "You also were included in Christ when you heard the word of truth, the gospel of your salvation. Having believed, you were marked in him with a seal, the promised Holy Spirit, who is a deposit guaranteeing our inheritance until the redemption of those who are God's possession—to the praise of his glory" (Ephesians 1:13-14).

Jesus Is Preparing Our Home

Where is our Groom now, and when will He return? Jesus has gone back to His Father's house, and He is preparing our new home. Even Jesus doesn't know when He will return. He is waiting for the Father to tell Him the bridal chamber is completed to His satisfaction. But when Jesus gets the signal, He will come as a "thief in the night" (1 Thessalonians 5:1-2) and whisk His bride away. He will give us plenty of warnings (Acts 2:19) to let us know the time of His return is drawing near.

"I dreamed about being a bride and played
dress-up bride all the time." Cathy

Jesus said, "In my Father's house are many rooms; if it were not so, I would have told you. I am going there to prepare a place for you. And if I go and prepare a place for you, I will come back and take you to be with me that you also may be where I am" (John 14:2-3). "No one knows about that day or hour, not even the angels in heaven, nor the Son, but only the Father" (Matthew 24:36).

The Bride Is Now Getting Ready

And what are we, Christ's bride, doing while He is away preparing our heavenly home? We're getting ready for His return! We are in a time of sanctification, and our ritual bath is the Word of God. Every time we read God's Word, He uses it to cleanse and purify us. As Jesus is making the house ready for His bride, God is making the bride ready for His Son.

So where are we now in the marriage process? We are betrothed, which was a legally binding contract and even more significant than the wedding day itself. Even though Christ's bride is not living with Him yet, our marriage contract is legally binding, and nothing can break that covenant. Jesus said, "No one can snatch them out of my hand" (John 10:28). We are now waiting for our Bridegroom to return to take us to our heavenly home to live in His presence forever. I can hardly wait!

An Unlikely Bride

While the story of the Jewish wedding ceremony is a lovely foreshadowing of Jesus and the bride of Christ, His encounter with a Samaritan woman shows the great lengths He will go to pursue and capture the heart of His beloved. In the Gospel of John, we find a story of a woman looking for Mr. Right in all the wrong places. Then one day Mr. Right came to her.

After Jesus had spent some time ministering in Judea, He decided to go back to His hometown of Galilee. Most respectable Jews would cross the Jordan River and travel along the east bank to avoid the despicable country of Samaria. The Samaritans were half-breeds, the result of Israelites who had intermarried with Gentiles, and the Jews didn't want anything to do with them. However, Jesus "had to go" through Samaria (John 4:4)—not because of geography of the land, but because His Father had sent Him on a divine appointment.

"I don't think I even considered the possibility I would not get married. I dreamed I would marry a young charming man like the ones I saw on TV. I did marry a charming young man, but things are not always as easy as they are for the fairy-tale princesses. Funny how we never see Cinderella or Snow White thinking about paying bills or towing cars." Kristi

---

Jesus had traveled ahead of His disciples and reached Jacob's well while the boys went into town to purchase some food. He was exhausted and sat down by the well's edge. After a few moments, a Samaritan woman came to draw her water for the day. Traditionally, the village women came to draw water early in the morning or at day's end to avoid the scorching heat of the noon sun. However, this particular woman did not want to associate with the other women...or, at least, they did not want to associate with her. She was tired of the searing stares, snide snickers, and the cutting remarks cast her way. For her, the scorching sun was easier to endure than the scorn of the village women. So she came to the well at midday.

When she arrived, she was surprised to see a man sitting by the well. A Jewish man. She tried to ignore Him, but as she prepared to dip her bucket in the well, He startled her by speaking to her.

"Will you give Me a drink?"

The woman was shocked that Jesus would make such a request. "You are a Jew and I am a Samaritan woman. How can you ask me for a drink?" (John 4:9).

It wasn't unusual for a thirsty traveler to ask for a cool drink of water, but it was scandalous for a Jewish man to carry on a public conversation with a woman, especially a Samaritan woman. It was unheard of for a Jewish rabbi to drink from the same cup as a Samaritan, male or female.

She gave her reply with a hint of sarcasm, but Jesus did not let that deter His mission. He was more interested in winning the woman than winning the war of words. He answered her, "If you knew the gift of God and who it is that asks you for a drink, you would have asked him and he would have given you living water…Everyone who drinks this water will be thirsty again, but whoever drinks the water I give him will never thirst. Indeed, the water I give him will become in him a spring of water welling up to eternal life" (John 4:10-14).

"I always dreamed about being a radiant bride. I had my wedding planned out my entire life. It was a huge affair filled with flowers and white dresses, just like a fairy tale." Lindsey

---

Living water. Never thirst again. Just the thought of never having to come to the well and face the townspeople again was enough to pique her interest. But Jesus had more for this woman than water for her parched body—He had satisfaction for her parched soul.

If ever there was a woman who wanted to be a bride, it was this woman. Yes, she had tried to satisfy the longing in her heart, but each marriage proved to be less than what she had hoped, leaving her feeling empty and disappointed. Five times she had been a bride, and five times divorce had shattered her dreams. When Jesus met her at the well, she was living with potential husband number six. Jesus knew all of this before she even spoke a word.

The woman said to him, "Sir, give me this water so that I won't get thirsty and have to keep coming here to draw water."

"Go call your husband and come back."

"I have no husband," she replied.

Jesus said to her, "You are right when you say you have no husband. The fact is, you have had five husbands, and the man you now have is not your husband. What you have just said is quite true" (John 4:15-18).

The light of the world had revealed her innermost darkness. She was amazed that Jesus saw right through her as if He had seen every day of her life. She believed Him when He said He was the Messiah. All her life she had been seeking fulfillment. She had gone from one man to the next, but her heart had remained as empty as the water pot she balanced on her head. However, on this day she met the only One who could satisfy her every longing. On this day she became the bride she had always wanted to be. No longer did she need her water pot, but she left it by the well as she ran into town to tell the villagers about Jesus, the Messiah, and bring them to the restorer and fulfiller of dreams.

To see how Jesus pursued this woman simply thrills my heart. He went to her. He waited for her. He wooed her.

I'm glad the woman in this story remained nameless, for she could be any one of us who has ever searched for our deepest longings to be fulfilled in another person but come up empty time and time again. Jesus "had to go" to Samaria to see this nameless woman, just as He "had to go" to the cross to seek for you—His bride.

A Fairy-Tale Ending

In the introduction I mentioned the beloved childhood fairy tale of Cinderella. Let's go back for a few moments and visit with this soot-covered beauty to see how she moved from the servants' quarters to the king's palace with the help of her fairy godmother.

The story begins with the words "Once upon a time." That phrase causes little girls and big girls alike to sit on the edge of their seats in anticipation. It awakens our senses, and we anticipate that something good is about to unfold.

"One Halloween I dressed up like a bride and couldn't understand why I couldn't take my baby doll around with me!" Maureen

---

You recall the story. This one so fair lived in a house with her evil stepmother and two wicked stepsisters. Her plight in life was to clean the house from top to bottom, wait on the terrible trio hand and foot, and live in seclusion from the outside world. She was relegated to reside next to the fireplace with her only true friends, the mice who loved her.

As a child I remember reading the story of Cinderella and gazing admiringly at the beautiful young girl with ashes on her fair skin and a smile on her ruby lips. It didn't matter that she wore a tattered dress and dingy apron. She was beautiful. But Cinderella didn't think she was beautiful at all. She believed her jealous stepmother and stepsisters, who told her she was ugly.

Why doesn't Cinderella just look into the mirror and see that she is much more beautiful than they are? I mused. *Look at their crooked noses stuck up in the air and their mean ol' sour faces.*

Not only was Cinderella beautiful on the outside, but her sweet disposition made her lovely on the inside as well. If it was obvious to me, surely she could see the truth. But her wicked stepsisters' voices were loud and convincing. She believed them.

One day an invitation arrived inviting all the young women in the village to a ball hosted by the king, at which his son would select a bride. The stepsisters laughed when Cinderella shyly suggested she might attend. After all, the invitation was extended to *all* the young unmarried ladies in the kingdom. She had just as much right to attend as they did. But Cinderella listened to their taunting and her tiny flicker of hope was extinguished.

"I used to wear my mother's wedding
dress around the house." Claire

But then her fairy godmother appeared, and with a wave of her magical wand Cinderella's rags were transformed into a shimmering ball gown, the mice were changed into a coachman and prancing horses, and a pumpkin became a carriage fit for a queen. Unfortunately, as John Eldredge said in his book *The Sacred Romance*, "When God's grace comes in the form of Cinderella's fairy godmother and dresses her in a beautiful gown, she does finally look in the mirror and sees clearly her great beauty, but she believes it is all due to magic."[2]

Of course, when the prince sees Cinderella, he realizes she is the woman of his dreams. He immediately recognizes her inner and outer beauty and knows he has found his one true love.

The one stipulation of the fairy godmother's magic is that Cinderella's good fortune ends at the stroke of midnight. She barely makes it out of the palace doors before the spell is broken, her gown changes back to rags, her coachman and horses back to mice, and the coach back to a pumpkin. However, in her race to beat the final stroke of midnight and her secret, she loses one of her tiny glass slippers on the palace steps.

With this one clue, the prince was determined to find the true love of his life. He searched the kingdom, and when he slid the glass slipper on Cinderella's slender foot, he knew he had found his bride. As the final page is turned, we read the words, "And they lived happily ever after."

Cinderella was doomed to a life in the ashes until her fairy godmother showed up. Ah, there's the gospel. "God demonstrates His own love for us in this: While we were still sinners, [covered in ashes of shame, clothed in tattered rags, taunted by lies of evil, destined to spend all of eternity in the furnace of hell] Christ died for us" (Romans 5:8). But God is no fairy godmother. He's our heavenly Father. And Jesus is more than a handsome prince. He's the Prince of the Ages.

Reading this story as an adult, I see Satan's fingerprints all over it. He bears a striking resemblance to the stepfamily that oppressed Cinderella and convinced her that she would never be anything but a homely house servant. Likewise, Satan tells us that we are worthless servants, when in reality we are princesses in the making. Satan tells us we are not worthy of going to the ball, when in reality we have a personal invitation. Satan tells us we belong in the ashes of shame, when in reality we have been set free by royal decree.

Satan tells us we deserve to wear the rags of condemnation, when in reality God is waiting to place the robes of righteousness on our regal shoulders. Satan tells us no one could possibly love us, when in reality God has gone to great lengths to show us how much He does. Satan tells us we are not beautiful enough to be a bride, when in reality God chose us from all others just for that very purpose.

"When I was a little girl, I dreamed of being a beautiful bride.
My girlfriends and neighbors and I used to play 'getting
married.' It was a dream I have yet to fulfill. I'm leaving
it in God's hands to pick me a husband if that is His will.
For now, I am His bride, and that's all I need." Karen

Our hearts are made for romance. But does "and they lived happily ever after" exist only in fairy tales? Surely not. Many women's hearts have grown cold, and their dreams lie in a broken forgotten heap, but the reality of a Prince who longs to make you His bride is a certain reality. "As a bridegroom rejoices over his bride, so will your God rejoice over you" (Isaiah 62:5).

An Easter Bride

It was a beautiful day for a wedding. The sun shone brightly as the daffodils danced in the gentle breeze, nodding their happy faces in conversation. A choir of robins, cardinals, and finches sang rounds of cheerful melodies, which floated through a clear blue sky that was a reflection of the bride's sparkling eyes. The air had that unusual crisp quality of spring, reminding us of the chill from winter's past and the warmth of summer's promise.

"I wanted to marry a man like Charles Ingalls
on *Little House on the Prairie*." Janet

The day was Easter Sunday 1997, the day the Groom had chosen to be joined to His beloved. As in the Jewish custom of old, He had proposed to His young maiden and then promptly gone away to prepare a home for her. On this day His Father had signaled that the home was ready and He could go to get His bride.

Iris had been waiting for her Husband to come and take her to the wonderful home that He had prepared for her. *How like Him to pick Easter*, she thought to herself. *My favorite day of the year.* She smiled as she heard Him coming, and her heart fluttered with the anticipation of seeing His face.

She wore a white dress with flecks of blue and carried a bouquet of pink carnations and white mums with a spray of asparagus fern as wispy as her baby-fine hair. A sweet smile spread across her face as she saw her beloved Jesus hold out His strong hand to help her cross the threshold of the temporal and into the hall of eternity. She walked into His loving embrace and drank in the loveliness of her surroundings which He had perfectly described in His many letters.

On Easter Sunday 1997, my husband's dear sweet 74-year-old Aunt Iris went home to be with the Lord. As we all gathered around to say our last goodbyes, I could not manage to be mournful. Yes, I was going to miss her, but Iris had never been married on this side of eternity, and the vision I had in my mind was of her joining the Lord as the bride of Christ. For me, it was not a funeral but a wedding. It was what she had always longed for…a dream come true.

In Isaiah 61:3 the prophet describes what God will do for the bride of Christ. He will bestow on her a crown of beauty instead of ashes, anoint her with the oil of gladness instead of mourning and place on her shoulders a garment of praise instead of a spirit of despair. Are you feeling brokenhearted because of broken dreams? Have you been in mourning because your dream of being a bride has not turned out the way you had hoped? God desires to blow away the ashes and place the crown of a royal bride on your head. So lift your head, dear one, and accept your crown from the King of kings.

The Groom's Perspective

I can't leave this section without taking one more look…but this time I want to focus on the groom. As I mentioned earlier, a woman never looks more beautiful than when she marches down the aisle to meet the man of her dreams. But what about the groom? Certainly he is not the focus of attention on such a day, but let's take just a moment to look in his eyes as he watches his bride come down the aisle. Come closer. Stand on your tiptoes if you have too. He won't mind. Look in his eyes. What do you see?

"I wanted to be a bride and a mother, but most of
all have someone who cherished me." Janet

If the light is just right and the angle of his head is just so, you will see what he sees. There, reflected in his eyes, is his bride. The vision of her fills his eyes as his love for her fills his heart. With each progressing step down the aisle, his heart pounds with anticipation. Go ahead, place your hand on his chest. Do you feel it? Strong, pounding, anticipatory. He loves her. He adores her. He can't imagine life without her. She is his, and he can hardly fathom this great prize that is for him alone.

Now, look a little closer. The bride is nearer now. You can see her face in the reflection of his eyes. Dear sister, the face is your face. You are the bride.

Jesus Christ has chosen you. He is wooing you, and He wants to take care of you as His precious bride. He's standing at the altar, just waiting for you to say, "I do."

Whether you are divorced with a heart broken by betrayal, widowed with a bed chilled by loneliness, single with still no promise of a ring on your finger, or happily joined to the man of your dreams, Jesus longs to take you in His arms, not "for as long as you both shall live," but for all eternity.

Wedding Feast of the Lamb

There is a place prepared for me
A table by the crystal sea
Where my Beloved bids me rest
And gently lean upon His breast
He dries my tears, He breaks my chains
He binds my wounds, He heals my pain

He soothes my tired and troubled soul
He fills my cup, it overflows
The finest wine, the choicest bread
By His own nail-scarred hands I am fed
He hides my shame in holy dress
He clothes me with His righteousness
He lifts my veil, He draws me close
Proclaims me His to the heavenly host
While angels sing His reverence
He leads me in a sacred dance
There is a place by the crystal sea
Where my Beloved waits for me.
He bids me come just as I am
To the wedding feast of the Lamb[3]

3

To Be a Mommy

I can still remember cuddling, rocking, and singing to my favorite baby dolls when I was a little girl. I'd love them until their nylon hair was matted, their outfits were tattered, and their painted cheeks were marred. I'd bandage their knees, kiss their heads, and teach them important life lessons.

Most little girls dream of one day being a mommy. In the hundreds of surveys I collected for this book, to be a mommy was the number one dream. And of all the dreams of a woman, this one can cause the most pain. Not being able to have children, the rebellion of the children we do have, or losing a child due to miscarriage, stillbirth, or untimely death can be one of the most heart-wrenching experiences of a woman's life. Motherhood hits at the very core of womanhood.

After I was married, my dream to be a mother began to grow. It seemed my arms ached to have a child to nurture, love, and pour my life into. When I was 26, Steve and I decided it was time to increase our family of two. We conceived on our first attempt, and nine months later, Steven Hugh Jaynes Jr. came screaming into the world. As I nestled that baby boy with a shock of thick black hair and long Bambi-like eyelashes against my breast, I knew I was holding God's first deposit in His great plan for my life—to be a mother. I had never felt more fulfilled in my life, and I was certain I was "born to bear." When Steven was about two-years-old, we began praying for baby number two.

"Steven," we explained, "God is the one who gives babies to mommies and daddies, so we are going to pray that He will send us another Jaynes baby so you can have a little brother or sister."

This sounded like a good idea to him, so he added "And, God, please send Mommy and Daddy another Jaynes baby" at the end of our family prayers each night. Conception happened so easily the first time that we thought this would be a wonderful opportunity to show Steven how God answers prayer.

Six months passed, and there was no news of another Jaynes baby on the way. Then one year passed with no news. Then two years passed with no news. During that time we began traveling down the frustrating road of doctor visits, infertility treatments, and timed intimacy (which is anything but intimate). We also began building our dream home with bedrooms for four children and a children's bathroom with two sinks so the brood wouldn't argue about whose turn it was. When the house was near completion, I walked from room to room. "Please, Lord," I prayed, "don't let us move into this house without the hope of children to fill it." My heart felt as empty as those bedrooms that seemingly would have no children occupying them.

"I wanted to have a huge family. The children I could not give birth to in the natural, God has given me by letting me mother other people's kids. My husband and I have conflicting blood types that makes it difficult for me to carry babies to term. We lost five children, have two biological children, and one adopted child." Rebekah

---

God did not answer my prayer as I had hoped. After many years of infertility treatments and heart-wrenching, faith-filled prayers, the children's bedrooms remained empty, the blankets unruffled, and the dream unfulfilled. It appeared there would be no more children. While Steven was everything I could have ever hoped for wrapped up in one package, my desire to have a houseful of little ones was not God's will.

Was I thankful for the child I did have? Absolutely, but that did not negate the desire in my heart to be a mother of many.

The inner turmoil associated with infertility is such a raw wound, and many women avoid discussing it. Each month the hopeful mother experiences a mini death, grieves her loss, and then by day 14 of the following month, rallies to hope once again. My friend Amanda Bailey wrote the following piece trying to explain her own personal struggle.

> It was eerily silent, this patch of ground in the eye of the storm raging only a half mile away from our home. The sound of the wind had been unimaginable with its roar like a plane engine and the occasional screech of splitting wood like a myriad of axes hammering in unison. My heart still vibrated, and the stench of burning plastic from overhead telephone wires set afire by lightning burned in my nostrils. The sparks had preceded the electricity outage by mere seconds.
>
> But here, in the eye of the storm, the grass was bright green with water droplets glistening in the rays, the sun was peeking through the dark clouds, and the fallen trees stood as still as soldiers on the battlefield with the standing ones keeping watch. Sensing a momentary peace, I expected the return of the storm, but my mind screamed for it to delay. "Not now! Not yet!" I cried. "It's too soon."
>
> As I turned to face the storm, I was startled by a small swatch of color moving over the bushes. The butterfly flitted up and off into the horizon where the orange sun set on the storm's dark horizon.
>
> My experience with infertility has been much like living through that hurricane so many years ago. The storm rages when the test proves negative. Then the eye of the storm comes around day 14 with renewed hope and a sense of calm. The calm continues as I think, *Perhaps this will be the month when my cycle will be interrupted and a baby will be conceived.* But when my period announces otherwise, I

once again hear the roar of the storm approaching, and I wonder why others around me can't hear it as well. The wind blows, lights go out, and life around me seems to fall apart.

But then there's the butterfly, which says "Hope again." And the eye of the storm returns.

I understand the storm and the hope that Amanda described. Weary from the ups and downs, I was relieved when Steve and I decided to stop trying to conceive and be content with our family of three.

Accepting When God Says No

Steven, however, continued to pray that God would give us another Jaynes baby. He prayed it every night. When he was about five years old, I thought it was time to tell him to stop. But how do you tell a child to stop praying a prayer? This was something God was going to have to do because I did not know how.

One day Steven and I were sitting at his miniature table eating our peanut butter and jelly sandwiches when he looked up at me and said, "Mommy, have you ever thought maybe God wants you to have only one Jaynes baby?"

You can imagine my shock at this statement coming out of the blue from a five-year-old. Once I regained my composure, I said, "Well, yes, I have thought that maybe that's the case. If it is I am so thankful, because He has given me all I have ever hoped for in a child wrapped up in one package—YOU!"

Then he cocked his little head like a robin and continued. "Well, what I think we ought to do is to keep praying until you're too old to have one. Then we'll know that was His answer."

What a great idea! Steven had no idea how old "too old" was, but he did know that God could do anything. If His answer was no, he didn't have a problem with that. I told Steven no many times, and he knew "no" did not mean "I don't love you." No meant no because I was his mother and knew what was best for him. I was the one having trouble with God telling me no.

The Lord taught me a great lesson that day. Through Steven's child-like faith, I saw an example of the attitude of trust I should have toward my heavenly Father who loves me and knows what's best, even when the answer is no. After all, if God said yes to every request, then He wouldn't be God at all...we would.

Trusting God in the Dark

Those years of infertility were a stormy time in my life, but then a few years later a tidal wave hit.

"Steve, can you meet me for lunch? I have a little surprise for you."

> "I wanted to be Harriet Nelson and have a
> home that was always clean." Verona

I was so excited to meet my husband and tell him this unexpected news. Even though we had arrived at a place of peace and contentment with our family of three, now it seemed Steven was going to have a little brother or sister after all.

I handed Steve a tiny wrapped package. He gingerly pulled back the paper and opened the lid to discover a baby pillow nestled in soft white tissue paper.

"Does this mean what I think it means?"

"Yes," I replied with tears filling my eyes.

> "I dreamed I would be a mother who rocked
> her children to sleep, read them stories, and
> cooked them meals and treats." Cindy

My dream was coming true! There would be more children after all. But even as the baby was growing well inside my womb and the nursery was being planned inside our home, the dream came to a screeching halt. The baby died. I had a miscarriage. For me it was not the loss of a child that was to be, it was the loss of a child that was. For months I grieved her loss.

There are still times today when I look at the portraits of our family of three and I can almost see a shadow of a fourth. But one day there will come a time when my little girl will not be a mere shadow. I will hold her in my arms. Until then it gives me great comfort to picture her healthy and whole and playing at the feet of Jesus.

During those summer months following our loss, a friend sang me this song.

> *God is too wise to be mistaken.*
> *God is too good to be unkind.*
> *So when you can't understand*
> *When you don't see His plan,*
> *When you can't trace His hand,*
> *Trust His heart.*[1]

I have learned much along this journey of trying to conceive and then losing a child. One thing I've learned is that I am not alone. In 2002 the National Center for Health Statistics estimated that 7.3 million women between the ages of 15 and 44 (11.8 percent), experienced an impaired ability to have children.[2] Also, at least 20 percent of first-time pregnancies end in miscarriage.[3] Miscarriage is not an uncommon problem, but there is nothing common about the pain. Because of my journey with infertility, God has allowed me to minister to many women who suffer the pain of empty arms through miscarriage, infertility, or an untimely death of a child. Perhaps there is no other life laboratory that affects the heart of a woman more than the issue of having or not having children—for God has placed a desire in our hearts to nurture and care for others.

God's Punishment or God's Plan

In the Old Testament, women who could not bear children felt great shame. They saw it as a curse from God. However, barrenness or infertility has been a part of God's plan for many women. Sarah was barren for 90 years before she miraculously gave birth to Isaac. She was called the "mother of nations," even though she only gave birth to one child (Genesis 17:15). Rachel, Hannah, and the Shunammite, all godly women, experienced infertility (Genesis 29; 1 Samuel 1; 2 Kings 4). We have no indication that Queen Esther, who saved the Israelite nation from annihilation, ever bore a child.

However, when someone experiences infertility or the loss of a child by miscarriage, the birth of a child with congenital defect, or the death of a child shortly after birth, many questions flood her mind: *Does God think I would be a bad mother? Is God punishing me for sin in my life? Is He punishing me for past mistakes? How could God really love me if He is withholding such a desire of my heart?*

"I dreamed about being a mommy. I was the oldest of five children and just loved mothering my younger siblings. My mother made being a mom look like the most rewarding job in the world." Cathy

---

To add to the pain of a woman's own personal fears and doubts, many times well-meaning friends come along with a bounty of advice that only accentuates the feelings of inadequacy: "You need to try to conceive every other day." "You need to try to conceive only on days such and such." "I think you exercise too much." "I think you don't exercise enough." "You're not conceiving because you are too thin." "Infertility treatment is not of God. If He wanted you to conceive, He would do it without medical intervention." "Try infertility treatment. If it's not God's will for you to conceive, it won't work anyway." "Try this." "Try that."

And then, when all the advice is rattling around in the woman's head, she hears, "You just need to relax and not think about it!" Confused? Imagine how the wounded woman feels as she tries to assimilate the bombardment of "wise counsel." This only adds fuel to the fire of a woman's feelings that her infertility is her own fault—she thinks she's just not doing something right.

Perhaps one of the most common misconceptions is when a woman feels God is punishing her with her barrenness. In Luke 1:5-7, the writer describes the barren couple Zechariah and Elizabeth as "*upright in the sight of God,* observing all the Lord's commandments and regulations blamelessly" (emphasis added). The New American Standard Bible describes them as "righteous." Eugene Peterson's paraphrase, *The Message,* says: "Together they lived honorably before God, careful in keeping to the ways of the commandments and enjoying a clear conscience before God." And yet they were without children. They were not being punished, but rather God had a specific plan for their lives.

"I dreamed about having 12 children
(that was until I had four!)." Cathy

I truly believe that if it is God's plan for a couple not to conceive children of their own, then He has a different but wonderful plan in mind. However, many times barrenness, as with all seemingly unfulfilled dreams, can so overshadow our lives that we are unable to see what God's dreams for us really are.

In John 9, Jesus' disciples asked Him about the correlation between a certain lost dream and sin. "Walking down the street, Jesus saw a man blind from birth. His disciples asked, 'Rabbi, who sinned: this man or his parents, causing him to be born blind?' Jesus said, 'You're asking the wrong question. You're looking for someone to blame. There is no such cause-effect here. Look instead for what God can do.'" (John 9:1-3 MSG).

When our dreams of becoming a mother don't turn out the way we had hoped, perhaps we need to make sure we are asking the right questions. Instead of, "Why me?" perhaps we should ask, "What now?"

Being Spiritually Fruitful

God fashioned women to bear children. Our wombs, breasts, hips, and hormones were uniquely designed for conceiving and giving life. There is an inborn nature to nurture, and while we may not give birth to our own flesh and blood in a delivery room, we can still—must still—be fruitful and nurture those in our sphere of influence.

When God created Adam and Eve, He commanded them to "be fruitful and multiply, and fill the earth, and subdue it" (Genesis 1:28 NASB). In the New Testament, we see another kind of fruitfulness as Jesus sent out the disciples. "Therefore go and make disciples of all nations" (Matthew 28:19). He could have said, "Be fruitful and multiply," which is exactly what they did.

In the last chapter we met the Samaritan woman at the well. After she realized that Jesus was the Messiah, she left her water pot, ran back to town, and brought an entire village to meet the man who told her everything she had ever done. As the mass of humanity came pouring over the hill to meet Jesus, He turned to His disciples and said, "I tell you, open your eyes and look at the fields! They are ripe for harvest" (John 4:35).

As a result of this woman's testimony, many Samaritans came to believe in Jesus as the Messiah. She was fruitful and multiplied, bringing many spiritual children into God's kingdom. The prophet Isaiah wrote, "Sing, O barren woman, you who never bore a child; burst into song, shout for joy, you who were never in labor; because more are the children of the desolate woman than of her who has a husband, says the LORD" (Isaiah 54:1). The woman at the well was a personification of Isaiah's prophecy—a desolate woman who had many children.

Think for a moment about why little girls want to grow up and become mommies. We want to cuddle and care for, rear and raise, share and shape, teach and train. We want to pour our love into another human being in the hopes that they will give that same love in return.

"I dreamed I would have two boys who were active in sports and one girl who would be active in piano, dance, and Girl Scouts. I have one boy who is not interested in sports and three girls. I dreamed of quiet evenings and noisy days, a big house with an upstairs with a room for everyone." Eva Marie

I asked more than 200 elementary school-age children to tell me why they thought their moms were great and why they thought their dads were great. My favorite response was, "My mom is a great mom because she takes care of me. My dad is a great dad because he lets me do things my mom won't let me do!" The overall bottom line response was…moms nurture and dads are fun!

God has created women with a desire to nurture, but I think it goes much deeper than just having children. Most long to invest their lives in something that matters. Most of the time that something is someone or someones. The Bible calls that being fruitful. Jesus said, "I am the vine; you are the branches. If a man remains in me and I in him, he will bear much fruit" (John 15:5). He also tells us that the true sign of a Christian is that they will bear fruit (John 15:8).

After Henrietta Szold lost the love of her life, she wrote, "Today it is four weeks since my only real happiness was killed." In her mind, her dream of happiness was lost. However, she went on to found Hadassah and, in the 1930s, involved the organization in a program that rescued 22,000 Jewish children from Hitler's concentration camps. Henrietta, who mourned her disappointment in never marrying and having children, became the mother of thousands. [4]

Sometimes, when our dream of motherhood is shattered, we have to let the dream die and allow God to birth other dreams in our lives. It is as if He is saying to us, "When you are letting go, remember that I am planting seeds of new life in you. Your grief is only for a season. My end is not death. It is always life. I am the author of life." [5] Whether it is the dream of having one child, the dream of having seven children, or the dream that a child will turn out a particular way, we must all eventually give that dream to God.

In my own life, I think of the woman who led me to Christ. She was a mother in my neighborhood who took me under her wing and nurtured, mentored, and discipled me. God used her to be my spiritual mother, and if it wasn't for her obedience to Him, I'm not sure where I would be today.

Several years ago my heart broke one day when I read about the pop star Madonna. She was known as the bad girl of MTV, Sean Penn's ex-wife, Dennis Rodman's born-to-be-wild girlfriend, David Letterman's foulmouthed guest. She's a movie star, the author of a sex book, and a woman who talked her personal trainer into inseminating her. During a television interview, the interviewer asked Madonna the usual shocking questions, to which she gave the regular shocking answers. The two of them were sitting there bantering questions and answers until the interviewer prefaced her next question something like this: "You're a woman who has it all. You're a singer, actress, and author. You have money, fame, and a place in American pop culture. You've been on the cover of almost every magazine. You're not just a global figure, you're a global force."

"Because I was adopted, I always dreamed about having babies who looked like me. I've never had anyone in my life resemble me, so I'd try to picture someone who had characteristics like mine." Annette

---

Meanwhile Madonna is sitting there, taking all this in and nodding her head—until the last question.

"Is there anything you would give it all up for?"

Suddenly Madonna's face froze. Her eyes filled with tears. Her lip quivered. She took a deep breath and answered.

"To have a mom."[6]

I never knew until I read that account that her mother died when Madonna was five years old. I wonder what she would be like today had someone come alongside her and been a mother to her. It could have made all the difference in the world.

Being a spiritual mother isn't limited to the spiritual birthing process but extends to nurturing a baby Christian as well. Karen said, "I am a first generation Christian and I don't know what a Christian woman is supposed to look like or be like. I don't know how to be a wife or a mother, and I'm feeling my way in the dark. I watch the women around me at church, but I need a mentor to show me how to follow Christ in my day-to-day living." What she needs is a spiritual mother, and someone brave enough to do it.

Birthing Spiritual Children

Let me share Beverly's story of her dream to become a mother and how God fulfilled it. For many years Beverly worked at Bank of America in the corporate lending group and was the personification of a young professional on the move up the corporate ladder. She was beautiful, intelligent, and articulate, and she had the reputation for accomplishing her well-thought-out goals. She married at 26, and the dream of having children began to bloom in both her and her husband's hearts. However, Beverly was born with only half of a uterus and one functioning ovary. While her doctors said conception would not be impossible, they warned the couple it could be difficult. The doctors' prediction proved to be true, and years of infertility treatments ensued.

One night at dinner, Beverly mentioned to a lawyer friend, "Dana, if you ever have the opportunity to place a child for adoption, I'd love to be considered."

"How serious are you?" Dana inquired.

"Very serious."

The next day Dana called with the news of a baby being released for adoption. With tears in her eyes, she described the birth parents to Beverly.

"The mother is five foot eight with a medium build and brown hair. The father is six feet tall with red hair, blue eyes, and fair skin," she described.

Dana could have been describing Beverly and Todd.

Four weeks later, little Todd Junior was placed in the loving arms of his adoptive parents. Three weeks later Beverly's dearly beloved father died of a massive heart attack at 55 years of age. With that loss, Beverly lost a large piece of her heart, which little Todd grew to fill. But Beverly still had a deep longing to bear a child of her own. The couple continued to pursue infertility treatments, even though each hopeful month ended in a mini death of that hope.

Finally, after several years of trying to conceive, a pregnancy test confirmed that Beverly was pregnant. And then a few months later, that dream was lost when she had a miscarriage.

"Oh, Bev," one of her friends consoled, "I feel God has other plans for you. Maybe God is calling you to birth children in another way."

That comment made Beverly angry. *I'm not sure what God's idea of birth is,* she thought to herself, *but mine involves a slap on a tiny bottom and the first breath of air from a new baby.*

"I dreamed of having one child (I had four sisters), but I have not been able to have one. Instead, I help raise my sisters' children. My unmarried sister had a baby and has come to live with us. The three of us are raising the child together." Martha

---

In the previous months Beverly had developed a relationship with a woman named Carol at the gym where they both taught aerobics. Carol was not a Christian and was curious to see how Bev would handle this loss in her life. Carol saw her pain, but she also saw her heart soften toward God and His will for her life.

"I'm amazed at how you've coped with the miscarriage," Carol commented.

"It's only because of Jesus Christ and the support of my friends that I could have gotten through this at all," Beverly replied.

Over the next weeks and months, Beverly began to share Christ with Carol by bringing her CDs, suggesting various books, and taking her along to women's events at her church. Even though Carol appeared to be confident and content, the gaping hole that can only be filled by Jesus Christ became evident. Beverly had never seen such a spiritual hunger before. Almost a year later, in a Wednesday night prayer service, Carol accepted Jesus as her Savior.

"I am so thankful for Beverly Spencer," Carol told the congregation. "For many months she shared Christ with me and allowed me to be a part of her life. She was willing to climb into the mud with me and help me work through all the dirt in my life. I never really understood the role that Jesus Christ plays in our lives until I saw Him guiding hers. I realize that Beverly has placed many parts of her life on hold in order to help me understand the eternal life that could be mine."

With tears in her eyes, Beverly felt God whisper in her ear, "Carol is My child that you have birthed."

"I wanted to be a different sort of mom than I had as
a child. I would not work, be home when my children
came home from school, volunteer in their classrooms,
and attend their extracurricular activities without
complaining. They would always know by my words
and deeds that they were loved and special." Mary

One year after Beverly's miscarriage, she and her husband decided to adopt again. After much prayer, the birth mother chose Beverly and Todd. Shortly after the adoption coordinator hung up the phone from telling them the good news, she called back again.

"Oh, I forgot to tell you the birth mother's name," she said. "It's Carol."

Beverly hung up the phone and fell on her knees thanking God for His presence in and providential plan for her life. In spite of her seemingly dashed dreams of bearing a child of her own, she had remained available to God to fulfill His dreams for her life. She allowed His truths to flow through her to one of His precious hurting children. As she was acting as a spiritual surrogate mother to birth His child Carol, He was forming her precious daughter in the womb of another by the same name. The story of two births will forever be woven together with the two precious Carols.

Arriving at a Different Destination

I love this piece Emily Pearl Kingley wrote after her child was born with Down's syndrome. She said it was like planning a fabulous trip to Italy, boarding the plane, and then hearing a disturbing welcome from the flight attendant as the plane touches down.

"Welcome to Holland!"

"Holland!" you exclaim. "What do you mean, Holland? I signed up for Italy! I'm supposed to be in Italy. All my life I've dreamed of going to Italy."

But there's been a change in the flight plan. The plane landed in Holland, and there you must stay.

The important thing is that they haven't taken you to a horrible, disgusting, filthy place, full of pestilence, famine, and disease. It's just a different place.

So you must go out and buy new guidebooks. And you must learn a whole new language. And you will meet a whole new group of people you would never have met.

It's just a different place. It's slower paced than Italy, less flashy than Italy. But after you've been there a while and catch your breath, you look around and begin to notice that Holland has windmills. Holland has tulips. Holland even has Rembrandts.

But everyone you know is busy coming and going from Italy, and they're all bragging about what a wonderful time they had there. And for the rest of your life, you will say, "Yes, that's where I was supposed to go. That's what I had planned."

And the pain of that will never, ever, ever go away, because the loss of that dream is a very significant loss. But if you spend your life mourning the fact that you didn't get to Italy, you may never be free to enjoy the special and very lovely things about Holland."[7]

No matter where you destination has taken you, or where it will take you in the future, I pray that you will begin to enjoy where you've landed. It might not be what you dreamed of, but it can have many wonderful features yet to be explored.

Seeing the Big Picture

In closing, I want to take you back to where we began with my own story. As you recall, I do have one incredible blessing in my son, Steven, but my dream to have a house full of children did not materialize as I had hoped. During one of my times with the Lord, I was studying in the Song of Solomon about being the bride of Christ. This is a very romantic book of the Bible about the courtship, engagement, and eventual marriage between a man and a woman. Many compare it to the relationship of Jesus with His bride, the church.

As I read Song of Solomon 2:1, God stopped me…

"I am a rose of Sharon…"

What was her name? God seemed to say.

"Sharon," I answered.

What is your name? He again seemed to ask.

"Lord, my name is Sharon," I whispered aloud.

Look it up, He prompted my heart.

I went to my Bible dictionary and looked up "Sharon." It meant a fertile valley near Mount Carmel. God was telling me that while my medical chart had INFERTILE written in its pages, He made sure that my name meant FERTILE before I was even born. No, I do not have a house full of children, but He has made me fertile in many other ways. Through writing, speaking, radio, and simply obeying Him when He nudges me to reach out to one of His own, God has allowed me to birth and nurture many spiritual children.

I dreamed of having a family and a white picket fence. I saw a boy and girl dressed in matching outfits playing on the white sandy beaches of Florida." Sue

---

God does not always give us the babies or husbands for which we've prayed, but He will always give us access to everything we need to have an abundant life filled with purpose, passion, and His provision. When God says no, we can rest assured there is a greater yes if we relinquish our shattered dreams to Him.

Someone asked me recently, "Would you rather have the house full of children or the ministry opportunities you have today?"

"I want exactly what God wants for my life—nothing more and nothing less," I replied. "Because I know that whatever He has planned for my life is much greater than anything I could ever imagine or conceive."

4

To Be Beautiful

I was sitting in a crowded restaurant with my family when she walked by in her full-length, white satin ball gown delicately trimmed in lace and studded with tiny "jewels." Crinoline swished as she moved across the room, a rhinestone tiara sparkled on her head, and pearl-studded slippers accentuated her feminine feet. Golden ringlets framed her rosy cheeks, and puckered lips glistened with a hint of gloss. She knew she was beautiful and glanced around at the admiring smiles of onlookers as she walked through the crowd. She was three years old.

I'm not sure when the dream to be beautiful enters a little girl's mind, but I do know when the dream ends—when the preacher says, "May she rest in peace." In my book *Becoming Spiritually Beautiful,* I told about my shenanigans as a little girl who wanted to be a grown-up beauty.

> I remember as a little girl sneaking into my mother's closet and slipping my child-size feet into her size seven high heels. I'd also stand on my tiptoes on a chair, pull a hat off the top shelf, and plop it on my head like an oversized lamp shade. Her satin evening jacket with sleeves that hug eight inches below my finger tips gave a nice elegant touch to my outfit. A lady going to a party would never be caught without "putting on her face," so I crept into the bathroom, opened the forbidden drawer, and created a clownish work

of art on the palette of my face. Red rouge circles on my cheeks, heaps of blue eye shadow on my munchkin lids, and smeared orange lipstick far exceeding the proper border were finished off with a dusting of facial powder with an oversized brush.

From the time a little girl stretches on her tiptoes to get a peek in the mirror, she desires to be beautiful—perhaps like her mommy. As the girl moves into the teen years, she experiments with makeup, delves into fashion, and attempts various hairstyles. Then it's on to makeover ideas in magazines and on talk shows. If one idea doesn't work— well, there's always next month.[1]

I believe the dream to be beautiful is not simply an American obsession, but something that lies at the very core of womanhood all around the world. *National Geographic* reported that on the border of Burma and Thailand, members of the Kayan tribe begin their beauty rituals at age five by wearing brass rings around their necks. As they grow older, more rings are added, and eventually their necks elongate to look like a giraffe's. For these women, the shiny brass rings are the ultimate sign of female elegance and status. Maori women in New Zealand consider it beautiful to tattoo their lips dark blue. Young girls in the Karo tribe in southern Ethiopia allow their elders to cut scars onto their stomachs, which they believe will make them more beautiful and able to attract a husband. In a West African country, Mauritania, they believe that bigger is better and have practiced the ritual of force-feeding young girls to plump them up. Interestingly, Dove posted on their Facebook page that only two percent of the women around the world describe themselves as beautiful.[2]

John Eldredge, in his book *Wild at Heart*, describes three longings that lie at the heart of every man: a battle to fight, a beauty to rescue, and an adventure to live. He also ventures to say that women have three longings of the heart as well: to be fought for, to share in an adventure, and to have her beauty unveiled.

Not to conjure, but to unveil. Most women feel the pressure to be beautiful from very young, but that is not what

I speak of. There is also a deep desire to simply and truly be the beauty and be delighted in. Most little girls will remember playing dress up, or wedding day, or "twirling skirts," those flowing dresses that were perfect for spinning around in. She'll put her pretty dress on, come into the living room, and twirl. What she longs for is to capture her daddy's delight.[3]

Created for Beauty

When I asked my three-year-old little friend, Brooke, what she wanted to be when she grew up, she tossed her head back, flipped her hair over her shoulder, and simply said, "Beautiful." We should never be ashamed of our dream to be beautiful. One travesty of the feminist movement is that it has tried to strip women of their femininity and make them more male. It is as if those in the movement were saying that being a woman wasn't good enough. They tried to make women into men by making them tough, independent, and rugged individuals who didn't need anyone or anything. But those who were banking on the tenets of feminism were left spiritually and emotionally bankrupt.

"I wanted to be beautiful, And when I was in school, that's all I ever thought about." Jean

A woman was and is one of God's most magnificent creations. As a matter of fact, she was the grand finale of God's creative genius and the inspiration for man's first poetry.

Bruce Marchiano paints a beautiful picture of God's intentional artistry in creating Eve:

> He shapes her frame and shades her skin. He molds her mind and measures her structure. He sculpts the contour of her face, the almonds of her eyes, and the graceful stretch of her limbs. Long before she even spoke a word, he has held her voice in his heart, and so he ever so gently tunes

its timber. Cell by cell, tenderness by tenderness, and with care beyond care, in creation he quite simply loves her."[4]

In the New Testament, Paul writes, "We are God's workmanship" (Ephesians 2:10). The Greek word for "workmanship" means "a work of art." Listen to these words as David describes the Creator at work:

> You created my inmost being; you knit me together in my mother's womb. I praise you because I am fearfully and wonderfully made; your works are wonderful, I know that full well. My frame was not hidden from you when I was made in the secret place. When I was woven together in the depths of the earth, your eyes saw my unformed body (Psalm 139:13-16).

Like an artist who sees the finished work in his mind's eye, God saw your unformed substance and then began to fashion you from head to toe. He made no mistakes but planned each detail of your being.

The Barbie Syndrome

Have you ever wondered what Eve looked like? I must admit, I've always pictured her looking a bit like Barbie. After all, isn't that what the artists always depict? Waist-length flowing tresses, hourglass figure, creamy smooth complexion, delicate feet begging for high heels... a perfect 10. Unfortunately, Barbie is the standard that much of our society has depicted as ideal beauty. That standard for beauty is being passed along to children, as it is estimated that a Barbie doll is being purchased for a young girl somewhere in the world every two seconds.[5] But is the Barbie image that realistic? If you blew Barbie up to life-sized proportions, her measurement would be 38-18-34, and she would be six feet tall.[6] The only blemish I can find is "made in Japan" stamped on the bottom of her otherwise perfect foot. Maybe I don't travel in the right circles, but I don't know anyone who fits that description. However, I do know many who try.

Americans spend more than 7 billion dollars a year on cosmetics.[7] Magazine racks bulge each month with periodicals promising dramatic makeovers for women of every shape, color, and size. They tell us how to thin thighs, firm flab, tuck tummies, build biceps, tighten tooshes, lengthen lashes, whiten teeth, and plump lips. We can learn the proper way to apply makeup, choose the best hairstyles to frame and flatter facial shapes, and determine what color wardrobe is best for our particular skin tone. Nearly 11.7 million cosmetic surgical and nonsurgical procedures were performed in the United States in 2007—that represents an increase of nearly 500 percent in the overall number of cosmetic procedures in the past ten years.[8] A recent study showed American women spent a half-billion dollars on shape-enhancing garments.[9]

"My princess dream started very young. Like most little
girls, I played dress-up, putting on long dresses and
high heels. My house was my castle, and I dreamed
of being rescued by a handsome prince who would
love me and take away all my hurts." Mary

In the U.S. and other modernized countries, obsession with outward appearance isn't limited to older women who have expendable income to fight the effects of aging and gravity. In the year 2000, American youths spent $155 billion on beauty products and trips to salons and spas—financed by willing parents.[10] In Mexico, nose jobs are the status gift for girls celebrating their *quinceañera*, the traditional coming-of-age fifteenth birthday party. In California, young girls are getting breast implants as high school graduation gifts.[11]

But when is all the manipulation enough? When are we ever satisfied? Today, more than ever before, women have unreal expectations placed on them by a society that glorifies youth and beauty. A few hundred years ago, women compared themselves to other women in their small villages. Today, women compare themselves to airbrushed models in magazines, on billboards, and on the silver screen. Most models admit they don't measure up to the pictures of themselves. Before a photo shoot, a model's hair is coiffed by a professional stylist, her face perfected by a professional makeup artist (they don't call them artists for nothing), and her image is captured under just the right lighting to make her eyes sparkle and lips glisten. Then, if she still isn't perfect, the photographer touches up the picture with digital manipulation to remove any flaws.

Another symptom that reveals how unsatisfied women are with their appearance is talk show hosts' most popular programs that feature makeovers. Viewers love to watch an artist transform a frumpy middle-aged housewife into a sophisticated cosmopolitan with just a few snips of the scissors, stroke of blush, and updated wardrobe. Silently we wonder, *Could they do that for me?*

"I dreamed about being a ballerina and twirling my way through theaters all over the world. I dreamed about living in the jungle with Tarzan. Looking back, these dreams appear quite the opposite, but actually they were quite similar. Both involved excitement and the physical rush of flying through the air and then falling into the arms of a handsome man. What could get any better!" Christie

---

I'm not saying I've never read a makeover article in a magazine or tried a few of its suggestions, but I do know this: No amount of skin cream, makeup, designer clothes, or exercise regimens will make a woman truly beautiful, for true beauty is an outward reflection of an inward glow.

Many men have married what they thought was a beautiful woman only to discover a contentious nagger when the honeymoon was over. King Solomon says, "A continual dripping on a very rainy day and a contentious woman are alike" (Proverbs 27:15). That outer beauty has a way of diminishing in importance when a woman's true self comes out. In *Beauty by the Book,* Nancy Stafford writes, "Beauty of form affects the mind, but then it must not be the mere shell that we admire, but the thought that this shell is only the beautiful case adjusted to the shape and value of a still more beautiful pearl within."[12]

I want to add something important here. I am not saying that a woman should ignore her appearance. When a wife doesn't care about how she looks, it is an affront to her husband and shows a lack of concern and respect for his feelings. In Willard Harley's book *His Needs, Her Needs,* he lists "To have an attractive spouse" as one of a man's five basic needs.[13] This does not mean he needs to have a beauty queen for a wife, but he does need a wife who takes care of her appearance, who doesn't let herself go, and whom he is proud to take out in public. I hear many women who ignored their appearance say, "But he should love me for who I am on the inside." He probably does. But would you put a diamond in a brown paper bag? No, you would put it in a velvet case! If we truly love our husbands, we will give them the gift of a wife he can be proud of. Don't be angry that your husband is a visual creature. God made him that way. It is most likely what drew him to you in the first place. Instead of resenting his God-given nature, seek to please him.

Many times I've spent all day writing in my workout clothes, my hair tied back in a ponytail and no makeup on. I'm sure I've scared the UPS man half to death by my ghastly appearance. However, at 4:30 I leave my office, put on something presentable, comb my hair, and apply a bit of makeup. Why would I do this so late in the day? Because I know that in a few moments one of my greatest gifts from God is going to walk through my door, and I want him to be glad he's home.

True Beauty

So where does real beauty come from? It comes from the heart. Rosalind Russell said, "Taking joy in life is a woman's best cosmetic." While joy in life is a *good* cosmetic, the peace that comes through a relationship with Jesus Christ is the *best*. As Thomas Watson wrote, "Oftentimes under silken apparel there is a threadbare soul."[14]

Peter wrote this about beauty:

> Let not yours be the [merely] external adorning with [elaborate] interweaving and knotting of the hair, the wearing of jewelry, or changes of clothes; but let it be the inward adorning and beauty of the hidden person of the heart,

with the incorruptible and unfading charm of a gentle and
peaceful spirit, which [is not anxious or wrought up, but]
is very precious in the sight of God (1 Peter 3:3-5 AMP).

I think the key word in the verses above is "merely"—which is
also used in the New American Standard Bible but omitted in the
New International Version. We can't depend on the outward appearance because what is on the inside will inevitably seep through. There's
nothing wrong with buying nice clothes, wearing jewelry, or applying
makeup, but we must not depend on those coverings to mask what
lies beneath. The Proverbs 31 woman wore purple and scarlet clothes,
which were very expensive in her day. She gave attention to her appearance, but what made her truly beautiful was her love for the Lord.

Doris Mortman said, "Until you make peace with who you are,
you'll never be content with what you have." [15] Until you understand
that you are God's workmanship, made in His image, a child of God
who resembles her Daddy, you'll never be content with the features He
has given you. Do you believe you are a happenstance mixture of your
parents' genes, or do you believe you were intentionally woven and knit-
ted together by God with a specific design in mind? What we believe
about our origin greatly affects what we believe about our destiny.

"I dreamed of being a model." Blair

And even though we become a new, righteous, and holy creation in
Christ the moment we believe, our souls become more beautiful each
time we spend time in God's presence. We become truly beautiful, not
by adding layers on the outside, but by removing layers on the inside.

Just as Moses' face glowed after spending forty days in God's presence, our faces will radiate the love of Christ when we spend time
with Him. King Solomon wrote, "Wisdom brightens a man's face and
changes its hard appearance" (Ecclesiastes 8:1).

Most women love the idea of spending a day at the spa and coming out a brand-new person. One of the best presents my husband ever

gave me was a day at the spa. My back was massaged, my hands were dipped in paraffin, my feet were kneaded, my nails were painted, my face was made up, and my hair was poofed. My makeover was on Friday, but by Monday the visit seemed like a distant memory. Dry flakes returned to my face, tension knots reappeared in my neck, red polish had chipped around my toes, and my white-tipped French manicure turned vibrant yellow after cleaning the bathroom without wearing gloves. My hair refused to submit to my commands, and I unwillingly exchanged the trendy new look for American housewife frump. Yes, a day at the spa can be fun, but there is only one beauty treatment that has lasting results.

You want to know the best beauty secret ever? You won't find it in a spa, at the cosmetic counter at the mall, or in a makeover article of a magazine. You will find it in the Word of God. We become more and more beautiful every time we sit at Jesus' feet. "We, who with unveiled faces all reflect the Lord's glory are being transformed into his likeness with ever-increasing glory, which comes from the Lord, who is the Spirit" (2 Corinthians 3:18) As my country grandmother used to say, we just keep gettin' purdier and purdier the more time we spend with Him.

A Princess Defiled

Let's visit Cinderella once again. She went from being held captive as a servant to being a captivating belle of the ball, from being covered with ashes to being crowned with jewels, from being abused by her wicked stepfamily to being adored by her entire village. We all love "And they lived happily ever after" endings.

In 2 Samuel 13, there is a story that somewhat reminds me of Cinderella's, but with two major differences: It is no fairy tale and the events occur in reverse. It is the story of Tamar, the lovely princess daughter of King David.

Tamar was one of the most beautiful young ladies in the entire kingdom. Her name meant "palm tree," a symbol of victory and honor. She had several siblings: sisters, brothers, half brothers, and half sisters. It was a royal blended mess.

"I wanted to be a teacher so I could wear pretty
dresses. I haven't gotten a degree or the chance to wear
pretty dresses or stand behind a podium." Tansy

One of her half brothers, Amnon, lusted after the beautiful Tamar to the point he couldn't sleep at night. At the advice of a wicked friend, Amnon plotted to lure Tamar into his bedroom with the help of their unsuspecting father. Amnon pretended to be sick and requested some of Tamar's special baked bread. He also requested that she feed it to him with her own hands. Tamar obeyed her father's request to tend to her brother. After she entered his bedroom, the supposedly sick Amnon commanded the servants to leave the room and lock the door behind them. Then he grabbed Tamar, threw her on his bed, and even though she begged and pleaded for him to stop, he stole her most treasured possession, her virginity. After he had his way with her and his lust was satisfied, Amnon tossed Tamar on the floor along with her hopes and dreams.

The distraught, devastated, and demeaned Tamar ran from Amnon's room crying out in anguish and despair. She tore her royal robes and ran the halls searching for her beloved brother, Absalom. When Absalom came to her rescue, he surmised what had happened and bid her to come to his house to live. "Shhhhh," he whispered, "don't worry; I'll take care of you. Now don't tell anyone what happened, just leave it up to me."

And even though Tamar was still a royal princess, she spent the rest of her days secluded in a darkened room, wearing sackcloth as if in mourning and placing ashes on her head in shame. Never again did she wear the royal robe that was rightfully hers or live as the princess she truly was. She lived the rest of her life believing she could never be restored.

This is not just the story of Tamar, but the story of many women I meet every day—hiding because of shame and feeling ugly and unworthy to accomplish God's dreams. Paul reminds us that when we come to Christ, He makes us a new creation (2 Corinthians 5:17) but many conceal or cover up that beauty with shame from past mistakes or abuse. It is as if they rise each morning and put a fresh dusting of ashes on their souls, the very ashes that Jesus came to wash away. And, dear sister, it is Satan who keeps the supply of ashes coming, and Satan who holds the box of ashes in his hand with the lid open ready for us to use.

Oh, we may not be walking around with ashes on our heads or dressed in burlap sacks, but we wear the mantle of shame that Satan has placed on our shoulders and secures with guilt-ridden deception and lies. I meet many women who have children, a husband, a successful career, and appear beautiful on the outside, but who are spending their days in desolation of the soul because Satan has convinced them that's where they belong. Wearing the cloak of shame because of past abuse, misuse, or mistakes, they don't realize that Jesus Christ has washed them clean, purchased a robe of righteousness made just for them, and is eager to place it on their shoulders.

Please don't let Satan deceive you into believing that you are anything less than a beautiful princess. Do not allow him to convince you your dignity cannot be restored. The truth is, it already has been. We simply need to start believing the truth.

The prophet Isaiah spoke of Jesus in these verses:

> He has sent me to bind up the brokenhearted, to proclaim freedom for the captives and release from darkness for the prisoners...to comfort all who mourn, and provide for those who grieve in Zion—to bestow on them a crown of beauty instead of ashes, the oil of gladness instead of mourning, and a garment of praise instead of a spirit of despair (Isaiah 61:1-3).

Jesus has the glass slipper in His hand. He's waiting for the princess to offer her foot—your foot. Don't let Satan tell you it doesn't fit. The One who made your foot has already decreed that it does.

The Beautiful Beloved

In the Song of Solomon, we meet a king who is riding though his kingdom and spies a young maiden working in the fields. He is captivated by her beauty and smitten by her form. Her hands are stained with grape juice from the vineyard, her skin is tanned from the midday sun, and her clothes are soiled from the dirt of the field, but the king sees beyond all that. While the king is enthralled with her beauty, she begs him not to stare at her. She does not feel worthy of such attention.

"I was the beautiful princess in my family but the other siblings came along and I had to share my crown." Christie

---

No matter what she thought of herself, the king was mesmerized and wooed her to become his bride. For centuries, commentators have noted a parallel between the Lover and the Beloved to Jesus and His bride. "The Shulammite maiden in the Song of Solomon represents you, and it will thrill your soul as you discover just how much Jesus loves you. You are His Bride, His Beloved. The same purity, faithfulness, and abandonment that Solomon, the earthy bridegroom desired for the Shulammite maiden, Jesus desires from you."[16] You may blush a bit, but listen to a few of the passionate pursuer's words about the woman of his dreams. Soak in his description of her beauty.

> Your cheeks are beautiful with earrings, your neck with strings of jewels (1:10).
>
> How beautiful you are, my darling! Oh, how beautiful! Your eyes are doves (1:15).
>
> Like a lily among thorns is my darling among the maidens (2:2).
>
> Your hair is like a flock of goats descending from Mount Gilead (4:1).
>
> Your teeth are like a flock of sheep just shorn, coming up from the washing. Each has its twin; not one of them is alone (4:2).
>
> Your lips are like a scarlet ribbon; your mouth is lovely. Your

temples behind your veil are like the halves of a pomegranate (4:3).

Your neck is like the tower of David, built with elegance (4:4).

Your two breasts are like two fawns, like twin fawns of a gazelle that browse among the lilies (4:5).

Your lips drop sweetness as the honeycomb, my bride; milk and honey are under your tongue (4:11).

How beautiful your sandaled feet (7:1).

Your graceful legs are like jewels, the work of a craftsman's hands (7:1).

Your waist is a mound of wheat encircled by lilies (7:2). [This is my favorite verse. A mound of wheat, mind you, not a flat plain!]

All beautiful you are, my darling; there is no flaw in you (4:7).

This woman's betrothed adored her rosy cheeks, her long neck, her flowing hair, and her ruby lips. He adored the fact that she had all of her teeth and shapely legs and small breasts. He even thought her *poochy* tummy was adorable.

But what did she think of herself? Not very much. "Do not stare at me because I am dark, because I am darkened by the sun. My mother's sons were angry with me and made me take care of the vineyards; my own vineyard I have neglected" (1:6).

"Did I dream of becoming a beautiful princess?
Well, I am a girl, Aren't I?" Vickey

She felt inferior to others because she was darkened by the sun. To be tanned in those days was not desirable. Women went to great lengths to shade their skin from the scorching sun. This woman, however, was very dark. Because she was forced to take care of her brothers' vineyards, she had neglected to take care of herself. But amazingly, in the end, she began to see herself as her bridegroom saw her. Oh, that we would do the same.

Is the Song of Solomon our song? I think so. Jesus, the lover of our soul, looks at us and thinks we are absolutely beautiful. However, we tend to look in the mirror and see our flaws. I read a quote once that said when a man looks in the mirror, he focuses on his best features. When a woman looks in the mirror, she focuses on her worst. I don't know how men see themselves, but I do know that most women focus on their negative features instead of their positive ones. We need to look into the only mirror that matters, the Word of God, and we will discover there that God thinks we are beautiful. I keep a card in my Bible with the following prayer: "Lord, help me see myself as You see me, no matter how beautiful it is."

"I dreamed I'd be beautiful, confident, and loved." Denise

Both the Shulammite maiden and Cinderella had difficulty seeing their beauty. Cinderella mistakenly believed her beauty was dependent on her dress and perfectly arranged hair. The Shulammite maiden mistakenly believed her beauty was dependent on fair skin and a tidy appearance. But in both scenarios, the prince knew differently. Jesus sees our true beauty and is captivated.

I can promise you this...nothing can convince a woman of her beauty more than being admired by her husband. While that may not be the case every day in our lives, we can be assured that as the bride of Christ, He sees us as altogether lovely.

Jesus desires to hear our voice and see our face. Both are His delight. "My dove in the clefts of the rock, in the hiding places on the mountainside, show me your face, let me hear your voice; for your voice is sweet, and your face is lovely" (Song of Solomon 2:14).

"The fruit of our love affair is our beauty; it is not something we can manufacture, manipulate, or control. Beauty springs entirely from the One who lavishes jewels and finery within our hearts. He sees our clamoring, hears our rage, knows our fear, and yet He runs to lift the veil from our face with His bloodstained hands. We are beautiful to Him."[17]

"I dreamed about being Miss America. I wouldn't ever miss this annual tribute, and after the newest lovely was crowned, I remember wrapping a towel around my head (they all had long hair, it seemed) and letting it trail down my back as I grabbed a hairbrush microphone and practiced introducing myself to the world. I loved it all: the hair, the dresses, the talent (I was sure this would be my downfall as I seemed truly devoid of possibilities here), the dance numbers, the drama, and the dreamy walk with the crown of diamonds. Ahhhh." Vickey

---

Mona Lisa

One summer I traveled to Paris and visited the Louvre. At the end of a long corridor lined with famous paintings, a crowd gathered to capture a glimpse of the famous *Mona Lisa*. I jostled for position to catch a glimpse and was disappointed at what I saw. Honestly, to me she looked rather plain. What was the draw? I didn't understand until I heard the tour guide explain her history.

No one is really sure of Mona Lisa's true identity, but many think her to be Francesco di Bartolommeo di Zanobi del Giocondo's third wife, Lisa di Antonio Maria di Naldo Gherardini. (Try saying that three times real fast. No wonder most just say, "We don't know who it is!") She was painted by Leonardo da Vinci between 1503 and 1507. The painting moved from King Francis I's castle, to Fontainbleau, to Paris, to Versailles, to Napoleon's estate, and ended up in the Louvre. However, on August 21, 1911, the *Mona Lisa* was stolen by an Italian thief. During that time, the Parisians placed another painting in her spot, but the citizens missed her terribly. Two years later, she emerged in Florence and was returned to Paris, where she remains in the Louvre behind bullet-proof glass.

"I never dreamed about being beautiful because I had too many brothers who assured me I wasn't." Carmen

---

Why is she loved today? Because once she was lost, but now she is found. She was stolen from her place of honor, but someone found her, paid the price for her, and placed her back in her rightful place. No wonder she's smiling.

So it is with us, dear friends. Once we were lost, but now we've been found, and as we have already established, we have been placed in our rightful place as children of the King. That makes you a princess. We're not in a museum, but our rightful position is in the King's eternal home.

David wrote, "The king is enthralled by your beauty" (Psalm 45:11). That means He is captivated, fascinated, enraptured, smitten, spellbound, and taken with you. You are beautiful.

5

To Have a Best Friend

Anne tipped the vase of apple blossoms near enough to bestow a soft kiss on a pink-cupped bud, and then studied it diligently for some moments longer.

"Marilla," she demanded presently, "do you think that I shall ever have a bosom friend in Avonlea?"

"A—a what kind of friend?"

"A bosom friend—an intimate friend, you know—a really kindred spirit to whom I can confide my inmost soul. I've dreamed of meeting her all my life. I never really supposed I would, but so many of my loveliest dreams have come true all at once that perhaps this one will, too. Do you think it's possible?"

"Diana Barry lives over at the Orchard Slope and she's about your age. She's a very nice little girl, and perhaps she will be a playmate for you when she comes home. She's visiting her aunt over at Carmody just now. You'll have to be careful how you behave yourself, though. Mrs. Barry is a very particular woman. She won't let Diana play with any little girl who isn't nice and good."

Anne looked at Marilla through the apple blossoms, her eyes aglow with interest.

"What is Diana like? Her hair isn't red, is it? Oh, I hope not. It's bad enough to have red hair myself, but I positively couldn't endure it in a bosom friend."

"Diana is a very pretty little girl. She has black eyes and hair and rosy cheeks. And she is good and smart, which is better than being pretty."

"Oh, I'm so glad she's pretty. Next to being beautiful oneself—and that's impossible in my case—it would be best to have a beautiful bosom friend. When I lived with Mrs. Thomas she had a bookcase in her sitting room with glass doors. There weren't any books in it. Mrs. Thomas kept her best china and her preserves there—when she had any preserves to keep. One of the doors was broken. Mr. Thomas smashed it one night when he was slightly intoxicated. But the other was whole and I used to pretend that my reflection in it was another little girl who lived in it. I called her Katie Maurice, and we were very intimate. I used to talk to her by the hour, especially on Sunday, and tell her everything. Katie was the comfort and consolation of my life. We used to pretend that the bookcase was enchanted, and that if I only knew the spell I could open the door and step right into the room where Katie Maurice lived, instead of into Mrs. Thomas's shelves of preserves and china. And then Katie Maurice would have taken me by the hand and led me out into a wonderful place, all flowers and sunshine and fairies, and we would have lived there happy forever after.

"When I went to live with Mrs. Hammond it just broke my heart to leave Katie Maurice. She felt it dreadfully, too. I know she did, for she was crying when she kissed me good-bye through the bookcase door."[1]

Anne of Green Gables is one of my favorite childhood stories. In the above scene, Anne shares her dream of having a lifelong bosom friend and echoes the hopes and dreams of most little girls—to have a best friend. Someone who understands your past, believes in your future, and accepts you just the way you are, warts and all.

When I was a little girl, I had the dream to have a bosom buddy or best friend. In the first grade my best friend was Kim. In the second, third, and fourth it was Pam. In the fifth it was another Kim. And in the sixth grade it varied from week to week as competition and coyness crept in to create havoc on the friendships of budding young adolescents.

Then there was Liz. From the seventh grade until the day we both walked across the stage to receive our high school diplomas, we were "bosom friends." But sometimes the flow of life has a strange way of causing friends to drift apart. Liz and I went away to different colleges and found our own separate circle of friends that did not include each other. Life choices, future goals, and personal passions grew in different directions like divergent streams, and a friendship that once flooded the banks evaporated to a mere trickle.

Even though I am now a grown woman and have been married for more than 30 years, I still love the idea of having a best girlfriend. I believe it is a longing that never dies.

"I had best friends growing up. Sometimes I think about that now. I am very family oriented and my parents, sister, and brother-in-law live thousands of miles away. My husband is very busy, And sometimes I long for a best friend to listen to all the daily things I want to express. I do talk to my husband, and I call my family quite a bit, but sometimes you just want empathy from someone in the same situation." Rachel

---

Little Girls' Friendships Are Different from Little Boys'

I have an adult son, and it was interesting to watch how boys' relationships and girls' relationships differed during his growing-up years. Little girls are more likely to be drawn to one or two best friends, and boys tend to be a part of a team or group. Little girls huddle to tell secrets, and giggle and chat about this or that, while boys huddle in dugouts and sidelines participating in group activities or team sports that usually involve some sort of ball.

Sociologist Janet Lever notes the differences between the relationships between girls and boys:

> There is usually an open show of affection between little girls, both physically in the form of hand-holding and verbally through "love-notes" that reaffirm how special each is to the other. Although boys are likely to have best friends as

well, their friendships tend to be less intimate and expressive than girls. Hand-holding and love-notes are virtually unknown among boys, and the confidences that boys share are more likely to be "group secrets" than expressions of private thoughts and feelings.[2]

In second grade, our principal (a woman) visited our classroom to have a heart-to-heart with the girls. "You need to stop walking down the hall with your arms around each other. Think how silly it would look if Mrs. Macon and I walked down the hall hand in hand or with our arms on each other's shoulders." At that point she and Mrs. Macon put their arms over each other's shoulders. We snickered. They did indeed look silly. But we were little girls, not old ladies (which is how we viewed the two). How sad I felt for them not to have a best friend the way I did.

Big Girls' Friendships Are Different from Big Boys'

Elliot Engel observed this female phenomenon in the relationships his wife had with other women. When he watched his wife and her best friend say goodbye before a cross-country move, he found that their last hugs were too painful to witness. He had to turn away and leave the room. He said: "I've always been amazed at the nurturing emotional support that my wife can seek and return with her close female friends…Her three-hour talks with friends refresh and renew her far more than my three-mile jogs restore me. In our society it seems as if you've got to have a bosom to be a buddy."[3]

Just as a woman's body was crafted to bear children, our hearts were crafted to "bear" friends. This is even evident in the cradle as studies show that girl babies are more likely than boy babies to cry (as if in sympathy) when they hear other babies crying.[4]

For most women, talking with friends is more than a pastime; it is essential to our well-being and a major way to connect on an intimate level. In fact, research has shown that women who enjoy close friendships are more likely to live longer and have fewer incidents of depression.[5]

Another interesting study showed the following:

> Friendships between women are special. They shape who
> we are and who we are yet to be. They soothe our tumul-
> tuous inner world, fill the emotional gaps in our marriage,
> and help us remember who we really are. But they may do
> even more. Scientists now suspect that hanging out with
> our friends can actually counteract the kind of stomach-
> quivering stress most of us experience on a daily basis.[6]

"When I was little, I always had a best friend. As
we got older, my best friend and I went separate
ways and lost contact. There are times now I
dream of having a best friend again." Tammy

And this:

> Until this study was published, scientists generally believed
> that when people experience stress, they trigger a hor-
> monal cascade that revs the body to either stand and fight
> or flee as fast as possible (a man's response)...It seems that
> when the hormone oxytocin is released as part of the stress
> response in a woman, it buffers the fight or flight response
> and encourages her to tend children and gather with other
> women instead. When she actually engages in this tend-
> ing or befriending, studies suggest that more oxytocin
> is released, which rather counters stress and produces a
> calming effect...In fact, the results were so significant, the
> researchers concluded, that not having a close friend or
> confidante was as detrimental to your health as smoking
> or carrying extra weight.[7]

I just knew those Frappuccinos with my girlfriends were good for
me!

After a draining week of ministry, I am refreshed by two hours of
conversation with a girlfriend at a coffee shop. On the other hand, after

a hard week at work, my husband is refreshed by four hours of golf and swing analysis with a foursome on the greens. When he comes home I always ask, "What did you guys talk about?" He looks at me with a strange expression and replies, "We talked about our game." You'd think I'd stop asking after a while.

Big Girls Need Friends Too

At almost every retreat or conference I speak at, a woman shares with me her hidden pain of not being able to develop deep endearing friendships. "I have been at this church for three years," Nancy shared. "I see women all around me who have best friends. I've tried everything I know—inviting others to lunch, offering my house as the place for Sunday school socials, and sending people cards from time to time—but it just seems like the women in the church already have established friendships and there's no room for me."

"I have dreamed of having a best friend of my very own my whole life. I dreamed we would grow old together after sharing our lives. Our kids would grow up together, and we'd live close by." Colette

---

Cammie dropped out of her Bible study after two years. "I've tried to be their friend, but not one of them has called me to go to lunch or included me in their weekend activities. I hear them talk about fun times involving shopping or going to the movies, and I feel so left out."

Wherever I go, women echo Nancy's and Cammie's heart cries. We long to be in relationship with one another. We thirst for a friend who knows what we need without even asking, who picks us up when we are down, who doesn't criticize our husband or children but encourages us to love them well, who is eager to hear our dreams for the future and is willing to help us make those dreams come true. We hunger for someone who doesn't ask how she can help but immediately begins to pitch in when our load grows too heavy. We yearn for a friend with whom we can be completely honest without the fear of rejection or ridicule, with whom we can share our victories and successes without the fear of jealousy or competition, and with whom we can confide our personal and spiritual struggles without fear of judgment or chastisement. We dream of a friend who is on our team, cheering us on as we run the great race of life and encouraging us to get up when we fall. We desire someone who will listen to our problems liberally and offer advice sparingly when asked, who dreams with and for us and then helps us accomplish those dreams, who looks for gifts God has given us and helps us unwrap and develop those gifts.

In my years of working with women, I have enjoyed witnessing clusters of friends. On one particular day, I had lunch with three dear women almost 20 years my senior who share a precious bond. I just sat back and observed as they reminisced, laughed, and chatted about first one thing and then another. It was just plain fun to watch.

I was with them, but I was not one of them. Oh, they love me dearly, but the three of them shared a special connection that was woven from many years of struggle, sadness, and sorrow; loss, laughter, and lunches; shopping, phone conversations, and prayer. It was a privilege and an honor to sip from the deep well they shared.

In 2002 clusters of women gathered in darkened cinemas with popcorn, soft drinks, and hopeful hearts to watch *Divine Secrets of the Ya-Ya Sisterhood*. I was among such a group. It is the story of four little girls who made a pact to be lifelong friends. We were allowed to follow their passing years and observe how that bond carried them through the difficulties of growing up, how they were *stretcher-bearers* during trying times, and how they loved and laughed through it all. But the reality is, lifelong friends like the four women in the *Ya-Ya Sisterhood* are very rare. To find *one* such friend is a treasure indeed!

Friendship Is God's Design

I believe God understands a woman's desire to have a bosom friend. He created us to be in relationship. In Luke 1, the angel Gabriel delivered some pretty incredible news to young Mary. While still a virgin, she was told that she was going to conceive a child by the Holy Spirit and give birth to the Savior of the world. Before Mary could catch her breath, the angel continued by telling her, "Even Elizabeth your relative is going to have a child in her old age, and she who was said to be barren is in her sixth month" (Luke 1:36). God knew the young girl was going to need the encouragement of a friend who would understand, and before she could even ask, He sent her to Elizabeth.

So Mary, probably around 16 years old, traveled a hundred miles from Galilee to Judea to spend three months with her friend. When Mary walked into Elizabeth's home, the older woman gave her a blessing. "Blessed are you among women, and blessed is the child you will bear! But why am I so favored, that the mother of my Lord should come to me? As soon as the sound of your greeting reached my ears, the baby in my womb leaped for joy. Blessed is she who has believed that what the Lord has said to her will be accomplished!" (Luke 1:42-45).

Can you imagine the turmoil Mary must have felt as she traveled to Judea? *No one is ever going to believe me,* she must have thought. *Joseph is going to put me away. And what will my parents think? I could be stoned for this.*

Can you imagine how Elizabeth's words of encouragement were a balm to the young girl's heart? God divinely revealed His plan to Elizabeth, and she in turn affirmed Mary before she even revealed her news. What a precious Lord we serve!

Jesus and His Friends

Jesus Himself had best friends. Think of graduated concentric circles like an archery target. His first and largest realm of influence was to the multitudes. Next, He gave special attention to 72 men whom He sent out to heal and cast out demons (Luke 10:1-16). Smaller still, Jesus gathered 12 men to be His good friends whom He closely discipled (Matthew 10:1-4). But then He chose an even smaller group of three to be His best friends: Peter, James, and John. These three men were privy to Jesus' transfiguration (Mark 9:2), His deep sorrow in the garden of Gethsemane (Mark 14:32-34), and the first at the empty tomb (John 20:3). But then there was a "place of deeper still"—the bull's-eye of friendship, if you will, that Jesus shared with no man. It was a place reserved for God alone.

Before His arrest, Jesus took Peter, James, and John with Him to Gethsemane to pray. However, He left the three and went a "little farther" (Mark 14:35) to be alone with His Father. It was a place where no man could join Him, no man could calm Him, and no man could comfort Him. He had to go alone.

"When I was young, I dreamed of having wonderful friends who would do special things for me like the popular kids at school." Donna

---

In *The Friendships of Women*, Dee Brestin says, "like gently moving streams joining into one river, we round the difficult bends of life together, strengthening each other with a fresh water supply. We are free and flowing and unconcerned with boundaries...We are afraid to run toward the ocean alone. We feel a sense of panic in solitude."[8] What a beautiful picture of the refreshing, refueling, and renewing power of friendship. However, our friends were never intended to meet our greatest need to be in relationship. No woman or man can fill all our emotional needs. If we look to one friend for everything, or even a few, we'll be doomed to disappointment. There is an empty place inside us that only Jesus can fill.

I have found that when I feel empty and try to grasp desperately at friends to fill the void, I come up emptier than before. At those low points, friendships seem to elude me. The more frantically I grasp, the more elusive true friendships become. However, if I go to Jesus and spend time in His presence, He fills me up! I move from depleted to replenished, defeated to reenergized, devastated to restored, and debilitated to rejuvenated. Rather than being a taker who sucks the very life from her relationships, I become a giver who pours into the lives of others. Then I find friendships are plentiful.

When God calls us to "come a little farther," to be completely alone with Him, but we go to friends instead, we will be sorely disappointed. People are a poor substitute for God.

So let's take a moment and look at the best friend a girl could ever have—Jesus Christ.

Jesus—Our Bosom Friend

One of the most intimate times Jesus spent with His 12 best friends occurred in the upper room the night before His arrest. He assured them, "Greater love has no one than this, that he lay down his life for his *friends*. You are my friends if you do what I command. I no longer call you servants, because a servant does not know his master's business. Instead, I have called you *friends*, for everything that I learned from my Father I have made known to you" (John 15:13-15, emphasis added).

No matter how close we may feel to our earthly friends, they will inevitably disappoint us. Human beings were never intended to fill the God-shaped void in our lives. Yes, we may have a bosom friend, as Anne of Green Gables described, but there is a place in our bosom that's meant for Jesus Christ alone. He is the friend of our dreams.

In the Old Testament, the mother in Proverbs 31:10-31 used an acrostic from the Hebrew alphabet to help her son remember what to look for in a wife who is worth more than rubies. Let's follow that example and see how Jesus is truly our best friend—from A to Z.

> Jesus *accepts* us just as we are. I'm always encouraged that He didn't tell the ones He called to change first and then follow Him. No, He told them to follow Him and knew they would change along the way as they stayed close to Him (Romans 15:7).
>
> He *believes* in us and encourages us to do even greater things than He did while He was on earth (John 14:12). He even appoints us to be His ambassadors or representatives here on earth (2 Corinthians 5:20).
>
> He *counsels* us when we have difficult decisions to make (Isaiah 9:6).

He *defends* us in spiritual warfare to make us more than conquerors (Romans 8:37).

He *encourages* us to walk in faith. "You give them something to eat," He encouraged the disciples as they looked on the hungry crowd of 5000 men plus women and children (Luke 9:13-14). "Go," He commanded His 12 disciples as He sent them out with authority to drive out evil spirits and heal every disease and sickness (Matthew 10:1).

He *forgives* us when we fail, just as He forgave Peter, who denied he even knew Him the night of His arrest (Matthew 26:69-75).

He *gave* His life for us. "Greater love has no one than this, that he lay down his life for his friends" (John 15:13).

He *helps* us when we call on Him. "The Lord is my helper; I will not be afraid. What can man do to me?" (Hebrews 13:6).

He *intercedes* for us, praying for us constantly (Romans 8:34).

He *jumps for joy* when we have victory in our lives. When the 72 disciples came back home telling how they cast out demons and healed the sick in His name, Jesus was *full of joy* (Luke 10:21). That Greek word for *joy* means "leap for joy or to show one's joy by leaping and skipping, excessive or ecstatic joy and delight."[9] It's not a picture depicted often of Jesus, but I dare say He jumps for joy over our triumphs!

He *keeps* us as His own and no one can snatch us out of His hand (John 10:28).

He *listens* to us. Even while dying on the cross, He took the time to listen to the thief being crucified with Him and offer him the promise of eternal life (Luke 23:43).

He *mediates* between God and man, bridging the gap between us forever. "There is one God and one mediator between God and men, the man Christ Jesus, who gave himself as a ransom for all men—the testimony given in its proper time" (1 Timothy 2:5-6).

He *nudges* us to step out in faith (Matthew 14:28-29).

He *opens* doors for our provision and closes doors for our protection (Revelation 3:7).

"I prayed and dreamed for a best friend to share with and grow in Christ with. I used to think God answered that prayer when He gave me the gift of my husband, but in recent years, I've realized that He answered that prayer when He gave me Jesus." Katie

---

He *promises* to never leave us nor forsake us (Hebrews 13:5).

He *quiets* our fears (John 14:27).

He *restores* our souls (John 4:10).

He *shepherds* us by prodding us with His staff when we are moving too slowly and pulling us back with the shepherd's crook when we start to stray (John 10:11).

He *tends* our wounds and broken hearts (Isaiah 61:1).

He *understands* our weakness because He was tempted in every way, just as we are, and lived in the confines of a human body (Hebrews 4:15).

He *varies not.* He never changes. He's the same yesterday and today and tomorrow (Hebrews 13:8).

He *warns* us when we are headed in the wrong direction (Luke 22:31-32).

He *eXchanges* our weakness for His strength, our weariness for His power, our sorrow for His joy, our darkness for His light, our burdens for His freedom, our sinfulness for His righteousness, our calamity for His calm, our confusion for

His clarity, our fear for His faith, our impossible situation for His possible solutions, our pain for His purpose, and our hurt for His hope (2 Corinthians 12:7-10).

He *yokes* us together and carries our burdens (Matthew 11:28-30).

He *zooms* in on us as if we were the only one in His sight (Luke 19:1-6).

What a friend we have in Jesus!

I don't know about you, but I'm absolutely crazy in love with Jesus, my best friend. I *do* know this about you; He's crazy in love with you!

"I dreamed about having a best friend who would be a loving, unconditional person that would lend me their ear at any given moment, hold me when I hurt, laugh with me when I am happy, and sit with me when words aren't necessary. I want to give that back in return." Annie

---

Anne Finds Her Bosom Friend

"Oh, Diana," said Anne at last, clasping her hands and speaking almost in a whisper, "do you think—oh, do you think you can like me a little—enough to be my bosom friend?"

Diana laughed. Diana always laughed before she spoke.

"Why, I guess so," she said frankly. "I'm awfully glad you've come to live at Green Gables. It will be jolly to have somebody to play with. There isn't any other girl who lives near enough to play with, and I've no sisters big enough."

"Will you swear to be my friend forever and ever?" demanded Anne eagerly.

Diana looked shocked.

"Why, it's dreadfully wicked to swear," she said rebukingly.

"Oh no, not my kind of swearing. There are two kinds, you know."

"I never heard of but one kind," said Diana doubtfully.

"There really is another. Oh, it isn't wicked at all. It just means vowing and promising solemnly."

"Well, I don't mind doing that," agreed Diana, relieved. "How do you do it?"

"We must join hands—so," said Anne gravely. "It ought to be over running water. We'll just imagine this path is running water. I'll repeat the oath first. I solemnly swear to be faithful to my bosom friend, Diana Barry, as long as the sun and moon shall endure. Now you say it and put my name in."

Diana repeated the "oath" with a laugh fore and aft. Then she said: "You're a queer girl, Anne. I heard before that you were queer. But I believe I'm going to like you real well."[10]

"Someone to call who will call me or I can call at
the drop of a hat. Someone with whom I can be
myself, who will love me and never stop being my
best friend. That's what I dream about." Helen

Women in the Bible
and Their Dreams

Sarah

A Woman Who Interfered with God's Dreams

S arai reclined on her scarlet-and-purple-tapestry-covered sofa and scanned the room, admiring her beautifully decorated surroundings. *Yes,* she thought to herself, *I have everything a woman ever dreamed of. I have a husband who adores me, which is more than most Hebrew women, who are treated like chattel, can boast. We have great wealth, even if some of our inheritance did come from my father-in-law's idol-making business. We have a beautiful cedar-and-stone home with servants to care for our every need. And, if I am to believe the accolades of the men and women in our village, I have beauty that seems to defy my years. Yes, I have everything a woman could want.*

Just then, Sarai heard a baby's cry carried on the wind and winging like an arrow to her heart. Suddenly, as quickly as an approaching storm cloud on a clear summer day, a longing deep within her soul overshadowed Sarai's sunny musings. There was one thing she did not have, one thing she would gladly give all her worldly possessions to obtain. She wanted to be a mother, to suckle a babe at her breast, and give her husband an heir.

Sarai was startled from her painful pondering by her husband, Abram, bursting through the front door.

"Sarai, I have some news."

"What is it, Abram, that you startle me so!" she said.

"God spoke to me today. He told me that we are to leave this place and go to a place He will show us."

"That's it?" she asked. "Just pick up and go? I'll tell you where later?"

"That's it. Just go," he answered. "Well, there was one more little detail. God said He would make of me a great nation."

The darkness returned. The word "barren" settled heavily on her heart. "How long will we be gone? Who will take care of your father? What will we do with all of our furniture? I am 65 and you are 75. It's time to start thinking about slowing down, not moving on to a new place and starting over! What are you thinking?"

"I don't know the answer to any of those questions. I only know what God said," Abram responded.

"What did God say—exactly?"

"He said, 'Leave your country, your people and your father's household and go to the land I will show you. I will make you into a great nation and I will bless you; I will make your name great, and you will be a blessing. I will bless those who bless you, and whoever curses you I will curse; and all peoples on earth will be blessed through you.' That is what He said."

So Sarai got up from her seat and began to pack. She could argue with Abram, but she knew better than to argue with God.

The couple bade farewell to their family and friends and began a journey to only God knew where. After Abram and Sarai settled down in their goatskin tent in the land of Canaan, God spoke to Abram again. "Look up at the heavens and count the stars—if indeed you can count them. So shall your offspring be" (Genesis 15:5).

This was the second of seven times God would speak to Abram. Each time, he "believed the LORD, and [God] credited it to him as righteousness" (Genesis 15:6). Sarai, on the other hand, grew tired of waiting on God and decided to take matters into her own hands.

On their wedding day, Sarai had promised Abram a son to carry on the family name. It was customary in those days, if a wife proved to be barren, that she would offer her maidservant to her husband to serve as a surrogate mother. So Sarai made Abram the offer. "The LORD has kept me from having children. Go, sleep with my maidservant; perhaps I can build a family through her" (Genesis 16:2).

"But God specifically said—" Abram argued.

"I know what God said," she interrupted, "but I'm 75 years old, for goodness' sake."

Abram believed God, but he was swayed by his beautiful wife. He gave the same answer to Sarai that Adam gave to Eve when she offered him the forbidden fruit—"Yes, dear."

Sarai's maid, Hagar, quickly conceived and began to act arrogantly toward her barren mistress. Sarai's interference had created a monster in Hagar (as our interference often does). Abram was taken aback when Sarai stormed into the tent in a huff.

"This is all your fault. I put my servant in your arms, and now that she knows she is pregnant, she despises me."

At a loss for words, Abram said, "Do whatever you think best." As she stomped away, he murmured, "You always do anyway."

Sarai began mistreating Hagar so severely that the servant girl ran away into the desert. But the Lord appeared to Hagar and encouraged her to go back to her mistress and submit to her. He also gave Hagar a promise regarding her son. "You shall name him Ishmael, for the LORD has heard of your misery. He will be a wild donkey of a man; his hand will be against everyone and everyone's hand against him, and he will live in hostility toward his brothers" (Genesis 16:11-12).

Hagar did return, and a few months later she gave the 86-year-old Abram a son. They named him Ishmael, just as God commanded.

Thirteen years later, God came to Abram again and reminded him of His promise to make of him a great nation through his wife, Sarai. This time Abram fell facedown and laughed (Genesis 17:17). He was 99 and Sarai was 89, and I think I might have laughed too.

Nevertheless, God reinforced His promise by establishing a covenant and changing Abram's name to Abraham, which means "father of many nations" or "father of a multitude." He also changed Sarai's name to Sarah, which means "princess and mother of many" or "one whose seed would produce kings."[1]

When the Lord appeared to Abraham a few months later, Sarah

overhead Him telling Abraham that Sarah would birth a child about that same time next year. This time, Sarah burst out laughing. The Lord confronted her, "Why did you laugh?"

"I did not laugh," she lied.

"Did too," He said.

"Did not," she lied.

Then the Lord asked, "Is anything too hard for the LORD?" (Genesis 18:14).

Sarah laughed at the news of her coming motherhood, but the joke was on her. One year later she gave birth to a bouncing baby boy and named him Isaac, which means "laughter." It was through this baby that God made Abraham a great nation, with more descendants than the stars in the sky. I'm laughing just thinking about the surprise!

And what of Ishmael? Ishmael was about 14 when Isaac was born, and he wasn't too happy with the competition for his father's affection. He mocked Sarah's son, and eventually she sent Abraham's firstborn and his mother away to the desert. On the verge of dehydration and starvation, God came to Hagar, opened her eyes to see a spring of water, and renewed His promise to take care of them both. In the end, Ishmael became the father of the Arab people, and Isaac became the father of the Jewish people. I have to wonder about the constant conflict we see between the two nations even today. What would have happened if Sarah had not interfered with God's dream for her life? It was a decision that has affected the entire world and will for many years to come.

What can we learn from Sarah, a woman who interfered with God's dream?

Our Interference Can Have Devastating Results

God had an incredible plan for Abraham and Sarah. While His plan was still accomplished despite Sarah's scheming, her interference caused much heartache and strife. Many times we have a tendency to run ahead of God when we feel He is not acting quickly enough. We connive, cajole, coax, and conspire. We hamper, hinder, hassle, and hurry.

Jeremiah 29:11 promises that God has a plan for each and every one of us. "'I know the plans I have for you,' declares the LORD, 'plans to prosper you and not to harm you, plans to give you hope and a future.'" He does not need our interference to accomplish that plan; He does require our obedience and cooperation.

I asked my Facebook friends to tell about a time when they interfered with God's plan:

Nichole: "I prayed that God would change my husband. I got tired of waiting, so I decided to take matters in my own hands and do it myself. I made a terrible mess of our marriage and the situation only got worse."

Deborah: "I prayed for a husband but got tired of waiting on God to bring him. I ended up dating a non-Christian, getting pregnant with twins, and was ultimately left all alone to raise them by myself."

Dorinda: "When I was 24, I got pregnant and had an abortion. I didn't trust God with the situation and took matters in my own hands. Years of nightmares, anxiety, guilt, and fear followed. I finally allowed God to walk me through to full repentance and redemption. I knew Christ at the time of the abortion, but I didn't believe He could help me get through the pregnancy. While I've dealt with the abortion physically, emotionally, and spiritually, and even share my testimony about God's forgiveness, I will never have the joy of raising that child."

Kimberly: "I lived with a man for 10 years. He partied all the time and didn't want to get married. I prayed that God would change him. Finally I prayed that God would change me and he moved out. I cried out to God, 'Why am I not enough for my boyfriend?' He answered, 'Why am I not enough for you?' Wow! I can honestly say that life with God in control is amazing. His ways have been by far the most exciting and fulfilling time of my life. Listen to His nudges, friends, and most of all, wait for His green light."

Irene: "I pushed my husband to take a job that moved us thousands of miles away from family and friends. Everything that could go wrong did go wrong. I know I interfered with God's plan by not waiting on Him to guide us. We are still suffering the consequences."

God has given us a free will and allows us to storm ahead, but He also allows the consequences of our interference to affect our lives.

No One Wins the Blame Game

After Sarai convinced Abram to sleep with Hagar and conceive a child, she then turned around and blamed Abram for the tension that was birthed between her and her maid. I read those words and shook my head. *How silly of her to blame Abram when it was her idea.* Then I read the words again and noticed a familiar ring to them.

How many times do we interfere with God's plans and then blame someone else for the negative consequences? We blame our imperfect parents, hard-hearted husbands, beastly boyfriends, brash bosses, and unruly children, but when we take a good look in the mirror, the blame many times lies squarely on our own shoulders and the decisions we made along the way.

When my son was young, I taught him how to ask for forgiveness and say, "I'm sorry." His tendency was to say "I'm sorry, but…" with the rationalization following close behind. However, in true repentance one takes full responsibility for his or her actions and commits to turn and go in the opposite direction.

Like Eve, many say, "The devil made me do it." But the devil never makes us do anything. He may make the suggestion, but we have the power to choose. The good news is that God promises He will never allow us to be tempted beyond what we are able to resist, but will always provide a way of escape (1 Corinthians 10:13).

If we've interfered with God's plan, we need to admit our guilt, tell Him we are truly sorry for our sin, and turn the situation back over to Him.

God Can Use What God Does Not Choose

The sexual relationship between a husband and a wife is a beautifully exciting act of love created and ordained by God. Sex was His idea, and He took great pains in creation to fashion our bodies to physically and emotionally become one. However, the Bible is very clear that sex outside of marriage is not His will and can have devastating results. Sex outside of marriage has caused insurmountable ills in our world today: broken homes, fatherless children, sexually transmitted diseases, depression, sterility, and infertility. One consequence of disobeying God in this matter is children born without the security of a mother and father living in a monogamous heterosexual relationship bound together by the covenant of marriage. But regardless of how a child comes into the world, God still loves that child and can use him or her in mighty ways.

There is a well-known story of some men in Scotland who had spent the day fishing. That evening they were having tea in a little inn. One of the fishermen, in a characteristic gesture to describe the size of the fish that got away, slung out his hands just as the little waitress was getting ready to set the cup of tea at his place. The hand and the teacup collided, dashing the tea against the whitewashed wall. Immediately an ugly brown stain began to spread over the wall. The man who did it was very embarrassed and apologized profusely, but one of the other guests jumped up and said, "Never mind." Pulling a pen from his pocket, he began to sketch around the ugly brown stain. Soon there emerged a picture of a magnificent royal stag with his antler spread. The artist was Sir Edwin Lanseer, England's foremost painter of animals.[2]

What a wonderful picture of God taking our mistakes and somehow creating a beautiful work of art. God can use what God did not choose.

God's Timetable Is Not Our Timetable

God is omnipotent (all-powerful), omnipresent (everywhere at once), and omniscient (all-knowing). And He often shows His power in the last moments of desperation, when the only option we have left is to trust in Him. God could have provided Sarah with a child when she was 40 or 50, but by waiting until she was 90, everyone knew that this was the work of God.

While working at a nonprofit ministry for ten years, I learned many lessons on trusting God for financial provision. We had many days when we didn't know how we were going to pay the next day's bills, and then a mysterious check would arrive in the mail.

On one particular occasion, we needed $3000 to meet the end-of-the-month bills. We prayed and I worried. I called the office and spoke to our executive director.

"Joel," I said, "I'm just going to write a check for the $3000."

"Sharon, God called you to this ministry, but He did not call you to fix every problem. I believe that we need to let Him handle this."

I was amazed at his faith, especially as he was in charge of the finances and my offer would have solved his dilemma.

The next day Joel called me.

"Sharon, guess what?" he said, a little choked up. "We got a check today from a church. It was for $3000."

What would have happened if I had interfered the day before? I'm not sure. But I do know that God did not need me to fix the problem.

God's timetable is not our timetable. It may seem as though He is moving too slowly, moving too quickly, or has forgotten our dream altogether. However, He has everything under control. Our job is to trust Him.

Naomi

A Woman Who Forgot Her Dreams

Naomi was a young woman when she met and married Elimelech. His name meant "God is King," and she knew he would
always serve the living God of Israel. She had always dreamed of living her days in the fertile land of Bethlehem, which meant "house of
bread." She also dreamed of having many strapping, robust sons; beautiful, wise daughters; and a passel of adoring grandchildren crowding
around her feet.

Time passed, and Naomi did have two sons, but they weren't quite
what she had expected. From the time they entered the world and gave
their first cries, Naomi could tell they were not going to be the strong,
stalwart boys she had always dreamed of. One boy she named Mahlon,
which meant "puny" or "weakling," and the other she named Kilion,
which meant "pining."

When the boys were still young lads, a devastating famine swept
through the area surrounding Bethlehem. In an effort to provide for his
family, Elimelech decided to pick up stakes and move them to Moab,
a grain-filled plateau east of the Dead Sea. It was not a land suitable
for farming, but he could raise goats and sheep on the plentiful grain.
The boys grew older, if not stronger, and eventually married Moabite
women. This was not Naomi's dream for her boys. She would have
dreamed that they marry Israelite women from her own country who

worshipped the one true God. But what could she do when Elimelech agreed to the unions?

Naomi made new friends and tried not to think of the homeland she left behind. But then her life took a drastic turn for the worse. Over a ten-year period her husband and both sons died. With the death of these three men, Naomi's hopes and dreams died as well. She felt discouraged, dejected, and depressed with no one to take care of her. She had two wonderful daughters-in-law, but without a husband or sons to bring children into the world and carry on the family name, her future was barren.

"Girls," Naomi announced one day after much contemplation, "I have heard news from my homeland. God has remembered Bethlehem and the famine has passed. There is no reason for me to stay in Moab, and I have decided to return to the land of my people. I want you both to go back to your mother's house and find other nice young men to marry. I pray God will be as kind to you as you have been to me."

Naomi kissed each of the girls as they wept loudly. "We will go back with you to your people," they cried.

"No, my daughters," Naomi answered. "Go back home. There's no reason for you to come with me. I know it is the custom for you to marry another son in a family if your husband dies, but I'm not going to have any more sons. Even if I did, I wouldn't want you to wait around until they were old enough to marry. Return home. That is the best solution. The Lord's hand has gone out against me. My dreams are buried with Elimelech, Mahlon, and Kilion."

The two women loved their mother-in-law dearly and clung to her robe with tears streaming down their cheeks. After what seemed like hours, one of the girls, Orpah, kissed her mother-in-law goodbye and turned to walk away. The other girl, Ruth, embraced Naomi and begged to go with her.

"Don't urge me to leave you or to turn back from you. Where you go I will go, and where you stay I will stay. Your people will be my people and your God my God. Where you die I will die, and there I will be buried. May the LORD deal with me, be it ever so severely, if anything but death separates you and me" (Ruth 1:16-17).

Naomi and Ruth both knew that most Israelites despised Moabites.

The Israelites had never forgiven the Moabites for hiring Balaam to place a curse on them after they left Egypt for the Promised Land many years before (Numbers 22–24). The women knew it would be dangerous for Ruth to live in Bethlehem. Yet, regardless of the opposition Ruth knew she would face, she still desired to go and take care of her friend. So Naomi conceded and allowed Ruth to return to Bethlehem with her.

After an arduous journey, the arrival of the two dusty and exhausted women caused quite a stir, and the townspeople began whispering among themselves. "Could this be Naomi? It looks like her...and yet it doesn't."

Naomi was so depressed, downcast, and discouraged that her very countenance masked the woman she had once been. She heard the whispers as she walked by and stopped in her tracks. "Don't call me Naomi (which means pleasant)" she told them. "Call me Mara (which means bitter), because the Almighty has made my life very bitter. I went away full, but the LORD has brought me back empty. Why call me Naomi? The LORD has afflicted me; the Almighty has brought misfortune upon me" (Ruth 1:20-21).

Ruth felt a pang in her heart at the words "brought me back empty." Part of her thought, *What about me?* But the other part knew Naomi was speaking out of her pain.

Naomi was a woman who had forgotten her dreams and saw no hope of finding happiness ever again. She was blinded by bitterness and didn't even recognize God's provision walking right beside her in the form of a Moabite girl, whose name meant "woman friend."

The next day Ruth went out to glean in the barley fields. It was customary for farmers to allow the poor to come behind the workers and pick up the barley that was left scattered on the ground after the harvesters had completed their work. Ruth and Naomi knew it would be dangerous for a Moabite woman to venture into the field because of the generational hostility toward them. However, Ruth took a chance in order to provide food for Naomi.

It just so happened that Ruth went to the field owned by a man named Boaz...

Wait—I hope you don't believe that for a second. I think the writer of this story was simply speaking tongue in cheek with a twinkle in his eye. "It just so happened" never happens in the kingdom of God. God *led* Ruth to this field just as surely as if He had taken her by the hand. He was in the process of restoring Naomi's dreams, and He placed Ruth smack-dab in the middle of a field owned by one who would make those dreams come true.

"Who is that young woman?" Boaz, the owner of the field, asked his foreman.

"She is the Moabitess who came back from Moab with Naomi. She said, 'Please let me glean and gather among the sheaves behind the harvesters.' She went into the field and has worked steadily from morning till now, except for a short rest in the shelter" (Ruth 2:6-7).

Something began to stir in Boaz at the sight of this one so faithful to the older woman who had lost so much. He had heard how she left her homeland and her people to care for her destitute and discouraged mother-in-law. Boaz called Ruth over to himself.

"My daughter, listen to me. Don't go and glean in another field and don't go away from here. Stay here with my servant girls. Watch the field where the men are harvesting, and follow along after the girls. I have told the men not to touch you. And whenever you are thirsty, go and get a drink from the water jars the men have filled."

At this, she bowed down with her face to the ground. She exclaimed, "Why have I found such favor in your eyes that you notice me—a foreigner?"

Boaz replied, "I've been told all about what you have done for your mother-in-law since the death of your husband—how you left your father and mother and your homeland and came to live with a people you did not know before. May the Lord repay you for what you have done. May you be richly rewarded by the Lord, the God of Israel, under whose wings you have come to take refuge" (Ruth 2:8-12).

Ruth had a very fruitful day of gleaning. She noticed that some of the workers she followed behind pulled out the choice barley from the bundles and left them on the ground for her to pick up. Boaz invited her to have lunch with him and his men, eating all the roasted barley she could hold and drinking their wine.

When she went back home that evening with arms overflowing with choice barley, Naomi's eyes lit up in surprise. "Where did you glean today to gather such a bountiful load?"

"His name was Boaz," Ruth replied. "And he was quite handsome, I might add."

"Boaz! I had forgotten all about Boaz! He is one of our relatives—one of our kinsmen-redeemers."

"What is a kinsman-redeemer?"

"In our customs, a kinsman-redeemer is a man who is responsible for protecting the interests of needy members of his extended family. He might provide an heir for a brother who has died, buy back land that a poor relative sold outside the family, or buy back a relative who had been sold into slavery."

Ruth noticed a spark in Naomi's eyes that she had not seen since the loss of her husband and two sons. They had a wonderful dinner, and Ruth feasted on Naomi's much missed chatter.

After the barley harvest had passed, Naomi devised a plan.

"Ruth, tonight I want you to take a long bath, put on your best robe, and splash on ample perfume. Then, after dark, go down to Boaz's threshing floor. Don't let anyone see you. After Boaz has had plenty to eat and drink and lies down for the evening, note where he beds down for the night. When you hear the heavy breathing that lets you know he is sound asleep, tiptoe over to him, uncover his feet, and lie down. He will tell you what to do when he wakes up."

"Is this another one of your Hebrew customs?" Ruth asked.

"Yes. Now listen carefully. When you uncover his feet and lie at the foot of his pallet, you are making known your desire for him to become your kinsman-redeemer and marry you. We call such a man as this a *go'el*. When he awakes, ask him to take the corner of his blanket and cover you. If he agrees, then he is agreeing to marry you."

"But suppose he doesn't want me?"

"Don't worry about that, child. From the rumors I've heard about the way he watches you in the fields, I don't think rejection is likely."

Ruth blushed at Naomi's comment and responded, "I'll do exactly what you say."

That night Ruth snuck on to the threshing floor where Boaz and his men slept to protect the harvested barley. Just as Naomi instructed, she waited until Boaz was asleep. Then she uncovered his feet and lay down to wait until morning.

During the night something startled Boaz, and when he woke up, he noticed a woman at his feet! "Who are you?" he asked, not able to recognize her in the darkness.

"I am your servant Ruth," she said. "Spread the corner of your garment over me, since you are a kinsman-redeemer" (Ruth 3:9).

"The LORD bless you, my daughter," he replied. "This kindness is greater than that which you showed earlier: You have not run after the younger men, whether rich or poor. And now, my daughter, don't be afraid. I will do for you all you ask. All my fellow townsmen know that you are a woman of noble character. Although it is true that I am near of kin, there is a kinsman-redeemer nearer than I. Stay here for the night and in the morning if he wants to redeem, good; let him redeem. But if he is not willing, as surely as the LORD lives, I will do it. Lie here until morning" (Ruth 3:10-13).

As soon as it was light, Boaz filled Ruth's shawl with barley and sent her back to Naomi.

"What did he say? What did he say?" Naomi eagerly asked as Ruth came bursting through the door.

"He thanked me! Can you imagine that? He thanked me for asking!" Ruth replied. Then she filled Naomi in on all the details and told her everything.

As God would have it, the other relative was not interested in becoming Ruth's *go'el*. This flung open the door for Boaz and freed Ruth to become his bride. What a joyous day when Boaz and Ruth became man and wife. Shortly thereafter, Ruth conceived, bore a son, and named him Obed. You might not have heard of Obed, but I bet you've heard of his grandson. His name was David—the most famous and powerful king in Israel's history.

I suspect Naomi told her friends to stop calling her Mara, for she was no longer bitter but beaming. Her friends proclaimed, "Praise be to the LORD, who this day has not left you without a kinsman-redeemer.

May he become famous throughout Israel! He will renew your life and sustain you in your old age. For your daughter-in-law, who loves you and who is better to you than seven sons, has given him birth" (Ruth 4:14-15).

What a glorious story. Naomi was a woman who forgot her dreams, yet God used a Moabite girl to restore them. He even placed her in the family tree of Jesus! Why do we ever doubt God's plans for our lives? He wants to give us exceedingly abundantly more than we could ever ask or think, and yet we tend to give up when times get tough. Admittedly, losing a husband and two sons is enough to devastate any woman, but Naomi's story is a wonderful reminder that God will never leave or forsake us. And as He did for Naomi, God provided a kinsman-redeemer for you and for me. His name is Jesus.

What can we learn from Naomi, a woman who forgot God's dream?

God Sometimes Uses Other People to Help Restore Our Dreams

Naomi had become very bitter, and that bitterness blinded her from seeing God's provision of love, loyalty, and life-giving nourishment through Ruth.

After I lost a child through miscarriage, I didn't want to be around anyone for several months. The only people I did want to talk to were those who had experienced the same painful broken dream. One particular friend, who had also lost a child, sent me the following poem.

He Makes No Mistakes!

My Father's way may twist and turn.
My heart may throb and ache.
But in my soul I'm glad I know
That He makes no mistake.

My cherished plans may go astray.
My hopes may fade away.
But still I'll trust my Lord to lead
For He does know the way.

Though night be dark and it may seem
That day will never break;
I'll pin my faith, my all in Him,
For He makes no mistake.

There's so much I cannot see,
My eyesight's far too dim;
But come what may, I'll simply trust
And leave it all to Him.

For by and by the mist will lift
And all things plain He'll make
Through all the way, though dark to me,
He made not one mistake.

A.M. OVERTON

God used Leigh Ann to help me remember that He does have a plan, and though I might not understand it, He makes no mistakes. God used a friend to help me remember my dreams.

God May Use Us to Restore Someone Else's Broken Dreams

When Naomi returned to town, her old acquaintances recognized that she was depressed and despondent because of her great loss. She had gone away married and wealthy and returned home widowed and poor. However, we see no signs that the townsfolk offered to alleviate her pain or minister to her in any way. Ruth gives us such a wonderful example of how to fan the dying embers of a friend's smoldering dreams. She didn't reprimand, rebuke, or remind Naomi why she needed to be thankful. She didn't criticize, correct, or tell her to stop feeling sorry for herself. She simply loved her unconditionally, cared for her unceasingly, and supported her unselfishly. She certainly lived up to her name, "woman friend."

In the South, when someone is hurting, we do what Ruth did—fix them a good meal. Whether someone has a baby, loses a loved one, or is sick for an extended period of time, it is common for us Southerners to whip up casseroles of every kind. This is what Ruth did for

Naomi—she made sure her mother-in-law had food to eat and plenty of it. But that was just the beginning. She carried Naomi's burdens too.

Paul encourages the Galatians to "carry each other's burdens, and in this way you will fulfill the law of Christ" (Galatians 6:2). The word "burden" here means "overburden," such as the loss of a child, a divorce, or a serious illness. These are all situations when burdens become simply too difficult to bear alone, and we need a friend to come alongside us for support. As a "woman friend," God may use us to restore someone's dreams by walking alongside them, taking care of their physical needs, tending to their emotional wounds, or trudging through the deep waters with them. When we allow God to use us this way, we, like Ruth, will be richly blessed.

In *Running on Empty,* Jill Briscoe writes, "Ruth was a wise woman. It is in companionship that gives itself unselfishly, without looking for returns, that we receive the very things we are looking for ourselves."[1]

God Desires for Us to Become Better, Not Bitter

Naomi blamed God for her afflictions. In one sense, she was correct. God is sovereign and in control of every aspect of our lives. However, He was not out to get her. His hand was not against her, as she claimed. Naomi became very bitter about what had happened to her, so much so that she changed her name. God never desires for us to become bitter. He longs to use the difficulties of our lives to make us better.

In Jesus' last words to His disciples, He compared their relationship to Him to that of a vine and its branches. "I am the true vine, and my Father is the gardener. He cuts off [lifts up out of the dust][2] every branch in me that bears no fruit, while every branch that does bear fruit he prunes so that it will be even more fruitful" (John 15:1-2).

When our dreams seem to be lost, it can feel as though God's giant gardening shears have lopped off a part of our lives vital to our existence. However, His desire is for us to bear as much fruit as possible, not become stunted by bitterness. In *Secrets of the Vine,* Bruce Wilkerson notes, "God isn't trying to just take away; He's faithfully at work to make room to add strength, productivity, and spiritual power in your life. His goal is to bring you closer to the 'perfect and complete' image of Christ."[3]

He goes on to say, "Not every painful experience is the result of pruning. Is your heart breaking because your teenager is experimenting with drugs and sex? God did not cause your son to do these things in order to prune you. Are you suddenly facing a future with diabetes or cancer? God isn't purposefully constraining your life just to see how you'll react. Yet every trial you face is an opportunity to let Him work in your life for abundance. If you invite Him into your circumstances, He will keep His promise to work everything together for your good (Romans 8:28)."[4]

Have you noticed the only difference between the words "bitter" and "better" is the letter *i*? When we stop focusing on the not-so-mighty "me, myself, and I" and start focusing on Almighty God, then we will begin to see our difficulties through the lens of God's perfect and perfecting plan. If He prunes away a dream, it is only because He has a greater dream in store that will produce more and better fruit.

"It Just So Happens" Never Happens in God's Economy

Divine providence is behind every twist and turn in the story of Ruth: the famine that led the family to Moab, the marriages to Moabite women, the deaths of Elimelech and Naomi's two sons, the lifting of the famine in Bethlehem, Naomi's return to her homeland, Ruth's gleaning in Boaz's field, Boaz's notice of Ruth, the refusal of the next in line to be Ruth's kinsman-redeemer, and Boaz and Ruth's subsequent marriage. These events are strung like pearls on the thread of God's providence and secured in place with the knot of His love.

Have you ever noticed such a stringing of events in your own life? Gayle experienced one particular series of events that were most definitely orchestrated by God. She started having trouble with her knees in her early thirties. Chronic pain in her right knee sent her to the doctor's office on a regular basis for cortisone injections. Because Gayle's mother had joint pain in her knees for most of her adult life, Gayle resolved herself to the same fate—arthritis. Her doctors never X-rayed the knee or performed an MRI to diagnose the problem, but instead prescribed treatment according to symptoms and a family history of joint pain.

One night after five years of cortisone injections, Gayle, her husband, Joe, and another couple attended a basketball game at their alma mater. On the way home, Gayle twisted around in her front seat to face the couple in the back. As they chatted, she noticed an 18-wheel semi-trailer truck's headlights rapidly approaching their car. *Surely he's going to stop,* she thought. But before she could even warn the other passengers, the truck plowed into the back of their car at 55 miles per hour. Gayle's knees were smashed into the dashboard.

The driver of the truck had fallen asleep at the wheel and never even applied the brakes before impact. Gayle and Joe's car, a heavy Lincoln Continental, was totaled, but no one in the car was hurt except Gayle. Her knees were black, blue, and swollen within a couple of hours.

When she went to the doctor the next day, he decided to take an X-ray to make sure there were no broken bones. "Gayle," he said, "I don't know how to tell you this, but you have a tumor in your right knee."

"A tumor? How long has it been there?"

"Well, this is a very slow-growing type of tumor which has probably been there for several years. The pain you've been experiencing in the past has most likely not been due to arthritis, but due to the tumor causing the bone to expand as it grows. We're going to have to remove it right away."

"I can't do it right away," she answered. "I have a two-week counseling course I'm going to next week. I've been on the waiting list for two years, so this tumor is going to have to wait. You did say it was slow growing, correct?"

"Yes," he answered, "but I wouldn't wait a day longer than necessary. You are a very lucky young lady. If you had not been in that car accident, we may have not found the tumor until it was too late."

Gayle smiled. Luck had nothing to do with it. God was in control.

She went to that counseling seminar. On the last night, 750 committed Christians gathered around her and prayed for her knee. The next day, when the doctor went in to remove the tumor, he was amazed to find that this slow-growing tumor had rapidly begun to shrink.

"Once again," the doctor said, "you are a lucky girl. According to today's X-rays, the tumor is smaller than it was two weeks ago."

Once again, Gayle knew luck had nothing to do with it. She then shared with the doctor about the 750 people who had prayed for her the night before.

Many times when something seemingly bad happens in our lives, we need to remember that God is the director of the drama. We may not understand the "whys" or the "what fors," but we can trust in the God who controls it all. Kathy Collard Miller said it so well. "Nothing that happens to the child of God is a coincidence, and when we look at every situation and encounter as God-directed, we will more easily fulfill His plan. This knowledge should also make each of us feel needed, valuable, and important: we are fulfilling God's purposes for His Kingdom."[5]

Just when it looks as though our dreams have been shattered, God picks up the pieces and creates a beautiful mosaic—a work of art which He had planned all along.

Esther

A Woman Who Fulfilled God's Dreams

Tucked between the Old Testament books of Nehemiah and Job
is the little book of Esther. We don't know much about Esther's
childhood, but I imagine her dreams were not that different from other
Hebrew girls growing up around 460 BC. She probably had dreams of
marrying a handsome Jewish husband and having a quiver full of children with names like Isaac, Mariah, Daniel, or Rebekah. I imagine she
dreamed of the day when her prospective groom would come to her
father, ask for his daughter in marriage, and promise an extravagant
mohar.

"And what will you pay for my daughter?" her father would ask.

"For one so lovely, I will pay 1000 sheep, 20 heifers, and 40 pieces
of gold," her handsome suitor would reply.

Perhaps Esther dreamed of having an inviting home filled with
lovely pottery, lively tapestries, and laughing friends. Perhaps she
dreamed of having her own well in the backyard—that would really
be a dream house.

But things didn't turn out the way she had imagined. We don't
know exactly what happened to her parents, but at some point in her
young life both mother and father died. When we meet Esther, she is
living with her cousin, Mordecai, who had taken her in and raised her
as his own daughter.

During this time in history, Esther's hometown of Susa was ruled by King Xerxes (Ahasuerus in the Hebrew). He was a powerful king who ruled over 127 provinces stretching from India to Ethiopia. While he was famous for his great wealth and territorial rule, he was most widely known for his grand parties that lasted for months on end.

As the book of Esther opens we find him throwing a party that lasted for 180 days. King Xerxes was planning to wage war against Greece, the only part of the known world not under his reign, and he hoped the lavish party showcasing his power and possessions would build confidence in his war plans among his peers. During the last seven days of the festivities, all the people from the least to the greatest in the citadel of Susa were invited to eat their fill and drink from hand-crafted golden goblets—no two alike. While the men were carousing in the gardens, Queen Vashti entertained the ladies at a party of her own in the palace.

On the final day of the festivities, King Xerxes sent word for Queen Vashti to come and parade before the drunken partygoers. Wearing her royal crown, he wanted to display her beauty before the men. Some commentators suggest that he commanded she parade before the crowd wearing nothing *but* her crown. However, the queen refused to be put on display before the revelers.

The king's attendant stood startled at the queen's reply, and the women gave out a collective gasp.

"But the king has ordered it!" the attendant sputtered.

"And I have refused," Vashti confirmed.

The servant returned to the king, and with a quiver in his voice delivered the news.

"What does she mean, she won't come!" the king exclaimed.

"She just said...no, sire."

The king was infuriated at the queen's refusal, but perhaps more than being angry, he was embarrassed and humiliated at his apparent lack of control over his own wife.

"What am I going to do about her insolence?" the king asked his counselors.

"Queen Vashti has done wrong, not only against the king but also against all the nobles and the peoples of all the provinces of King Xerxes. For the queen's conduct will become known to all the women, and so they will despise their husbands and say, 'King Xerxes commanded Queen Vashti to be brought before him, but she would not come.' This very day the Persian and Median women of the nobility who have heard about the queen's conduct will respond to all the king's nobles in the same way. There will be no end of disrespect and discord" (Esther 1:16-18).

The king's counselor then suggested that Queen Vashti be removed as queen and the crown be placed on someone more deserving. The king agreed to the suggestion and issued a royal decree to search for a new queen. Among the young virgins brought to the palace was Esther. She was entrusted to Hegai, a eunuch who was in charge of the king's harem. Immediately, Esther won Hegai's favor. He was impressed not only by her outward beauty, but her inner beauty as well. However, there was one little detail Esther and her cousin failed to mention.

She was a Jew.

Esther spent one year at the royal spa before being presented to the king—six months with oils and six months with perfumes and cosmetics. She was also assigned seven maids to take care of her every need. At the end of her beauty treatment, King Xerxes chose Esther to be the next queen. She was not only beautiful in form and feature, but gentle and kind. If there had been a Miss Susa contest, Esther would have won the crown and Miss Congeniality at the same time. After he selected Esther as the queen, the king gave a great banquet in her honor and proclaimed a holiday throughout the provinces.

Now, lest we think being Xerxes' queen sounds like a dream come true, there are a few details we need to understand. Esther was not a cherished wife as she had hoped to become. She was just one of many wives and concubines who served as the king's possessions and objects of sexual satisfaction. Kings in those days collected young virgins the way modern-day stamp collectors collect stamps. Most likely, Esther would never be a part of the outside world again but live within the palace confines for the rest of her life. As part of his harem, she would rarely see the king. She did not live with her husband as you and I think of a marriage relationship today. She could only approach the king safely when summoned. If she approached the king uninvited and he was not pleased, he could have her put to death. Also, Esther would never carry on her Jewish heritage by having a quiver full of Hebrew children. King Xerxes was a Gentile—not what she had dreamed.

But God had another dream for Queen Esther: to save the entire Hebrew nation. A few months after Esther was named queen, her cousin, Mordecai, overheard a plot to kill the king. He reported this to Esther, who reported it to the king. The would-be assassins were caught and hanged, and Mordecai's name was recorded in the record books for saving the king's life.

Sometime later Haman, one of the king's officials, was elevated to a place of honor above all the other nobles of the empire. "I command all the royal officials at the king's gate to kneel down and pay honor to Haman when he passes by," the king proclaimed. But because Mordecai bowed only to the one true God of Israel, he refused to bow to Haman. If Haman had been king, he would have possibly bowed, but Haman was an Amalekite, an enemy to the Jews. This infuriated Haman, and he began to plot Mordecai's demise.

"Who is this man who refuses to bow before me?" Haman raged. "I'll have him killed! Better yet, I will have his entire race exterminated! Every Jew in the nation will be killed because of this man's insolence."

Haman went before the king and explained, "There is a certain people dispersed and scattered among the peoples in all the provinces of your kingdom whose customs are different from those of all other people and who do not obey the king's laws; it is not in the king's best interest to tolerate them. If it pleases the king, let a decree be issued to destroy them, and I will put ten thousand talents of silver into the royal treasury for the men who carry out this business" (Esther 3:8-10).

The king, feeling very indifferent toward Haman's request, took his signet ring from his finger and gave it to Haman. "Keep the money," the king said, "and do with the people as you please" (verse 11).

As the news of the Jews' impending extermination spread across the land, the king and Haman sat down to eat, drink, and be merry, but the city of Susa was in an uproar. When Mordecai heard of the news, he tore his robe, put on sackcloth, sprinkled ashes on his head, and went about the city wailing loudly.

Esther heard of her cousin's strange behavior at the city gate and sent one of her attendants to find out why he was in mourning. "Mordecai, what is wrong?" the eunuch inquired. "The queen has heard about your deep sorrow. She has sent me to bring you clothes instead of the sackcloth you are wearing."

"I cannot accept them," Mordecai answered through his tears. "The king has issued a royal decree to have all the Jewish people annihilated. He is doing this at the request of Haman because I refused to bow before that pompous Amalekite. Here, this is a copy of the actual decree. Take this back to Esther. Tell her she must go before the king and plead for her people."

The eunuch went back and reported to Queen Esther all that Mordecai had said. She sent him back to Mordecai with this message: "All the king's officials and the people of the royal provinces know that for any man or woman who approaches the king in the inner court without being summoned the king has but one law: that he be put to death. The only exception to this is for the king to extend the gold scepter to him and spare his life. But thirty days have passed since I was called to go to the king" (Esther 4:11).

Upon hearing Esther's response, Mordecai sent back the following reply: "Do not think that because you are in the king's house you alone of all the Jews will escape. For if you remain silent at this time, relief and deliverance for the Jews will arise from another place, but you and your father's family will perish. And who knows but that you have come to royal position for such a time as this?" (verses 13-14).

Then Esther sent back a reply to Mordecai: "Go, gather together all the Jews who are in Susa, and fast for me. Do not eat or drink for three days, night or day. I and my maids will fast as you do. When this is done, I will go to the king, even though it is against the law. And if I perish, I perish" (verses 15-16).

So Esther, along with all the Jews of Susa, fasted and prayed. Then, after three days, she bathed, dabbed on perfume, slipped into her royal robe, and went before the king. The king was sitting on his throne and facing the entrance when he saw her approach the forbidden inner court. At her appearing, he was pleased and extended the gold scepter. Esther approached the king and touched the tip of the scepter.

"What is it, Queen Esther?" he asked. "What is your request? Even up to half the kingdom, it will be given you" (Esther 5:3).

"If it pleases the king," replied Esther, "let the king, together with Haman, come today to a banquet I have prepared for him" (verse 4).

Esther knew the best way to the king was through his stomach. After dinner she invited him to join her again the following evening. By now the king was curious. He knew Esther had a request, and she promised to reveal it on the second evening. Of course, Haman felt quite smug being invited to dine with the queen not once but twice.

When the king and Haman joined her the following evening, Queen Esther announced her petition and reason for disturbing the king.

"If I have found favor with you, O king, and if it pleases your majesty, grant me my life—this is my petition. And spare my people—this is my request. For I and my people have been sold for destruction and slaughter and annihilation. If we had merely been sold as male and female slaves, I would have kept quiet, because no such distress would justify disturbing the king" (Esther 7:3-4).

"Where is this man who has dared to do such a thing?" Xerxes asked (verse 5). (He had never even asked Haman who the people were he wished to exterminate.)

Esther turned and pointed across the table. "It is Haman!"

Furious, the king stood from the table and marched into the garden to let his burning anger cool. Haman threw himself at the queen as she reclined on the couch. "Please spare me, my queen!" he begged.

Haman's timing couldn't have been worse. The king entered just as Haman threw himself at the queen. "What! Will you even dare to molest the queen while she is in the palace?"

"I wasn't—"

"Silence!" the king shouted.

The next day Haman and his sons were hanged on the gallows that Haman had built to hang Mordecai. While the king could not revoke a royal decree, he issued another decree that allowed the Jews the right to assemble and protect themselves; to destroy, kill, and annihilate any armed force of any nationality or province that might attack them and their women and children; and to plunder the property of their enemies. Thus, on March 7, 473 BC, the entire Hebrew nation was spared. Even to this day, the Jews celebrate the feast of Purim to commemorate Queen Esther's brave act.

Esther had dreams for her life. They were perhaps very simple—a husband, children, a home, and a quiet and peaceful existence. However, God had a much larger dream for this little orphaned girl. He had a dream to make her a queen and an instrument to save an entire nation—the nation from which the Savior of the world would be born. It is interesting that God's name is not mentioned once in this small book of the Bible, but His fingerprints are on every page. William M. Taylor noted, "It was not needful that the name of God should be introduced into it, because his hand is everywhere so manifest throughout it."[1]

Esther experienced fear in her high calling, but she overcame her fear through faith in God's protection, provision, and perfect timing. She was a woman who fulfilled God's dream.

What can we learn from Esther, a woman who fulfilled God's dream?

God Has Bigger Dreams for Our Lives than We Could Ever Imagine

Can you imagine what young Esther would have thought if someone had come up to her at the market when she was gathering produce for her cousin and told her she was going to be the next queen of Persia and save her people from annihilation? I imagine she would have laughed or run for cover from the lunatic making such a prediction. But God had a plan. He took a lonely orphan girl and used her to rescue the Jewish nation.

If someone had come to me in my teen years and told me I would be spreading the gospel through an international radio program, speaking at women's conferences, and authoring several books, I would have quickly informed them that they had a serious case of mistaken identity.

My voice was too Southern, my confidence was too shattered, and my brain was wired for math and science. As a matter of fact, when God did begin opening doors for ministry, I reminded Him of all my short-comings and why He had the wrong girl for the job. But as I began to take those first baby steps of obedience, He began to show me glimpses of His great plan.

Our dreams are always too small when compared to the magnifi-cent dreams God has planned for His girls. While God has probably not called you to save an entire nation from destruction, He has called you to be a woman He can use. Missionary Amy Carmichael wrote, "Often his call is to follow in paths we would not have chosen."[2]

"'For my thoughts are not your thoughts neither are your ways my ways,' declares the LORD. 'As the heavens are higher than the earth, so are my ways higher than your ways and my thoughts than your thoughts'" (Isaiah 55:8-9).

Whether God is calling us to be a catalyst for saving someone from physical death or be a catalyst for saving someone from spiritual sep-aration from God, when we move forward in obedience, empowered by His strength, bolstered by His power, and confident in His provi-sion, we will see Him accomplish great and mighty works through us. How marvelous that He allows us to participate and be the hands and feet through which He works.

"We are God's workmanship," Paul reminds us. "Created in Christ Jesus *to do good works*, which God prepared in advance for us to do" (Ephesians 2:10, emphasis added). God created Esther for a purpose, just as He has created you and me for a purpose…"for such a time as this."

God's Dreams Require Courage to Fulfill

Hearing God's call on our lives is the first step. Obeying that call is the second. Making the leap between hearing and obeying may be one of the most difficult moves of our lives. Because of Esther's willing-ness to transcend her fears, the nation was saved and she was the vehi-cle through which an amazing miracle transpired.

Anne Graham Lotz, one of Billy Graham's three daughters, was comfortable being the wife of a dentist and mother of three. But God had a different dream for Anne—not to replace her role as wife and mother, but to add to it. Several years ago, on a visit to southern India, a group of people took her to a soccer stadium full of thousands of expectant people. They asked her to deliver an evangelical message the way her daddy did. Anne explained to her hosts that this is not what she did. Yes, she spoke to Bible studies and to smaller crowds, but not to large arenas. Nevertheless, God had a call on Anne…a dream for her life. She laid her fears aside, stepped into the pulpit, and preached.

"I was sitting there thinking, 'I'm an American housewife, I don't belong here,'" she recalled. "But I just stepped aside and let God take over. And it's amazing what he can do."[3]

Mary Slessor, at the beginning of her remarkable missionary career in Calabar, which is now part of modern Nigeria, once prayed, "Lord, the task is impossible for me but not for Thee. Lead the way and I will follow. Why should I fear? I am on a Royal Mission. I am in the service of the King of Kings."[4]

God Can Take a Painful Childhood and Turn It into a Purposeful Adulthood

Reading the story of Esther gives me so much hope as I listen to story after story of painful childhood memories of men and women today. While we don't know much about Esther's parents, we do know that she was an orphan who was raised by her cousin, Mordecai. As far as we can tell, she had no feminine influence in her life, and yet she grew to be a gracious lovely woman who won the favor of everyone she encountered.

Perhaps your childhood was less than ideal. Perhaps you had an alcoholic father, an absent father, an abusive mother, or an aloof mother. Perhaps you lived in poverty or grew up in an orphanage, a foster home, or with parents who felt you were a bother instead of a blessing. But let me assure you of this. No matter what your childhood memories hold, God can and will use every bit of it for His purposes and for His glory…if you let Him. It doesn't matter how you started; what matters is how you finish.

Paul said, "One thing I do: Forgetting what is behind and straining toward what is ahead, I press on toward the goal to win the prize for which God has called me heavenward in Christ Jesus" (Philippians 3:13-14). Paul had to put his past behind him to accomplish what God had called him to do in the present. Likewise, when we put our painful pasts behind us and obey what God is calling us to do in the present we will experience a fruitful, fulfilling, fascinating adulthood. He can take those miseries of the past and turn them into ministries in the present. He can take our messes in life and turn them into messages of hope. God took a frightened orphan girl and used her to accomplish a great mission. He did it for Queen Esther. He wants to do it for you.

God's Power Follows Our Obedience

If God said, "I'm looking for a woman to help accomplish My plans and fulfill My purposes," would you feel qualified? Not many of us would raise our hands and shout, "Pick me! Pick me!" But here is something we must always remember: God doesn't necessarily call the qualified, but He always qualifies the called. When the angel of the Lord came to call Gideon to be the leader of the Israelite army, Gideon was hiding in a winepress threshing wheat. Now, you don't thresh wheat in a winepress. You thresh wheat by throwing it up into the open air and letting the chaff blow away and the heavier grain fall to the ground. So why was Gideon in the winepress? He was hiding. That's right. He was so terrified of his encroaching enemies that he was hiding. And yet, when the angel of the Lord addressed Gideon, he said, "O valiant warrior" (Judges 6:12 NASB). I imagine Gideon looked first to his left and then to his right before asking, "Are you talking to me?"

God doesn't see as we see. We tend to look at what we can accomplish in our own strength, but He looks at what we can accomplish in His. Consider this: Jacob was a deceiver, Joseph was a brat, Moses was a stutterer, Sarai was barren, David was a shepherd, Rahab was a harlot, Peter was a fisherman, Paul was a murderer, Mary Magdalene was a transformed demoniac, the Samaritan woman was a five-time divorcée, Timothy was timid, and Priscilla was a tent-maker. Even though they might not be who the world would choose to lead a great nation or movement, these were a few of the men and women God chose to fulfill His purposes in their lifetime through His power.

"God chose the foolish things of the world to shame the wise; God chose the weak things of the world to shame the strong. He chose the lowly things of this world and the despised things—and the things that are not—to nullify the things that are, so that no one may boast before him" (1 Corinthians 1:27-29). I don't know about you, but that fits me to a T. And here's even better news, "I can do everything through Him who gives me strength" (Philippians 4:13).

When Dreams and Life Collide

Shattered Dreams

Steve and I were enjoying a quiet evening with our good friends from college days, Larry and Cynthia Price. It had been almost a year since we had last seen them, and I was eager to hear of the latest family news about their children: Daniel, Julianna, and Laura Beth. While the four adults feasted on grilled teriyaki chicken, baked potatoes, and tossed salad with homegrown sliced tomatoes, the kids ran out the door to attend the Friday night high school football game. For more than an hour conversation and sweet tea flowed. We were just finishing the last bites of chocolate silk pie when our laughter was interrupted by the ringing phone.

"Hello," Cynthia answered.

I could only hear one side of the conversation, but it was obvious something was terribly wrong.

"Daniel, calm down! What's wrong? Talk slower," she urged. Then, "Oh, no. Okay, Daniel. We'll meet you at the hospital."

An ashen-faced Cynthia turned to her husband and could barely force the words out of her mouth. "Larry, Daniel said Will took a bad hit at the football game. He went in for a tackle. Then he stood up, fell on the ground, and didn't get back up. They are taking him to the hospital in Clinton."

"Cynthia, you two go on to meet them," I said. "Don't even think twice about us. I'll clean up and take any calls that come in."

"Are you sure? I hate to leave you here."

"Absolutely. Now scoot!"

Before they left we all held hands and prayed for Will; his mother, Luanne; his dad, Bob; and his two brothers and little sister, who were all at the game.

"My dream of being a mother was much more romantic
than reality. I thought it would be a lot more fun and
that my kids would think I was great." Mary

As Larry and Cynthia disappeared down their mile-long driveway, my mind rushed back to another time, 14 years earlier, when I first met Luanne Johnson. She was Cynthia's best friend in the sleepy rural town of Rose Hill, North Carolina, 200 miles from our home. She had just given birth to her third child, Bailey. Bailey was born with a hole in his heart. When he was seven months old, Luanne kissed his cheek before the doctors and nurses rolled him into the operating room to correct the defect. The physicians assured the Johnsons that the procedure had a 98 percent success rate and there was no cause for alarm. While Bailey came through the surgery just fine, he developed complications a few days later and had to go back in for a second procedure. When Luanne kissed Bailey on the cheek just before releasing him to the attending nurse for the second surgery, she had no idea it would be the last time she would see her child alive. Bailey died on the operating table on his brother Will's third birthday. And now this.

I pictured Luanne riding in the ambulance or perhaps following in a car close behind the blaring sirens. I recalled the words I had penned in another book, "There is an inexplicable bond that exists between a mother and her child. Even though the umbilical cord is severed in the delivery room, a cord of love connects them for the rest of their lives."[1] Luanne already had one deposit in heaven. The thought of a second was almost too painful to imagine.

Oh, he'll be okay, I thought. I'd grown up in a small North Carolina town where high school football was a part of community life. When

I was in elementary school, I went to Friday night games and played under the bleachers, paying very little attention to the pigskin on the field. When I was a teenager, I was a cheerleader and knew just enough about the game to know which cheers to yell when. My father-in-law had been a football coach off and on for more than 35 years. Boys were constantly "down on the play." But they always got up, didn't they?

I'm not sure how much time passed, but Cynthia's phone call startled me from my musing.

"Sharon," Cynthia began, "Will didn't make it. He died before he even got to the hospital."

Somehow the news spread through the quiet little town that Will Johnson had been hurt at the football game. All through the night I fielded calls that came to the Prices' home. Cynthia was Luanne's best friend, and Daniel had been Will's. Townsfolk knew where to call for the latest update.

The next day the newspapers all around the state reported the story. Will had gone in to make a tackle, and instead of grabbing his opponent at the waist, he hit the boy carrying the ball much too high. His opponent's helmet crashed into Will's chest, causing a concussion of the heart. He stood up and said, "Coach, I think I need to come out." Then he collapsed and his heart never beat again.

I was just a visitor from 200 miles away. I didn't know most of these people, but one thing was clear. What affected one, affected them all. A mother's dreams had been shattered and the entire town mourned.

"I am disappointed with my life. I had hoped to be a better mother and wife. I spent my life doing everything on my own strength instead of relying on God." Collette

Shattered dreams are a part of life. Children die, husbands leave, jobs are lost, cancer tests come back positive, proposals are rejected, teenagers rebel, houses burn, and terrorists attack. Part of the pain is the feeling that God has forgotten us, grown deaf to our cries, lost our address, or simply doesn't care. Isaiah wrote: "The LORD has forsaken me, the Lord has forgotten me" (Isaiah 49:14). David cried, "My God, my God, why have you forsaken me? Why are you so far from saving me, so far from the words of my groaning? O my God, I cry out by day, but you do not answer" (Psalm 22:1-2). Even Jesus called out from the cross, "My God, my God, why have You forsaken me?" (Matthew 27:46).

"One month after I completed high school, I became pregnant (unexpectedly) and married my high school sweetheart in August. Four days after the wedding, I miscarried. I had just started college, but my husband was in the service and stationed six hours away. By October I was clearly realizing that you can't make a marriage work with those ingredients, and I felt conviction to try to make the marriage a success. So I dropped out of college, left my dreams of becoming a doctor behind, and moved to be with my husband. Within a month, he had decided that the demands of being a husband and trying to do military schooling at the same time were not easy for him, so he sent me back home for a time. Six months earlier, I had been just another teenager with hopes and dreams and plans. Now, I felt as though my entire life was a failure overnight. Within three years, my marriage had failed, I was 1300 miles away from home, had a young daughter, and a job that wouldn't even make the rent." Wendy

---

I have cried, "Where are You, God? How could You do this to me? Have You forgotten all about me? Don't You care?" Then He answers, "Can a mother forget the baby at her breast and have no compassion on the child she has borne? Though she may forget, I will not forget you! See, I have engraved you on the palms of my hands" (Isaiah 49:15).

Ah, the string around His finger, the nail scar on His palm, the brand upon His heart. No, He doesn't forget.

Mary and Martha's Shattered Dream

In the New Testament, we find a story about two sisters whose dreams were shattered by a death in the family. Jesus received word that one of His best friends, Lazarus, was sick. The sisters sent this message to Jesus. "Lord, the one you love is sick" (John 11:3). Lazarus wasn't just any friend. He was so close that Jesus would know of whom they were speaking when they simply said, "The one you love."

John goes on to tell us that Jesus also loved Martha and her sister (verse 5), and then he writes, "*Yet* when he heard that Lazarus was sick, he stayed where he was two more days" (verse 6, emphasis added). It was as if John were saying, *I just didn't get it. He loved them, but He waited. If He would stop to help a stranger, certainly He would travel to heal a friend. But He waited!*

Jesus didn't go at once because God had a greater plan. It would have been a miracle on a small scale to heal a sick friend. It would be a miracle on a grand scale to raise him from the dead. It is difficult to wait on God when our dreams are falling apart, but He wants to make sure we understand that we are absolutely helpless in our own strength so that we will understand the greatness of His.

Two days later God gave Jesus the signal. It was time to go to Bethany. By the time Jesus arrived, Lazarus' decaying body had been in the tomb for four days. His death shook the entire village, and many Jews from surrounding cities went to mourn the loss. For these two women, this was more than the loss of a brother; it was the loss of their future dreams. With no father, no husband, no children, and now no brother, they would have no one to take care of and protect them in a culture in which it was difficult for women to provide for their own needs.

When Martha heard that Jesus was coming, she left the mourners and ran to meet Him.

"Lord," Martha said to Jesus, "if you had been here, my brother would not have died" (John 11:21). Can you relate to Martha? She was disappointed in Jesus. Her internal battle between the realities of her brother's decaying body and of knowing that Jesus could have prevented his death in the first place battled for supremacy.

Have you ever cried, "Lord, if You had been here, this would not have happened to me"? Have you ever asked, "Where were You? Where are You now?"

"I tried not to have dreams when I was young because
I did not want to be disappointed." Kelly

Then it is as if she thought better of the words that had escaped her lips, and she said, "But I know that even now God will give you whatever you ask" (verse 22).

Jesus said to her, "Your brother will rise again."

Martha answered, "I know he will rise again in the resurrection at the last day."

Jesus said to her, "I am the resurrection and the life. He who believes in me will live, even though he dies; and whoever lives and believes in me will never die. Do you believe this?"

"Yes, Lord," she told him, "I believe that you are the Christ, the Son of God, who has to come into the world" (verses 23-27).

Martha went back to her home and told Mary Jesus was asking for her. Like Martha, Mary ran to meet Him and said, "Lord, if you had been here, my brother would not have died" (verse 32). Do you see a pattern? Once again, *If You had been here, this would not have happened to me. Where were You?*

Do you think God hurts when we hurt? Oh, yes, dear sister, God hurts. Jesus wept when He saw the pain of those around him. He wept for the two sisters. He wept for the mourners. He wept for the ravages of sin and resulting death that Satan ushered into the world. He was so moved that He didn't even offer a condolence but simply asked, "Where have you laid him?" (verse 34). And what happened when Jesus arrived at the tomb? Two simple words: "Jesus wept" (verse 35).

Jesus ordered the stone to be rolled away from the mouth of the cave that served as Lazarus' tomb. Then He looked up and said, "Father, I thank you that you have heard me. I know that you always hear me, but I said this for the benefit of the people standing here, that they may believe that you sent me."

When He had said this, Jesus called in a loud voice, "Lazarus, come out!" (verses 41-43).

And he did.

Jesus resurrected Lazarus, and He resurrected Mary and Martha's dreams as well.

Those of us who have lost a loved one may be thinking, *Yeah, but God didn't bring my brother back. God didn't save my child. God didn't resurrect my dead marriage. God didn't bring Will back to life.*

Let's go back to Will for a moment. Did resurrection power take place after Will's death? His mother would say a resounding yes.

Luanne shared with me that just days before Will's final football game he had said, "Mom, I'll be glad when this is all over. Now that I'm older, I see just how unimportant all this sports stuff is."

As Luanne knelt beside her boy on that football field, she begged him to keep breathing. But then, as she felt him take his last breath, his words echoed in her heart, "I'll be glad when this is all over."

"It's all over, son," Luanne whispered. "Go on home."

"People in my life destroyed the dreams of a little girl. My dreams turned into nightmares." Tansy

---

At Will's funeral a few days after his death, Luanne stood and shared the gospel message about the Jesus Will loved so. What was the result? Thirty people attending the service committed their lives to Christ or renewed their passion for serving Him.

"Mrs. Johnson, I gave my life to Christ today."

"Luanne, I haven't been following Jesus like I should. I recommitted my life to Him today, and I'm going to get serious about my relationship with God."

"Luanne, our family was in a shambles and I was thinking about leaving my husband. But after today I have decided to make our marriage work. I see how important family is."

"I have been putting my family on the back burner and letting everything and anything come before them. After today, I'm putting my family second only to God."

The following week Luanne spoke to an assembly at the school

Will's team had been playing against at the time of the accident. She shared the gospel, and the crowd marveled at her faith. Hands shot up all around the gymnasium when Luanne asked if anyone would like to accept Jesus Christ as their Lord and Savior.

The Johnson family continues to minister about the power of Jesus Christ that sustains us when our dreams are shattered. Because of Will's death, hundreds have come to Christ and many family relationships have been restored.

The Bible says that before we know Jesus Christ, we are spiritually dead. However, when we accept Jesus Christ as our Savior, God gives us a new heart and a new spirit that is fully alive (Colossians 2:13). That is resurrection power at its best.

The Death of the Disciples' Dream

If ever there was a group of people who lost their dream, it was Jesus' disciples and the women who ministered to and with them. They had such high expectations that He would be the next political leader in Israel. They had witnessed His power in feeding 5000 men plus women and children with two loaves and five fishes. They had felt the waves beneath their tiny boat subside at His command. They had witnessed Him resurrect a lifeless child during a funeral procession, restore rotting flesh of lepers' limbs, render sight to a man blind from birth, and release a man bound by demons. They had seen Him walk on water, outwit the Pharisees, and win the lost.

In their small dreams for a political leader, they missed the bigger picture of a spiritual Savior. While Peter realized Jesus' identity, he did not understand His destiny. Peter was shocked when Jesus explained that He had to go to Jerusalem, suffer, be killed, and on the third day rise from the dead. He even took Jesus aside and began to rebuke Him. "Never, Lord!" he said. "This shall never happen to you!" (Matthew 16:22). Suffering was *not* part of Peter's dream.

Jesus turned and said to Peter, "Get behind me, Satan! You are a stumbling block to me; you do not have in mind the things of God, but the things of men" (verse 23).

Call me stupid, but don't call me Satan. Yet that is how Jesus sees it when we try to block God's plans. It is amazing that one minute Peter could be a building block and the next a stumbling block. But that's the trap we all fall into when we have our minds set on our own agenda rather than God's.

"I went through an abusive marriage for 12 years. It hurts now and probably always will." Janet

---

Does that mean we give up our dreams? I can promise you this, whatever dreams you have for your life, God's dreams for you are greater. The power of the Holy Spirit the disciples received after Jesus' resurrection, and the impact they made on the world thereafter, was beyond their wildest dreams. That's what happens when we align *our* dreams with *God's* dreams. That's what happens when we give our shattered dreams to God.

Our Reaction to Shattered Dreams

Even though Jesus forewarned the disciples of His death and resurrection, they fled when the soldiers came to arrest Him and failed to appear when they hung Him on a cross to die. As Jesus' battered and torn body was sealed away in a borrowed tomb, their hopes and dreams were sealed away with Him.

Virtually every day I receive e-mails from women with shattered dreams. A husband has an affair, becomes addicted to pornography, abuses the children, or deserts the family. A child gets caught with drugs, becomes pregnant, or dies in a car accident. Parents divorce, friends betray, careers come to an abrupt halt. The list is endless. So what do we do when our dreams are seemingly destroyed? What do we do when dreams and life collide? The answer to those questions will shape the rest of our lives.

The book of Job is about a man who lost his dreams. One day Satan came before God "from roaming through the earth and going back and forth in it" (Job 1:7). God asked him, "Have you considered my servant

Job? There is no one on earth like him; he is blameless and upright, a man who fears God and shuns evil" (verse 8).

Satan responded with, "Does Job fear God for nothing? Have you not put a hedge around him and his household and everything he has?" In other words, "Of course he loves You—You give him everything he wants!"

"My beautiful dream wedding became a reality, but three years later, the man I married chose to become a homosexual." Jane

---

Satan continued, "But stretch out your hand and strike everything he has, and he will surely curse you to your face" (verse 11). God allowed Satan to strike Job. He lost his ten children, his wealth, and his health. Just about the only thing Job didn't lose was his nagging wife, who told him to curse God and die. All through the book of Job we see a man who was beaten down by life but refused to turn his back on God. In the end, God, the restorer of dreams, blessed Job, made him prosperous again, and gave him twice as much as he had before (Job 42:10).

Satan, the Destroyer of Dreams

Did you notice a common theme with Sarah, Naomi, and Esther? With each woman the Jewish nation and the family tree of Jesus Christ was at stake. Sarah gave birth to Isaac, who was the second patriarch in Jesus' family line. Naomi's daughter-in-law Ruth gave birth to Obed, who was the father of Jesse, who was the father of David, who was the father of Solomon, and after many more "who was the father ofs," we get to Jesus. Esther saved the Jewish nation from annihilation by the Persians.

As I look at each one of these women and their dreams that teetered on the brink of extinction or fulfillment, I'm drawn to these questions: Who was the real enemy? Who was trying to destroy their dreams and the Jewish nation? Who was trying to destroy God's plan to bring the Savior of the world through the Hebrews? I believe there was only one antagonist in each of these stories. It wasn't Ishmael, Hagar, or Haman. It was Satan himself. Just as God's fingerprints are throughout the book of Esther, so are Satan's claw marks on the words and schemes of Haman. Likewise, as we begin to think about the dreams God has for our lives, we need to realize we have an enemy who tries to prevent those dreams from coming to fruition—the roaring lion that prowls around looking for someone to devour, someone's dreams to destroy (1 Peter 5:8).

Circumstances exist in each of our lives that cannot be reconciled other than by trusting that God's ways are not our ways. However, Satan is an opportunist who takes advantage of our vulnerable moments, twists and turns our thoughts, and tries to destroy our future hope. He taunts us with: *If God loved you, He would not have let that happen to you. If He cared for you, He would give what you want: A husband who would meet your needs, children who would obey your rules, and a career that would satisfy your goals.*

Satan has one basic weapon to destroy our dreams: lies. The Bible describes him as "a murderer from the beginning, not holding to the truth, for there is no truth in him. When he lies, he speaks his native language, for he is a liar and the father of lies" (John 8:44).

"I always wanted to be a mother. As much as I loved having four babies, they were much harder to deal with and more time consuming than I thought they would be." Cathy

---

While lies are Satan's primary weapon of choice, causing us to doubt God is his primary goal. During my years of struggling with infertility and the loss of a child, Satan taunted me with lies: *If God loved you, He would answer your prayer. You must not be a very good mother for God not to give you other children. You are a failure as a woman. You are a failure as a Christian. Believing the promises of God works for other people, but apparently they aren't meant for you.* On and on he spewed lies. Unfortunately I believed many of them.

Eve was a woman who had everything a girl could ever hope for. She was physically perfect, spiritually unified with God, emotionally one with Adam (the only perfect husband who ever existed). She had no clothes to wash, no groceries to buy, no house to clean, and she walked with God in the cool of the evening. And yet Satan slithered into the garden and told her that God was holding out on her. He told her that she would be happy if she did the one thing God told her not to do, eat of the tree of the knowledge of good and evil. "You will not surely die," he lied. "For God knows that when you eat of it your eyes will be opened, and you will be like God, knowing good and evil" (Genesis 3:4-5). Eve believed the lie, and it cost her her life.

Satan tempted Jesus the same way; not in a garden, but in a desert. However, each time he offered up a temptation that would have destroyed God's plan of redemption, Jesus refused it with the truth. His response to each of Satan's temptations was, "It is written" (Luke 4:4,8,10).

Author Neil Anderson said this about how to win the spiritual battles we face with Satan: "You don't have to out shout him or out muscle him to be free of his influence. You just have to out truth him."[2]

He whispers lies even though he knows the truth. Satan doesn't doubt God's control or God's power; he just wants to cause you to doubt. He says to the woman sitting alone in church, *Look at that family in the pew in front of you. Dad, Mom, and two spit-shined children. Why hasn't God blessed you with a family like that? You could be happy with a home like theirs.*

What you don't know is that the father just lost his job with no new employment opportunity in sight. The mother just this morning discovered a lump in her breast. One child got caught at school for lying, and the other was caught going on the Internet where he shouldn't have been. And yet, the enemy whispers…even though he knows the truth.

If Satan can get us to doubt God's justice and divine plan, then he knows we will be more easily swayed to try and make our own dreams come true in our own way. He still roams the earth looking for someone to devour with his lies. Even when he left Jesus in the desert, the Bible tells us, "He left him until an opportune time" (Luke 4:13). He would be back. He's always looking for the opened door, the unsecured window, the unsuspecting mind.

"It was in my mid- to late-twenties that I started worrying
that God might not give me my ideal 'picture of life.' That ideal
was a middle-class, American picture: a husband who loved
me, healthy children, and at least one dog and cat. And we
would live in a cozy home with a fireplace. I had been a little
fearful before, but my fear was increasing with my age. The
older I got, the more I feared I might not marry." Mariana

In any war a key defense tactic is to send in a spy to discover the enemy's battle plans. When we know what's coming, we can better prepare. It's often the surprise attacks that catch us off guard and defeat
us. This was never more evident than the Japanese attack on Pearl Harbor, December 7, 1941. While the U.S. secretary of state was meeting
with two Japanese diplomats in Washington, DC, discussing peace,
the Japanese military had already launched the attack on the U.S. military base at Pearl Harbor. Vice Admiral Chuichi Nagumo led a 33-ship
Japanese strike force under cover of night and launched 350 airplanes
against the U.S. fleet anchored in the peaceful waters of Oahu, Hawaii.
The attack killed 2388 people and wounded approximately 2000 more.
One ship, the *U.S.S. Arizona*, still sits upright on the bottom of the harbor with more than a thousand men entombed aboard.

As I walked through the *U.S.S. Arizona* Memorial in eerie silence
and read the names of those who died, I was reminded of how the
enemy still attacks us when we least expect it. Even today, bubbles of
oil rise to the surface where the *U.S.S. Arizona* lies in its watery grave to
remind us what can happen when we are caught off guard by the enemy.

Pain with a Purpose

Our shattered or unfulfilled dreams undoubtedly will cause
us great pain. However, that pain can be used for a great purpose.
Like Naomi, we can decide to become bitter or better. The choice is
ours. Hopefully, a shattered dream will stir our appetites for a higher
purpose or a higher calling or a higher love or a higher trust. Can
we love God no matter what? Will we trust Him regardless of our

circumstances? Do we believe He has greater dreams for our lives than we ever imagined?

Author and counselor Larry Crabb writes, "Shattered dreams open doors to better dreams, dreams that we do not properly value until the dreams that we improperly value are destroyed. Shattered dreams destroy false expectations, such as the 'victorious' Christian life with no real struggle or failure. They help us discover true hope. We need the help of shattered dreams to put us in touch with what we must long for, to create a felt appetite for better dreams, and living for better dreams generates a new, unfamiliar feeling that we eventually recognize as joy."[3]

Listen to Noni Joy Tari's perspective on shattered dreams recorded in Florence Littauer's book *Dare to Dream*:

> Because God loves us so much, He only uses two alternatives in how He ministers to us regarding our dreams: He turns them into fertilizer or He brings them to fruition.
>
> When people have broken dreams or dreams die, it is one of the most painful experiences in a person's life. But God never simply buries our dead and broken dreams because He'd be burying our hearts along with our dreams. Instead, He creatively turns our failures into fertilizer for an even more wonderful dream, a dream with even more potential to come to fruition.
>
> In my own life I have learned that I never need to be afraid to wish and hope and desire and dream big. Because when I honestly tell the Lord about my dreams, one of two positive things will happen. Either the dream will become fertilizer for something even better, or the Lord will give me the gumption and oomph to bring my dream to fruition. I can't lose either way![4]

Time and time again I have seen God take the most painful circumstances in my life and use them for His perfect purposes. Inevitably, I see that He had a greater dream in mind than I had ever imagined. Just as a seed needs the darkness of the earth to germinate and sprout, many times we need the darkness of pain to cultivate a new and deeper walk with God. But oh, the flowers that bloom in the soil of a fertile heart.

In the Garden of Gethsemane on the lower slopes of the Mount of Olives, Jesus cried in such anguish that drops of blood beaded on His forehead. Physicians tell us that in times of intense anguish, the body faints as a defense mechanism to prevent capillaries from bursting. In His angst, Jesus did not faint; thus His capillaries broke and blood spilled from the pores of His brow. Did He want to go to the cross? Three times He cried out to God, "My Father, if it is possible, may this cup be taken from me. Yet not as I will, but as you will" (Matthew 26:39).

The cup did not pass from Him, and Jesus obediently went to the cross. He didn't like the pain, but He endured it for God's eternal purposes.

God's greatest desire is for us to be conformed to the image of His Son. Like Michelangelo, who chipped and chiseled a block of stone to reveal the magnificent statue of David, God uses the chisel of life's circumstances to remove the unnecessary or excess in our lives to reveal the image of Christ within. As Bible teacher Beth Moore notes, "We cannot often refuse the fire, but we can refuse to be refined by it."[5] Let's look at a few verses that reveal how trials or shattered dreams can refine us.

Trials test our faith. "In this you greatly rejoice, though now for a little while you may have had to suffer grief in all kinds of trials. These have come so that your faith—of greater worth than gold, which perishes even though refined by fire—may be proved genuine and may result in praise, glory and honor when Jesus Christ is revealed" (1 Peter 1:6-7).

Trials mature our character. "Consider it pure joy, my brothers, whenever you face trials of many kinds, because you know that the testing of your faith develops perseverance. Perseverance must finish its work so that you may be mature and complete, not lacking anything" (James 1:2-4).

Trials purify our souls. "He knows the way that I take; when he has tested me, I will come forth as gold" (Job 23:10).

Trials bring eternal glory. "Our light and momentary troubles are achieving for us an eternal glory that far outweighs them all. So we fix our eyes not on what is seen, but what is unseen. For what is seen is temporary, but what is unseen is eternal" (2 Corinthians 4:17-18).

Trials keep us dependent on God. "To keep me from becoming conceited because of these surpassingly great revelations, there was given me a thorn in my flesh, a messenger of Satan, to torment me. Three times I pleaded with the Lord to take it away from me. But he said to me, 'My grace is sufficient for you, for my power is made perfect in weakness.' Therefore I will boast all the more gladly about my weaknesses, so that Christ's power may rest on me. That is why, for Christ's sake, I delight in weaknesses, in insults, in hardships, in persecutions, in difficulties. For when I am weak, then I am strong" (2 Corinthians 12:7-10).

Trials conform us to the image of Christ. "I consider that our present sufferings are not worth comparing with the glory that will be revealed in us" (Romans 8:18).

Yes, there is great purpose in the pain. I pray we won't miss it!

Letting Go of Shattered Dreams

One day my son was turning flips on the monkey bars on the playground and got a piece of bark in his eye. "Get it out! Get it out!" he cried. He was in pain and desperately wanted me to remove the bark. At the same time, he wouldn't remove his hand to let me do it. He vacillated between "Get it out!" and "Don't touch it!" for 45 minutes. Finally the pain overcame his fear and he decided to trust me. It took me 45 minutes to convince him to remove his hand and 10 seconds for me to remove the piece of bark from his eye.

In my frustration God whispered to my heart, *Are you really any different?*

I heard a story about a little boy who had his hand caught in a valuable vase. His parents pushed and pulled, tugged and twisted, but they couldn't get him free. Finally, they resolved to break the vase. But before the hammer came crashing down on the beautiful porcelain, the boy's father coaxed him one last time. "Son, I want you to open your fingers and spread them apart, draw them together at the tips, and try one more time to slip your hand out."

"I know the Bible has dreams for my life, but it is hard for me
to have faith because I've had so many disappointments." Janet

"I can't open my fingers like that, Daddy," the boy replied. "If I do,
I'll drop my penny!"

How about you? Are you hanging on to disappointment, to an
unfulfilled or shattered dream? Listen to the words of this poem by
Faith Mitchner.

> *Just as my child brings his broken toys*
> *with tears for me to mend,*
> *I took my broken dreams to God*
> *because He was my Friend.*
> *But then instead of leaving Him*
> *in peace to work alone,*
> *I hung around and tried to help*
> *with ways that were my own.*
> *At last I snatched them back and cried,*
> *"How could You be so slow?"*
> *"What could I do, My child?" He said,*
> *"You never did let go."*

Are you clinging to something that is worth about as much as a
penny compared to what God wants to give? Oh, my friend, God has
such great plans for you. You are His child. Let's let go of the penny,
let go of our broken dreams, and be free to become all He has created
us to be.

10

Restored Dreams

In 2002 my family traveled to Europe and visited one of the greatest artistic masterpieces in the history of man: the Sistine Chapel. Many artists contributed to the paintings, tapestries, and sculptures within its walls, but the most magnificent feat is the ceiling painted by Michelangelo. From 1508 to 1512, Michelangelo lay on his back and painstakingly painted one gigantic spiritual, historical, and biblical account of man. But almost as soon as the paintings were completed, they began to fade. After years of fading, ill-conceived attempts to cover the paintings with varnish added to layers of smoke and dirt, and the original masterpiece was barely visible.

The Italian proprietors of this historical and spiritual international treasure decided to test a new process for cleaning the murals that lined the walls and ceilings. In 1981, a special cleaning solution called AB-57 was developed. When years of filth and grime were gingerly removed inch by painstaking inch, the proprietors were surprised by the vibrant colors that emerged. The process of cleaning the ceiling took eight years, twice as long as it had taken Michelangelo to paint it. Artisans were awed at the inspiring beauty, the ingenious craftsmanship, the intense colors, and the intricate details as the paintings were brought back to life. For the first time in nearly 500 years, spectators saw the masterpiece the way it was originally intended.

But not everyone was pleased with the restoration. Some local folks

153

rebelled at the newly restored works of art. They had become accustomed to the dulling filth and grime left by years of pollution. "We want our paintings back!" they cried.

It was difficult for me to fathom anyone not appreciating the vivid colors that the artist originally intended. Then God reminded me of His desire to restore our faded dreams with the vivid colors He intended. Yet some of His children are much more comfortable with the filth and grime that mar His original works of art. Yes, God has dreams for our lives, but many times years of disappointment diminish those dreams until they are no longer recognizable. God desires to restore our forgotten dreams to a beauty beyond our wildest wonderings. Can we bear the beauty? Are we ready for the vibrant colors? Dare we dream again? I hope your answer is yes!

"Since I am now a single mother who struggles to make ends meet and get it all done, it is definitely not the life of my childhood dreams. But through it all, I have seen the hand of God work and move in my life. I do not regret for a minute that I am now in the relationship I am in with the King of kings. I have a wonderful child, and we live in the presence of the Lord." Sue

---

Let's look now at God, the restorer of dreams, and prepare for a breathtaking view of His masterpiece, an original work of art...you.

But God

One evening I had the opportunity to be the speaker at a fundraiser banquet for a women's and children's homeless shelter. The afternoon before the event, I went to the shelter to visit with some of the ladies who temporarily lived there. I listened to their dreams, and I noticed that theirs were no different than those of the women I spoke to who had six digit incomes and lived in grand estates.

When Sherry was a little girl, she dreamed that she would live in a blue house with a white picket fence. Darla dreamed she would marry, have three children, and live in a small bungalow. Patty dreamed she would become a nurse and work in the local hospital. Betty dreamed she would be a veterinarian. Rose dreamed she would be an ice-skater and teach other people how to skate. Not one of the women, in their wildest dreams, imagined they would be living in a homeless shelter, sharing a bathroom with seven other women, addicted to alcohol or drugs, running from an abusive boyfriend, or unable to keep a job.

"I wanted to be a career woman and not be someone who stayed home and cleaned the house. Now, I am so pleased that I am able to stay at home, take care of my family, and clean my house!" Kristie

---

But here they were. How were they going to make it in the world again? One thing was sure—they needed to learn how to dream again. They needed vision to imagine their lives differently than their seemingly hopeless situations portrayed. The counselors at the homeless shelter gave the women more than food stamps, a ten-step program, or a roof over their heads. They introduced them to Jesus, the restorer of broken lives and shattered dreams.

The Bible is filled with stories of seemingly hopeless situations that serve as a backdrop for God's miracles. The escaping Israelites are trapped between the Red Sea on one side and encroaching Egyptian soldiers on the other. Joseph is thrown into a pit, taken into slavery, and tossed into prison. The Israeli army is defenseless against the giant the Philistine named Goliath with no one brave enough to challenge him. Jesus is arrested, beaten, and crucified by the very people He came to save. Just when dreams are seemingly shattered God miraculously shows up and intervenes. That's who He is...the restorer and fulfiller of dreams.

"God called Jesus Christ to what seemed absolute disaster. And Jesus Christ called His disciples to see Him put to death, leading every one of them to the place where their hearts were broken. His life was an absolute failure from every standpoint except God's. But what seemed to be failure from man's standpoint was a triumph from God's standpoint because God's purpose is never the same as man's purpose."[1]

I've noticed that many times man's hopeless situations and God's divine interventions are connected by the little word "but." The words "but God" have become two of my favorite words in Scripture.

In Luke 9, after Jesus, Peter, James, and John returned from the Mount of Transfiguration, they were met by a desperate father whose dreams were being destroyed one seizure at a time. For years his only son had been gripped by demons and thrown into convulsions accompanied by foaming at the mouth and ear-piercing screams. "It scarcely ever leaves him and is destroying him," the father explained (Luke 9:39).

The nine disciples who had remained behind during Jesus' absence were unable to cast out the demon. They had been empowered to do so, but with their most positive influences absent (Jesus, Peter, James, and John), and their most negative influences present (the Pharisees and unbelievers), they lacked the faith. So Jesus asked the father to bring the boy to Him.

"Even while the boy was coming, the demon threw him to the ground in a convulsion. *But Jesus* rebuked the evil spirit, healed the boy, and gave him back to his father" (verse 42, emphasis added). In one short verse, a father and son's hopeless situation and God's divine intervention were bridged by the powerful words "but Jesus."

If you're like me, you may read the story of God's intervention and restoration in Luke 9 and think, *But could He do that for me? Could He intervene in my hopeless situation, lift the fog, give me clear direction, and restore the years I've lost through poor decisions?*

Mark tells us this same story, but he gives us some insight into the father's heart that Dr. Luke omitted. Again, it involves the word "but."

Jesus asked the boy's father, "How long has he been like this?" "From childhood," he answered. "It has often thrown him into the fire or water to kill him. *But* if you can do anything, take pity on us and help us." "If you can?" said Jesus.

"Everything is possible for him who believes." Immediately the boy's father exclaimed, "I do believe; help me overcome my unbelief!" (Mark 9:21-24, emphasis added).

Oh, my. *But if you can?* I cringe at the father's words, and yet those unspoken words are too often the underlying current of my own prayers. I remember when I was fourteen years old and a brand-new Christian, praying for my unsaved dad. My prayers went something like this: "God, I'm praying for my daddy. Now, Lord, he's a bad man. He drinks, chases women, gambles…(I continued to enumerate his more colorful and less honorable activities so God would realize the gravity and bleakness of the situation.) And, Lord, I know You saved Saul of Tarsus and spoke to him through a blinding light on his way to Damascus, but my daddy is probably worse than Saul. So, if You can, will you save my daddy too?"

"I was told when I was 12 years old that I could not be an actress or author because I wasn't good enough or smart enough. I was 40 before my husband convinced me that I had enough talent and drive to see my dreams become a reality." Eva Marie Everson—author

---

And, praise God, He did. I didn't have a very strong faith at the time, but like the boy's father in Mark 9, I had enough.

Remember what the Lord said when he overheard ninety-year-old Sarah laughing at the prophecy that she would have a baby in her old age. "Is anything too hard for the LORD?" (Genesis 18:14). The boy's father said, "If you can do *anything*" and Jesus assured him God could do *everything.*

Restoring Sight to the Blind

One day Jesus was traveling down the road from Jericho when two blind men began to call out after him, "Lord, Son of David, have mercy on us!" (Matthew 20:30). Many blind men and women traveled to

Jericho with the hopes of obtaining the plentiful balsam used for eye defects.[2] However, the dream of regaining their vision was nowhere in sight, and they continued to stumble in darkness. And now hope was walking their way.

When these two men cried out to Jesus, the crowd rebuked them and warned them to be quiet, but the men continued to cry, "Lord, Son of David, have mercy on us!"

Jesus stopped and called to them. "What do you want me to do for you?" (verse 32).

(I have to stop right here. Can you just imagine Jesus showing up at your door and asking, "What do you want Me to do for you?" It gives me shivers just to think about that. I wonder how many times I've missed His still, small voice asking me that very question. Now back to our two blind friends.)

When Jesus asked the question, the men didn't have to think of a response. They immediately replied, "Lord, we want our sight" (verse 33).

"Moved with compassion, Jesus touched their eyes; and immediately they regained their sight and followed Him" (Matthew 20:34 NASB). The New International Version says they "received" their sight, but the New American Standard Bible better translates the word, "regained," meaning they saw again. They had not been born blind but once had seen the sparkle in a child's smile, the vibrant yellow of a desert flower, and the incandescent hues of a sunset. At some point, the two men had seen, but because of illness or circumstance they had lost their vision. With one touch from Jesus, their dreams of seeing again were restored.

Have you lost your sight? Jesus is asking, "What do you want Me to do for you?"

Oh, Lord, help us to see again.

From the Pit to the Palace

Some dreams are shattered by what has happened to us, and some dreams are shattered because of what has happened through us because of the choices we have made. Let's take a look at both and see how God is the restorer of dreams regardless of the origin of the circumstance.

First, let's look at a dream that was nearly shattered because of something done *to* someone.

The story of Joseph is recorded in Genesis 37–50. Joseph was the second youngest and most favorite of Jacob's 12 sons. Perhaps he's most well known for the coat of many colors his father made for him. Joseph's brothers were jealous of this tattletelling Daddy's boy and couldn't speak a kind word to him.

When Joseph was about 17, he had a vision regarding his future. In this vision, he saw himself and his brothers binding sheaves of wheat in a field. Suddenly Joseph's sheaf stood upright, while his brothers' sheaves gathered around his and bowed down. Unfortunately, the young Joseph did not keep this dream to himself but shared it with his brothers. This only added fuel to the fire of their hatred.

Then Joseph had another vision of eleven stars, the sun, and the moon all bowing down to him. He hadn't learned from his first mistake, and he told his brothers this dream as well. Even his father became angry at the idea of he, Joseph's mother, and his brothers all bowing down to him.

> "When I met my husband, he drove a BMW, owned his own business, and was the picture of success and security. Through a business downturn and a number of poor decisions, we lost everything but our Suburban and each other. Because the Lord finally turned me to surrender it all to Him, our marriage is better than ever and our family is strong." Dorothy

Sometime later Joseph's father sent him to check up on his brothers, who were with the sheep several miles away from their home. When his brothers saw him coming, they plotted to take his life. "Let's kill him and throw him into one of these cisterns and say that a ferocious animal devoured him. Then we'll see what comes of his dreams" they schemed.

One of his brothers, Reuben, talked the others out of actually killing Joseph and instead throwing him in an empty cistern alive. Rueben was secretly planning on getting him out later and taking him back home. But before he could rescue Joseph, one of the other brothers noticed an Ishmaelite caravan approaching. "I have a better idea," Judah said. "Let's sell Joseph to these slave traders for 20 shekels of silver. That way his blood won't be on our hands." So the brothers pulled Joseph out of the well, handed him over to the caravan, and waved goodbye as he was carted off to Egypt. Then they killed a goat, spread its blood on Joseph's coat, and told their father he had been killed by a ferocious animal.

But God had a dream for Joseph, and ten jealous boys couldn't stop it. Things did not go well for Joseph for quite some time. He was falsely accused of attempted rape by his master's wife and thrown into prison. While incarcerated, he became known as an interpreter of dreams. Through several twists and turns of events that only God could orchestrate, Joseph was called on to interpret one of Pharaoh's dreams, which predicted seven years of abundance followed by seven years of famine. His interpretation gave Pharaoh the foresight to prepare for the coming drought by storing up enough grain to feed the Egyptians as well as those in the surrounding countries. As a reward, Pharaoh made Joseph the governor of Egypt to oversee the entire rescue mission.

During the famine, guess who showed up to purchase some grain? Joseph's brothers. They didn't recognize him, but I wonder if visions of eleven sheaves of wheat bowing down to one standing upright danced in their heads.

God had a dream for Joseph. Yes, en route he traveled from the pit to the prison before finally reaching the palace, but God's purposes were accomplished nonetheless. When I read the story of Joseph, I'm always struck with one thread throughout. He always did the best he could in every circumstance and did not let bitterness or resentment stymie his activity or love for God. When he was a servant, he was the best servant he could be. When he was a prisoner, he was the best prisoner he could be. And when he was governor, he was the best governor he could be.

Unlike most of us, he had a very clear picture of what God had planned for his life. God had revealed it in an actual dream. And yet

Joseph never once did anything to try to make that dream come to fruition on his own. He simply did his best at each step along the way and waited on God to direct his path. And what of his attitude toward his brothers when they came begging for help?

Once Joseph revealed that he, the governor of Egypt from whom they came to buy grain, was their long-lost brother, they fell down in terror. "We are your servants," they cried. But Joseph said to them, "Do not be afraid, for am I in God's place? And as for you, you meant evil against me, but God meant it for good in order to bring about his present result, to preserve many people alive" (Genesis 50:18-20 NASB).

While many were at work to destroy the plan that God had for this young boy, God, the restorer of shattered dreams, fit each piece of the puzzle together to create a magnificent masterpiece of faith, forgiveness, and overriding power to fulfill His plans. Oh, that we would have the same attitude as Joseph when the twists and turns of life take us to difficult, dark places.

So what does Joseph's story have to do with you and me? Everything. God has a plan for each and every one of His children. "No eye has seen, no ear has heard, no mind has conceived what God has prepared for those who love him" (1 Corinthians 2:9). People may abuse, misuse, and mistreat us. Tragedy may trail behind us. And yet God's dreams will be accomplished when we cooperate with Him.

Beth Moore wrote:

> Every little girl has dreams; and, if she trusts Christ with all her heart, nothing can disable God from surpassing a childhood reach with a divine reality. The suicide of her husband could not keep God from surpassing Kay Arthur's dreams. Her sudden paralysis could not keep God from surpassing Joni Eareckson Tada's dreams. Her horrifying stay in a Nazi concentration camp could not keep God from surpassing Corrie Ten Boom's dreams. Her world of poverty and suffering could not keep God from surpassing Mother Teresa's dreams. God surpasses our dreams when we reach past our personal plans and agendas to grab the hand of Christ and walk the path He chose for us. He is

obligated to keep us dissatisfied until we come to Him and
His plan for complete satisfaction."³

Perhaps your life has not turned out the way you had planned. Perhaps you are at a place you did not expect to be. Remember this, even though we may have been thrown in a pit or tossed into a prison, God can use every bit of our pain to get us to the palace He planned all along.

From the Penthouse to the Pigpen

You may be thinking of the times you've let God down by denying Him, disobeying Him, or dishonoring Him. You may be thinking of the dreams in your life that were shattered because of *your* poor decisions. Many times I've cried out, "Oh, God, how could You love me? I'm not worthy of being called Your daughter! I'm not worthy to fulfill the dreams You have for my life. I've strayed. I've taken control of my own life. And I've made a mess."

God knows all about wayward children who think they know what's best for their own lives. To help us understand just how God feels about His children when they stray, Jesus told a story about a rebellious son and the unrelenting love of his father (Luke 15:11-24).

"My biggest dream developed out of the fact that I was the only one in my family who went to church and had any interest in God. In my teen years, I always felt like an outsider at church because I was always alone. Everyone was gracious and included me, but it wasn't my family. I remember falling on my knees at age 15 and asking God if I could just be on the inside sometime in my life. I married a pastor who planted a church that has grown from 17 people in 1971 to 2400 in 2002. God answered!" Gayle

---

"There was a man who had two sons. The younger one said to his father, 'Father, give me my share of the estate.' So he divided his property between them" (verses 11-12).

When the young man asked for his inheritance a bit early, it was if he were saying, "Father, I wish you were dead. Go ahead and give me what's coming to me now." The father could have refused and tried to protect the boy from making a bad decision, but instead he chose to let his son learn from his mistakes.

The prodigal went to the big city and lived it up in the penthouse with his new friends, but it wasn't long before his money ran out. As his wealth disappeared, so did his friends and his dreams. And then we see the turning point in this young man's life. Luke 15:14 says, "He began to be in need." With no money, no food, and no place to lay his head, the boy went to work for a farmer taking care of pigs. For a Jew, simply touching a pig would render him unclean, and here was this young man tending them the way a Hebrew tends sheep. Not only did he take care of the pigs, he was so hungry he wanted to eat the pigs' food himself, but "no one gave him anything" (verse 16).

When he came to his senses, he said, "What am I, crazy? Even my father's hired hands are treated better than this. They have plenty to eat, and I'm out here starving to death. I'm going back home, beg my father for forgiveness, and ask for a job!"

So he got up and went to his father. What do you think his father was doing all this time? I think he was praying. I know he was expectantly watching. Here is my favorite part of the story:

> While he was still a long way off, his father saw him and was filled with compassion for him; he ran to his son, threw his arms around him and kissed him. The son said to him, "Father, I have sinned against heaven and against you. I am no longer worthy to be called your son." But the father said to his servants, "Quick! Bring the best robe and put it on him. Put a ring on his finger and sandals on his feet. Bring the fattened calf and kill it. Let's have a feast and celebrate. For this son of mine was dead and is alive again; he was lost and is found." So they began to celebrate (verses 22-24).

I can just picture the father scanning the horizon day after day, praying for his son to return. Then one day it happened. He caught a glimpse of his son coming across the field. The father didn't stand stoically waiting for an appropriate apology. There was no, "I told you so." Instead, when he saw his son in the distance, he pulled up his robe, ran shamelessly to embrace him, and smothered him with kisses and tears of joy. He placed a robe meant for an honored guest on his shoulders, slipped a ring signifying authority on his finger, and fitted the sandals of a freed man on his dusty bare feet. Then they had a big party!

Even though the son did not deserve forgiveness, even though he had squandered his inheritance, even though he had rejected his family, the father restored the son and his squandered dreams…and our heavenly Father will do the same for us. Whether you are the son in this parable or the parent who is praying for a prodigal to return, Jesus paints the picture of God's unrelenting love and His desire to restore shattered dreams.

Even when our dreams are shattered by our own poor decisions? Even then.

In my Bible, this parable is titled "The Parable of the Lost Son," but for me a better title would be "The Parable of a Father's Unrelenting Love."

Prodigal Patty

Perhaps you know a prodigal. Perhaps you *are* the prodigal. Let me share a story of a prodigal that is dear to my heart. We'll call her Prodigal Patty. Patty and I will tell you her story together.

When Patty was a little girl, all she wanted to be when she grew up was a mommy and a wife. Like me, she pretended on many occasions to be a bride and played dress-up to prepare for the big day. Patty's father was a preacher, and her upbringing was very strict: no television, no radio, no swimming with people outside of her immediate family, no wearing of pants. Even dark-colored clothes were considered too masculine. But while the family was very religious, Patty knew her parents fought a lot and sensed the tension in their home. When she was fifteen years old, she woke up one morning and her father was gone. It was then she discovered that this man she adored was having an affair.

"My mother lost a husband, and my sister and brother lost a father, but I lost the one person in the world who loved me more than any other," she said. "I was a daddy's girl, and I lost the most important person in my life."

Patty's family went from being incredibly close to one another to each man for himself. They were in survival mode, fighting a similar battle but on individual battlefields in their own hearts and minds. Her father left the pastorate, and unfortunately her mother forbid him to see the children. Patty recalls him leaving a birthday present on the porch for her sixteenth birthday.

"I caught a glimpse of his taillights as he drove away. I was encouraged that he remembered my birthday, but when the lights of his car were out of sight, I felt the light in my own life go dim."

Patty's father married the woman with whom he had the affair, and her mother remarried six weeks after the divorce was final. Both parents divorced their second spouses and married a third some years later. Patty never shed a tear during this incredible time of loss, but her heart bled as each arrow struck its tender chambers. Her sister turned to a lifestyle of partying with her friends, her brother turned to drugs, and Patty turned to anyone who would love her, accept her, and make her feel important. Ultimately, she turned to other women. Patty joined the homosexual lifestyle.

"For ten years I lived a life of homosexuality, not only as a mere participant, but as a vocal supporter for the coalition for gay and lesbian rights. I volunteered at a gay and lesbian helpline center and counseled gays on issues they were dealing with at the time. I was the sick and hurting leading the sick and hurting. I later became in charge of a newsletter for the gay and lesbian coalition. It was a life of absolute immorality, and yet I continued to pray and ask God to not let go of me and turn me over to my own way of thinking. I hurt my parents badly, and I even demanded that if my mom wanted to see me, she would have to let me bring whomever I was with at the time home with me, including holidays. Oh, how my mother must have loved me and the complete heartbreak this must have been for her. Being in that lifestyle is so all-consuming and such a brainwash. Unless you have been there it is hard to explain. Satan twists your thinking to where you whole-heartedly believe that your friends are your true family. "

Patty knew she was a prodigal. She knew what she was doing was wrong. But she did not have the strength or willpower to break free. Satan took one step of desperation made by a hurting young girl and turned it into a walk of bondage. But God—here come my favorite words again—*but God* didn't let go of Patty. Just as the prodigal son's father scanned the horizon day after day searching for his son, Patty's heavenly Father was watching and waiting for His daughter's return.

"I went from one relationship to another searching for true love to mend whatever hurts I was feeling instead of looking to God. I was feeding off of others who were searching as well. The change of address stickers on my mail started mounting up until little yellow stickers covered the envelopes. As odd as it seemed, I attended a church for gays, hoping God would approve of what I was doing, even though I knew it was an abomination to Him. Oh, how faithful He was to me."

Just like the prodigal son in Luke 15, God allowed Patty to continue in her rebellious lifestyle until she hit rock bottom. And just like the prodigal son, she began to be in need and came to her senses.

Patty moved to another state with one of the leaders of the gay movement in the area. During one of their retreats, her entire group of friends turned against her and accused her of lying about a certain matter. Each one turned their back on her and asked her to leave their circle. This was the final rejection. Crying uncontrollably, Patty left and headed back to her hometown. She doesn't remember how she got there. Amazingly, when she arrived home, she had a small spare tire on her wheel, but she didn't remember having a flat or anyone changing it along the way. (I suspect an angel took care of Patty.)

When she arrived home, she was unable to speak but simply rocked back and forth or lay in a fetal position. She was admitted to a counseling facility to undergo intense treatment. When Patty arrived, she had not showered, eaten, slept, or combed her hair in days. She was unresponsive to therapy, and the staff suspected she would die. After a week of no change, someone came into her room and placed a book, *The Search for Significance*, on her nightstand. She picked it up and began reading about her life on every page. God began to whisper His loving words into Patty's heart. He began wooing her back to spiritual, emotional, and physical health. And even though she wasn't listening to the counselors, her heavenly Father scanned the horizon and began calling out her name. With tears streaming down her cheeks, she responded to His voice and turned to run into His arms. I can just see God now, picking up the hem of His robe and running to meet her!

"I was on my way back," Patty said. "The Lord had to strip me of my home, my job, and all my friends in order to save me from myself. What Satan meant for evil, God is using for good. Oh, what mercy. What grace. I am amazed that God chose to save me, bless me, and now use me in His kingdom."

"God has confirmed that my life has purpose—that I am important to His kingdom—whether or not I'm married. He has helped me shift my self-identity from being 'not married' to being a servant in His kingdom. Consequently, I believe that once I shifted my focus, I was more open to some incredible ministry opportunities God had in store for me. One of those was a trip this past summer to the Czech Republic to teach English and share Christ at a summer camp. God had helped me shift my focus from 'I want to be married' to 'I want to serve God.'" Mariana

---

Patty's life is a portrait of restoration and redemption. Her dreams of being a wife and mother have come true. She is a beautiful young woman with a very masculine handsome husband and two lovely children. God is using Patty to help families with prodigals living in the gay lifestyle and encouraging them to not lose hope. Patty came back to the Father, and He came running to meet her. He placed a royal robe of righteousness around her shoulders and proclaimed, *Let's have a feast and celebrate. For this daughter of mine was dead and is alive again; she was lost and is found!* And God, with all the angels, threw a big party to celebrate her return.

No matter what has been done *to* you or what has been done *through* you, God can take the pieces of your shattered dreams and make a beautiful mosaic of your life. There is no place so far from Him that His mercy cannot save and use for His glory. He is the restorer of dreams.

What You Was Made For

I sat in a darkened theater watching the movie *The Legend of Bagger Vance*. Now, I know the theology wasn't correct, but one scene caused tears to stream down my cheeks. It was during a time when I was struggling with some issues in my past that were blocking my ministry in the present. Let me take you to the scene.

As a young man, Rannulph Junuh was an incredible golfer who showed great promise. But right in his prime, he was called away to war. During one particular battle, his entire company was killed. Junuh was the lone survivor, but he did not survive very well. When he returned home, he lost his dream of becoming a professional golfer and lived in an abandoned old house in seclusion from the rest of the world. Through a series of events, he was challenged to play in a golf tournament and represent the city of Savannah, Georgia. Along with the challenge came a certain fellow, Bagger Vance, who would be his caddy. Bagger, as it turned out, was supposed to be a type of angel sent to help Junuh rediscover his dreams. In one final scene, Junuh is trying to recover from a bad shot by hitting a ball out of the woods. Standing alone among the trees, the horrors of war return and he cannot go any further. He hears the gunfire and sees the soldiers falling all around him. Trembling hands. Pounding heart. Sweaty brow. Fearful eyes. Tormented screams. Rapid fire. Exploding bombs.

Then Bagger appears in the woods and interrupts Junuh's vision of the past. Listen to this scene:

> **Junuh:** "I can't do this. You don't understand."
>
> **Bagger:** "I don't need to understand. Ain't no soul on this entire earth ain't got a burden to carry he didn't understand.

You ain't alone in that. But you been carrying this one long enough. Time to go on an lay it down."

Junuh: "I don't know how."

Bagger: "You got a choice. You can stop or you can start."

Junuh: "Start?"

Bagger: "Walkin'. Right back to where you always been and then stand there. Still…real still…and remember."

Junuh: "It was long ago."

Bagger: "No, sir. It was just a moment ago. Time for you to come on out of the shadow, Mr. Junuh. Time for you to choose."

Junuh: "I can't."

Bagger: "Yes, you can. But you ain't alone. I'm right here wich ya. I been here all along. Play the game. The one that only you was meant to play. The one that was given to you when you came into this world."

(Junuh takes his stance and places his hands on the club.)

Bagger: "Ready? Take your stance. Strike the ball, Junuh, and don't hold nothin' back. Give it everythin'. Let yourself remember…remember your swing. That's right. Settle yourself. Now is the time, Junuh."

Rannulph Junuh took his stance, clutched the club, and knocked the ball out of the woods and onto the green. He also came out of the darkness and remembered who he was and what he "was made to do."

Now, I'm not a golfer, but I was standing right there in the woods with Junuh. With sweaty palms and racing heart…remembering the pains of the past…remembering past failures…remembering past defeats…remembering the battles lost and the wounded left behind. Then God came and whispered in my ear, *Sharon, take your stance. It's time for you to come out of the shadows. Don't be afraid. You do what I have created you to do. The plan that I set in place for you before you came into this world. Don't let the memories of the past hold you captive. I'm right here with you. I've been here all along.*

Are you ready to come out of the shadows? Are you ready to tackle that thing God has placed in your heart to do? Settle yourself. Now's the time. Come on now, and let's discover God's dreams for our lives together. But first let's take a brief intermission.

Interrupted Dreams

Most of us have had shattered dreams. Many of us have had restored dreams. But I dare say there are a number of us who are in between, waiting for God to move in our lives or tell us where to move instead. Oh, I've been there, my friend. Just like waiting through a long intermission in the middle of a play, I've sat in the dark waiting for the curtain to rise and for God to show me the rest of my story.

Moses—now, he was a man who experienced an intermission. A 40-year intermission. When God began to show me glimpses of the dreams He had for my life, I reacted much the way my friend Moses did. God's sneak preview left me sputtering a long list of reasons why I wasn't qualified for the job. And, like Moses, I began a series of what-ifs that revealed just how weak my faith really was. But I'm getting ahead of myself. Let's start at the beginning.

Moses was born during a time when the Israelites were slaves in Egypt. All day long they were under the whip of taskmasters who forced them to make bricks from mud and straw. But instead of breaking their spirits as Pharaoh had hoped, the heavy labor only made them stronger. Pharaoh was concerned that the Israelites were becoming too numerous and could potentially try to take over the country, so he made a decree that every newborn Hebrew baby boy must be thrown into the Nile. During this time, a woman named Jochebed became pregnant.

"Mommy, what will we do if the baby you are carrying is a boy?" her seven-year-old daughter asked.

"We will remain calm and pray that God will show us what we are to do. I have a strange feeling about this child. I do not believe God will allow him to die."

At the proper time, Moses was born and his mother hid him in their mud-thatched home for three months. Jochebed had a dream for her son. It was very simple, really. She had a dream that her son would live. During that time, I believe she prayed and asked God for clear direction and divine intervention. Soon He began to weave a plan in her mind, and with nimble fingers she wove reeds into a basket and covered it with pitch to make it watertight. Then she obeyed Pharaoh's command and placed the baby into the alligator-infested Nile River, only Moses was set afloat in his own personal ark. While he bobbed over the surface of the water, his mother prayed that someone, anyone, would come by and save her precious child. Meanwhile, his sister, Miriam, hid in the bulrushes to see what would happen.

"I wanted to live in the jungle with Tarzan. My dreams have been fulfilled in a different way than I expected. I work in television (definitely a jungle with animals, in a sense) and I teach worship dance at my church. The greatest aspect is that it is all much more fulfilling because the Lord is involved in every area. How boring my dreams would have been without Him to fulfill them. Now I swing through the jungle of life with Him, get rescued from the cannibals by Him, and dance for Him!" Christie

---

As God would have it, someone did come along. Well, not just someone, but the only one in the entire kingdom who could do whatever she wanted—Pharaoh's daughter. God answered a mother's prayer exceedingly abundantly more than she could have ever asked or imagined (Ephesians 3:20 NKJV).

"Oh, this must be one of the Hebrew babies," the princess said as her attendants drew Moses out of the water. "Look how beautiful he is."

On cue, Miriam magically appeared out of the reeds and asked, "Shall I go and get one of the Hebrew women to nurse the baby for you?" (Exodus 2:7).

"Yes, go," she answered. "And I will pay her."

Talk about a dream come true! Jochebed must have been ecstatic! She was going to nurse her baby and get paid to do it.

After Moses had been weaned, somewhere between two to three years old,[1] Jochebed delivered him to Pharaoh's daughter, and he became her son. "Moses was educated in all the wisdom of the Egyptians and was powerful in speech and action" (Acts 7:22). He learned reading, writing, arithmetic, and perhaps one or more of the languages of Canaan.[2]

We don't know how, but sometime before age 40, Moses discovered that he was not an Egyptian after all, but a Hebrew. (Charlton Heston discovered this when he found his baby blanket!) At that point Moses devised a dream for his life. He decided he was going to be the deliverer of the Hebrew nation. Now this is crucial. Moses decided *what* he was going to do. Moses decided *when* he was going to do it. Moses decided *how* he was going to do it. He planned a work and then set out to work the plan. It was all his doing.

One day Moses saw an Egyptian and a Hebrew fighting. *This will be a good day to begin my plan of freeing the Hebrews from bondage*, he must have thought to himself. So Moses killed the Egyptian and hid him in the sand. One down, several million to go.

The next day, Moses saw two Hebrews fighting. "Why are you hitting your fellow Hebrew?" Moses asked the one in the wrong.

The man said, "Who made you ruler and judge over us?" (That was a good question. Who *had* made him ruler and judge over them? Certainly not God.) "Are you thinking of killing me as you killed the Egyptian?" (Exodus 2:13-14).

Moses knew then that his act of murder was widely known and he was terrified. When the Pharaoh heard about it, he tried to have Moses arrested and killed. So Moses fled to the land of Midian. He probably thought his dreams were shattered and lost forever. In truth, he just needed an intermission.

Moses went from riches to rags in one day. In Midian he married a woman named Zipporah and spent the next 40 years tending her father's smelly sheep.

Moses had a dream. It was a good and noble dream. It was a dream to save the Hebrew nation from slavery and bondage. However, he ran ahead of God and tried to make his dream a reality in his own way, in his own time, and in his own strength. The result was disastrous. After a while, he forgot his dream altogether.

The Moses we see 40 years after he fled from Egypt is not the same ostentatious Moses we saw earlier. After 40 years of tending sheep, Moses had become so insecure that he had developed a speech impediment. No longer was he powerful in speech and actions but now pitiful without confidence or courage. No determination. No drive. No dreams.

Moses' mother had placed him in the river to save his life. God had placed him in the desert to save his soul. Now, God had him right where He wanted him—at the end of himself. A. W. Tozer said, "The reason why many are still troubled, still seeking, still making little forward progress, is because they have not yet come to the end of themselves. We are still giving some of the orders, and we are still interfering with God's working within us." Moses had come to the end of himself, and when he had, God was waiting there to embrace him.

"I wanted to be a missionary in India to help children
in the orphanages. I've never make it to India, but
I am a guardian for abused and neglected children
going through the court system." Annette

One day while Moses was tending his sheep on Mount Horeb, he saw a bush that was burning but not being consumed. When the Lord saw that Moses had turned aside to see the bush, God spoke to him.

"Moses! Moses!"

"Here I am," Moses replied.

Then, from the midst of the burning bush, God told Moses that He had a dream for his life. He had heard the cry of the Hebrews in Egypt, and He was going to use Moses to deliver them.

But Moses argued with the Lord. "Who am I that I should go to Pharaoh? Who am I going to say sent me? What if they don't believe me?" With each point of Moses' argument, God's answer was the same: "I will be with you."

In one last plea of desperation, Moses said, "O Lord, I have never been eloquent, neither in the past nor since you have spoken to your servant. I am slow of speech and tongue" (Exodus 4:10). Essentially he was praying, "O Lord, please send someone else to do it."

God grew angry with Moses and allowed him to take his brother Aaron along as a mouthpiece. And oh, the problems his brother caused.

I hope you'll go back to the early chapters of the book of Exodus and read the rest of the story. But let's stop right here and make a few observations. Did you notice that God's dream for Moses was the same dream Moses had for his life 40 years earlier? Yet Moses had forgotten the flame that burned in his heart so many years before—to free the Hebrew people. He had forgotten his passion, his purpose, and his preordained preparation for the task. However, God had not forgotten. He was simply waiting for Moses to get ready.

Where did Moses go wrong? He went ahead of God. Anabel Gillham writes, "Moses wasn't wrong in his vision or in his goal. He was wrong in his method. His perception of how God worked and of God's ways was wrong. Moses didn't really know what God wanted him to be, and it took another 40 long years for God to build new patterns into Moses and bring him to that understanding. God wanted a man who was aware of his inadequacies; a man who, of necessity, would draw from God's strength, wisdom, and power; a man who would recognize God's ability through his own weakness."[3]

So many times, when we think we are ready, we aren't. Then when we think we aren't ready, we are. So what does it mean to be ready to fulfill God's dreams for our lives? We are ready when:

- We are willing to pray for God to accomplish His dreams for our lives rather than our own.

- We realize that we can accomplish nothing in our own strength, talents, and abilities, but are totally dependent on Him to work in and through us.

- We understand that God wants to accomplish God-sized dreams in our lives.

- We are willing to accomplish God's dreams in God's ways in God's timing.

God interrupted Moses' dreams and waited for him to learn a new method for success. God speaks. Moses obeys. God accomplishes what He purposes to do.

Time in the Desert

Many times when we experience what we think is a shattered dream, it is in reality an interrupted dream. Sometimes God takes us to a place of intermission to develop our character, strengthen our faith, and deepen our understanding of who He is or what He has prepared for us to do. Many times that place feels like a desert wasteland. Moses grew up as a boy in Egypt, but he became a man in the desert. The Israelites spent 40 years in the desert. Jesus spent 40 days in the desert. The desert is not always welcomed, but it is always profitable. God doesn't take us into the wilderness to see if we have what it takes. He leads us into the wilderness to reveal to us what is truly in our hearts.

Think of how we train our own children. When my son was born, after spending nine months swimming about in my warm cozy womb, he emerged to the shocking reality of lights, cameras, and action. He didn't like the fact that the world actually had a schedule, and he balked at the inconvenience of having to sleep during the night and be awake during the day.

I can still remember sitting on the edge of my bed with tears streaming down my cheeks as I listened to him cry at night. I imagined he was thinking, *Where is she? Doesn't she care about me? Isn't someone going to come and get me out of this crib?*

I did love that little bundle of joy—every single ounce of him. But I had to let him cry a few nights so he could learn when to sleep. It wasn't selfishness on my part. I was awake during his entire struggle. It would have been much easier to let him have his way and stop his crying. But that wouldn't have helped him learn. What made it more difficult was that I couldn't explain the process to him. He was too young to understand. Likewise, when we are struggling, I think many times God has tears streaming down His cheeks. He has to let us struggle to learn our lessons. And more often than not, if He tried to explain, we wouldn't understand. "I am the LORD your God, who teaches you what is best for you, who directs you in the way you should go" (Isaiah 48:17).

In the Bible, when God wanted to get someone's attention, many times He sent them into the desert. In our own lives, when He wants to get our attention, He may send us into the desert as well. It may even come in the form of a shattered dream or an interrupted dream. Don't waste the dry times. Take advantage of the intermissions. Deepen your relationship with God by spending time with Him. And at the proper time, when the curtain rises, you'll be ready to play the leading role in the grand drama God has planned for your life!

Interrupted by Self-Sufficiency

Suzi was a gifted speaker. Her bubbly personality and quick wit kept her audiences entertained, encouraged, and enlightened. After a few speaking engagements, Suzi began to feel very comfortable in her calling as a conference speaker. At the conclusion of her events, crowds came up to her and showered her with accolades.

"Suzi, you were great today!" "Wonderful job tonight, Suzi. You are hilarious." "Suzi, you really blessed me with your words tonight. I hope you'll come back another time."

Pretty soon, Suzi began to believe her own press. *I am pretty good*, she thought to herself. *This isn't going to be as hard as I thought. I love being in front of people, and I guess I inherited my father's quick wit because I sure can make them laugh. This must be God's will for me.*

Suzi became very comfortable in her new calling—too comfortable. One particular church enjoyed her so much at their retreat that they invited her back again for the next year's event. Suzi spent very little time in prayer, preparation, and planning or asking for God to fill her, use her, strengthen her, and guide her. Instead, she went into the battle alone and ill-equipped.

The women laughed on cue, smiled, and seemed to enjoy themselves, but there was an emptiness to the weekend. There was no substance, no moving of the Holy Spirit, no anointing. The women's director felt it, the women in attendance felt it, and Suzi felt it.

On the way home, Suzi turned to her friend who had attended with her and asked, "I blew it, didn't I?"

"Yes, you did."

God interrupted Suzi's plans and she stopped cold in her tracks.

Like Moses, Suzi cringed at her failure and ran away to the desert. No, she didn't run to a literal desert, but she vowed to never speak again. She felt shame at her utter lack of dependence on her heavenly Father and attempt to do ministry in her own power.

"I'm done," she said. "I'm not going to do this anymore."

But God (there are those words again) wasn't finished with Suzi. Now He had her where He wanted her. She spent two years in the desert, and then He came to her and called her back into ministry. She was reluctant at first, but like Moses, she had learned the secret to effective ministry—total dependence on God. Let me clarify a bit. Suzi did not become a speaker again. Suzi allowed God to speak through her again.

Interrupted by Betrayal

Suzi's interruption came as a result of her own actions. However, sometimes our interruptions come because of the actions of others that inevitably affect our lives. Let's visit with Belinda and let her tell us her story:

> As far back as I can remember, I really wanted only two things in life: to make a loving, warm, nurturing home for my family and others that crossed our paths, and to be used by God. I always

thought I, as a woman, was called to be the "heart" of Jesus to others; that to be a wife and mother was a calling. I would make our home inviting, safe, and fun for my husband and family, and a shelter from the cold, cruel world. When I met my husband, it was with this idea in mind. He had come through incredibly difficult circumstances and had never known true love. God and I would love him and multiply that love in our home and to the world. At least that was the plan.

For 29 years I battled for that home. We had three children and were active in our church. We were a committed Christian family. I played the piano for worship services and led a middle-school choir. My husband was a leader in church, sang in the choir with me, and became a deacon. It was a dream come true.

For most of that time, however, there was an unwelcomed undercurrent troubling our home. I did everything I could to keep our Christian family afloat. Of course, it was what God wanted me to do. My husband didn't understand God's love or mine. There was a cancer growing in our marriage: My husband was a sex addict and had lived a double life since he was a teenager. To be a sex addict includes being a chronic liar, and I believed many, many lies. I watched my dreams sink to the depths of hell and couldn't do a thing about it.

Months of anguish and wrestling before God opened my heart to the reality of my life. My dream seemed so godly, so biblical, so right, but I had made a Christian marriage and home my idol. It was my dream, even though it was a facade. It was a pretense I kept holding together with all my strength. Gradually, God held my heart in His loving hands and said, "Trust me enough to let go of your dream and let Me show you the dream that I have for you. It is nothing like what you have made."

My dreams died. My warm, loving, nurturing, sheltering home had not been enough for my husband. Detaching from the rescue effort was excruciating for me. Now, when I am tempted each day to tenaciously grasp my life, I stretch out my hand and hold it open toward heaven. "God, may I not grasp anything in my life, but hold it up to You. Place in my life what You choose. Remove from my life what You choose."

Christ has taught me that He is all I need, that to spend my life dancing with Him is enough. As my dreams have been reduced to a pile of ashes, I've let go of them. I sift through the dust to gather any precious remains. Even in two years of brokenness and loss, God has used my home and kitchen to nurture many people both physically and spiritually. As I write this, I am thrilled and amazed that a friend of my son is going to church with us tomorrow morning. He came to Christ last weekend and wants to know more about God. What joy in the midst of sorrow. How like my Lord to use broken, struggling beggars to show another one where to find bread, to bring life even in death. What a dream come true!

Interrupted by Unforgiveness

After I had gone to college for two years, I returned to my hometown to work as a dental hygienist. But the following spring, I felt a tug to return to college and continue my education. I prayed and looked into various programs, but I couldn't get clear direction from God. Not to decide *is* to decide, and I did not return to college. The following spring, I began to feel the same tug and the same cloud of confusion. Along with my disturbing uncertainty, I began to have flashbacks of violent childhood memories.

One night I visited one of my mentors and asked him to pray with me about what I was to do with my life. In the course of the conversation, I also mentioned the flashbacks. After listening to my dilemma, Mr. Thorp began our prayer time by turning to various scriptures. First he read Matthew 6:8-15:

> Your Father knows what you need before you ask him. This then, is how you should pray: "Our Father in heaven hallowed be your name, your kingdom come, your will be done on earth as it is in heaven. Give us today our daily bread. Forgive us our debts as we also have forgiven our debtors. And lead us not into temptation, but deliver us

from the evil one." For if you forgive men when they sin against you, your heavenly Father will also forgive you. But if you do not forgive men their sins, your Father will not forgive your sins."

Then he turned to Matthew 18:19-22:

"Again, I tell you that if two of you on earth agree about any-thing you ask for, it will be done for you by my Father in heaven. For where two or three come together in my name, there am I with them." Then Peter came to Jesus and asked, "Lord, how many times shall I forgive my brother when he sins against me? Up to seven times?" Jesus answered, "I tell you, not seven times, but seventy times seven."

Each time Mr. Thorp turned to a passage about God answering prayer, there was a verse about forgiveness either before or after it. "Sharon," he said, "I sense God is telling you that you have unforgiveness toward your father. It that true?"

I wanted to say, "Wait a minute. I came here to pray about my future, not about my past." But God was showing me that unforgiveness in my past was impeding His work in my future.

At that time in my life, I had been a Christian for seven years, and my dad had become a Christian just the year before. I did not even realize that I had not forgiven him for the pain he had caused in my childhood. Now, when he made a mistake, all those old feelings I had toward him resurfaced like hot lava lying beneath a dormant volcano waiting to explode.

God was showing me that in order to get out of this intermission stage of my life, I needed to forgive my dad. Until I obeyed, my dreams were going to be interrupted by His hand.

That night I forgave my father for everything he had ever done. Even the ashes were blown away, and God replaced the bitterness with tender, inexplicable love for my dad. When I forgave my dad, God set *me* free.

Interestingly, the next day the cloud of confusion lifted. I applied to college in late spring, even though the head of the department told me it was too late and the program I desired to enroll in was full. I was told that the only way I could get in was if someone were to drop out, which was very unlikely. Confident that this was God's plan for me, I resigned from my job and looked for an apartment near the college campus. Ten days before the start of the fall semester, the head of the department called and said, "You won't believe this, Sharon. This never happens, but someone dropped out of the program. We'd like you to come in the fall if you can make the arrangements."

"Husband number one thought making babies with other women when he was married to me was okay. It wasn't. Husband number two became terminally ill. But, finally, number three is a peach, a man of God who adores me. I never wanted to be married three times, but I'm not disappointed with my life. Had I not had to go through all I did, I would not be a writer, I possibly would not be a believer, and I would not be able to support so many hurting people through my singing, speaking, and books." Carmen

---

I could believe it, and the arrangements were already made. I enrolled in the fall and met Steve six weeks later. Nine months after that, I became his wife.

I am not saying that when you forgive those who have hurt you, you'll strike it rich, find the man of your dreams, or live happily ever after. However, I do believe that unforgiveness can be a dam that stops the flow of God's power in our lives and the wellspring of His blessings.

The Greek word for forgiveness, *aphiemi*, means "to let go from one's power, possession, to let go free, let escape."[4] Bible teacher Beth Moore explains, "In essence, the intent of biblical forgiveness is to cut someone loose. The word picture drawn by the Greek term unforgiveness is one in which the unforgiven is roped to the back of the unforgiving. How ironic. Unforgiveness is the means by which we securely bind ourselves to that which we hate most. Therefore, the Greek meaning of forgiveness might best be demonstrated as the practice of cutting loose the person roped to your back."[5]

Unforgiveness is a roadblock to fulfilled dreams. Paul warns that when we don't forgive, Satan has outwitted us and a root of bitterness begins to grow (2 Corinthians 2:10-11; Hebrews 12:15). Amazingly, every time I type the word unforgiveness into my computer, my spell-checker underlines it in red, implying that it is not a word. How like Satan to tell us that unforgiveness is not a problem! It is, my friends. Oh, it is.

Forgiveness has nothing to do with whether the person deserves to be forgiven. Most of the time he or she does not. It has everything to do with the person doing the forgiving and his or her desire to be free. And let me tell you a little secret. The person or people we hold a grudge against—the person or people we're not forgiving—they don't care. That's right. Most of the time they don't care and, more often than not, they don't even know we are walking around with the albatross of unforgiveness hanging around our necks. It is as though we're banging our own heads against the wall and saying, "Here, take that!" The only person hurt by unforgiveness is the person choosing not to forgive.

I must always remind myself of how much Jesus has forgiven me. My offenses have been many. How can I not forgive others? When we take someone off of our hook and place them on God's hook, we are setting ourselves free. It is a gift we give ourselves!

Forgiveness is not easy. When Jesus told the disciples to forgive their offenders seven times a day, they immediately said, "Increase our faith!" (Luke 17:5). But friends, the price for not forgiving those who have hurt us is very costly. It can cost us our dreams.

Intermission over. Let's get on with discovering God's dreams for our lives.

Dare to Dream Again

12

Discovering God's Dreams

Now let's dare to dream together! The question is, how do you discover God's dreams for your life? How do you know His will? That is an age-old question men and women have asked for thousands of years. While I am not going to pretend to be an expert on discerning God's will, I do want to share some helpful steps I've learned along the way.

First and foremost, I want to emphasize what Henry Blackaby says in *Experiencing God.* God's will for your life is to follow Christ. Jesus said, "I am the way and the truth and the life" (John 14:6). He does more than show you the way. He *is* the way! And following Jesus will lead you right down the road of God's perfect plan and powerful purpose for your life.

With that said, let's take a look at how to discover God's dreams for your life. I've listed my points in a way you can remember them: D-R-E-A-M-S.

D—Dare to Dream God's Dreams for Your Life

God chooses to do extraordinary work through ordinary men and women who trust in Him. In *Experiencing God Day by Day,* Henry Blackaby writes, "Would you dare to believe that God, who called you to Himself and equipped you with His Spirit, could work mightily through you? Have you made the connection between the time and place in which you live and God's call upon you? World events never catch God by surprise. He placed you precisely where you are for a purpose."[1]

"If I had to do it all over again, I would have pursued my dreams sooner rather than making them chase after me." Eva Marie

---

Blackaby goes on to say, "There will be times when obeying God will lead you to impossible situations. If you look at your own skills, knowledge, and resources, you will become discouraged. However, when you become a Christian, God placed His Spirit within you. You now have the resources of heaven at your disposal. The success of your endeavors will not depend on the way you use your own resources but on how you obey the Spirit of God."[2]

"'Not by might nor by power, but by my Spirit, says the Lord Almighty" (Zechariah 4:6). God wants to make more than our simple dreams come true. Our dreams, like the disciples' dreams, are always too small. When we say yes to His God-sized dreams, we experience the abundant life He had planned all along. Jesus said, "I came that they might life, and have it abundantly" (John 10:10 NASB). Another Bible translation quotes Jesus as saying, "I came that they may have *and* enjoy life, and have it in abundance (to the full, till it overflows)" (AMP). As you begin to pray about your dreams, consider these questions:

- What interests are you most afraid to admit to others?
- What would you do if you knew you couldn't fail?
- What would you do if financial constraints were not an issue?
- What stirs your heart and makes you excited to get out of bed in the morning?
- What would you regret not having done if you knew your life was ending tomorrow?

When we ask God to show us His dreams for our lives and merely think on the small scale of what we can accomplish on our own strength, it is like going to the ocean with a teaspoon. We at least need to come with a bucket! Then when He reveals His plan, we will be able to dip into His vast resources and pour His blessings onto those around us. "No eye has seen, no ear has heard, no mind has conceived what God has prepared for those who love him" (1 Corinthians 2:9).

R—Remember Who God Is and Who You Are

Once God has revealed His dreams or purposes for your life, what you do next will reveal what you believe about His ability to accomplish them. What you do next will determine whether or not you will experience His mighty power working through you. When we believe that nothing significant can happen through us, we are saying more about what we think about God than what we think about ourselves. "Not that we are sufficient in ourselves to think of anything as being of ourselves, but our sufficiency is from God, who also made us sufficient as ministers of the new covenant" (2 Corinthians 3:5-6 NKJV). The key is remembering who God is and who we are as His children.

Who God Is

In chapter 1 we looked at several names of God. Of all the names of God mentioned in the Bible, perhaps the most powerful description of God was given in His reply to Moses. "I AM WHO I AM. This is what you are to say to the Israelites: I AM has sent me to you" (Exodus 3:14). Whatever you need, dear friend, God is.

Here are a few words that Pastor Shadrack Lockridge used in a sermon to describe our Lord: He's enduringly strong. He's entirely sincere. He's eternally steadfast. He's immortally graceful. He's empirically powerful. He's impartially merciful. He's unparalleled. He's unprecedented. He's supreme. He's preeminent. He supplies strength to the weak. He's available to the tempted and the tried. He sympathizes and He saves. He heals the sick. He cleanses the lepers. He forgives sinners. He delivers the captive. He defends the feeble. He's the wellspring of wisdom. He's the pathway of peace. He's the roadway of righteousness. He's the highway of holiness. He's the gateway of glory. He's the captain of the conquerors. His light is matchless. His goodness is limitless. His mercy is everlasting. His love never changes. His grace is sufficient. He's incomprehensible. He's invincible. He always has been and He always will be.

Friend, there is nothing our God cannot do! We looked at Moses earlier. Remember his response when God called him to lead the Hebrews out of Egyptian bondage? "I can't do it. Please send someone else!" he cried.

> "I dream of serving God with my husband and children. I have dreams of making a significant impact in the lives of countless women for God through speaking, writing, and just being available. I dream of seeing God do more than I could ever imagine or fulfill on my own." Vickey

---

Now let's compare Moses' response to that of a young shepherd boy named David, who faced a giant challenge of his own. When David, most likely in his teens, came upon the Israelite army caught in a standoff with the Philistine army, they were shaking in their sandals. It appeared the enemy had a secret weapon named Goliath. Each day, Goliath came before the Israelites, taunting and challenging them. No one, absolutely no one, would fight this nine-foot tower of power… until David arrived on the scene. His response to the situation? "Who is this uncircumcised Philistine, that he should taunt the armies of the living God?… *The* LORD who delivered me from the paw of the lion and the paw of the bear, *He will* deliver me from the hand of this Philistine" (1 Samuel 17:26,37 NASB, emphasis added). So David gathered five smooth stones and a sling. With his first attempt, he ran at the Philistine, flung the stone, and landed it right in the middle of Goliath's forehead. I can only imagine the rip-roaring cheers that went up when the giant fell facedown in the dirt. Did you get that? Facedown. Seems to me if someone gets hit in the forehead, he would fall backward, but this giant fell forward. Why? Because David threw the stone, but God gave the push from behind that killed the giant!

I am so excited right now! I hope you are too. Remember who God is. If He can conquer giants for a little shepherd boy, think what He can do for you.

Who You Are

When God called me to speak and write to encourage and equip women, we had quite a discussion. I reminded Him of all my short-comings, failures, and how ill-equipped I was for the job (as if He didn't know those things already). But while I resisted, God persisted. He reminded me that He chose a prostitute to rescue the spies in Jericho, a seamstress to start the first church in Ephesus, a five-time divorcee to evangelize an entire Samaritan community, a teenage girl to bear His only Son, and a delivered demonic to be the key witness to the most important event in all of history—His resurrection. He reminded me that He chooses the weak things of the world to shame the strong and the foolish things of the world to shame the wise (1 Corinthians 1:27). The very fact that you are aware of your inadequacies makes you a prime candidate for effective ministry.

The truth is, when we come to Christ, we get a whole new identity! We become new creations (2 Corinthians 5:17) who are equipped by God, empowered by the Holy Spirit, and enveloped in Jesus Christ! Here is just a taste of who you are as a child of God.

Salt of the earth	Matthew 5:13
Light of the world	Matthew 5:14
Valuable to God	Matthew 6:26
Child of God	John 1:12
Chosen by God	John 15:16
Justified by Christ	Romans 5:9
Free from condemnation	Romans 8:1
Joint-heir with Christ	Romans 8:17
Accepted by Christ	Romans 15:7

Temple of God	1 Corinthians 3:16
A saint	Ephesians 1:1
Blessed with every spiritual blessing	Ephesians 1:3
Righteous and holy	Ephesians 4:24
Able to do all things through Christ	Philippians 4:13
Dearly loved by God	Colossians 3:12

In order to accomplish God-sized dreams, we must move past who we think we are and start believing who God says we are. You have a daddy who loves you, a groom who adores you, spiritual children waiting to be born, beauty that makes God's heart skip a beat, and a best friend who's always available for you.

E—Examine God's Word to Learn His Character and His Ways

Now that we are daring to dream God-sized dreams and remembering who God is and who we are in Christ, we need to sift our dreams through the filter of God's Word. How do you know if the ideas in your mind are from God, Satan, or of your own making? That is a very valid and common question. Plain and simple, we must know the truth. Every thought, every idea, must be filtered through the sieve of God's Word. Is what you are hearing consistent with God's character? Is it consistent with God's ways? Is it consistent with His Word?

When someone is training to become a bank teller, he or she is taught how to recognize counterfeit money. However, the instructors do not teach what counterfeit bills look like. Rather, they teach what genuine money looks like. The tellers study the markings, coloring, and feel of real money so when the counterfeit comes along, they can recognize it. D.L. Moody once said, "The best way to show that a stick is crooked is not to argue about it or to spend time denouncing it, but to lay a straight stick alongside it."[3]

God has given us His Word, in which are hidden the keys to wisdom and knowledge. The more time we spend with Him, the more familiar we become to that still, small voice, and the quicker we recognize it.

"I would like to go to India and work in an orphanage." Annette

---

I don't know about you, but God hasn't spoken to me through a burning bush lately or guided me by a moving star in the east. God hasn't written a warning on my wall with His finger or spoken to me through a donkey. But He does speak to me through His Word on a daily basis. Examine God's Word to learn His character and His ways. "All Scripture is God-breathed and is useful for teaching, rebuking, correcting and training in righteousness, so that the man of God may be thoroughly equipped for every good work" (2 Timothy 3:16).

A—Ask God to Reveal His Dreams for Your Life

We already imagined Jesus appearing at the door and asking, "What would you like for Me to do for you?" And yet that really did happen to several people during His time here on earth. "What do you want me to do for you?" He asked the blind men on the road from Jericho (Matthew 20:32). "What do you want me to do for you?" He asked James and John (Mark 10:36). "What do you want?" Jesus asked Andrew and his friend (John 1:38). Here is a mystery: God knows everything, and yet He longs for us to ask for what we need.

Jesus said,

> Ask and it will be given to you; seek and you will find; knock and the door will be opened to you. For everyone who asks receives; he who seeks finds; and to him who knocks, the door will be opened. Which of you, if his son asks for bread, will give him a stone? Or if he asks for a fish, will give him a snake? If you, then, though you are evil, know how to give good gifts to your children, how much more will your Father in heaven give good gifts to those who ask him! (Matthew 7:7-11).

When we pray and ask God to reveal His plans for our lives, we are saying we want nothing more and nothing less than what He desires for us. It is not asking Him to merely bless our plans, but asking Him to show us His. We are placing our lives in the palm of God's hand for Him to accomplish His purposes in His power with His provisions. His bountiful resources are limited only by our willingness to receive them.

"I guess my dreams were unrealistic. They have not come true. I don't feel disappointed that these dreams were not realized. They were just dreams...how could they come true?" Yvonne

---

In 2000 Bruce Wilkerson's little book *The Prayer of Jabez* took the world by storm. It was based on the prayer of a man in the Bible who prayed a very simple prayer: "Jabez called on the God of Israel saying, 'Oh, that You would bless me indeed, and enlarge my territory, that Your hand would be with me, and that You would keep me from evil, that I may not cause pain!' So God granted him what he requested" (1 Chronicles 4:9 NKJV). I believe part of the success of this book was that it stirred people to dare to dream again. But *The Prayer of Jabez* is not about getting what you want. Dr. Wilkerson never intended it to be. He wrote:

> Notice a radical aspect of Jabez's request for blessing: He left it entirely up to God to decide what the blessings would be and where, when, and how Jabez would receive them. This kind of radical trust in God's good intentions toward us has nothing in common with the popular gospel that you should ask God for a Cadillac, a six-figure income, or some other material sign that you have found a way to cash in on your connection with Him. Instead, the Jabez blessing focuses like a laser on our wanting for ourselves nothing more and nothing less than what God wants for us. When we seek God's blessing as the ultimate value in life, we are

throwing ourselves entirely into the river of His will and power and purposes for us. All our other needs become secondary to what we really want—which is to become wholly immersed in what God is trying to do in us, through us, and around us for His glory.[4]

After Jesus' resurrection the early church experienced phenomenal growth. Luke wrote, "The Lord's hand was with them, and a great number of people believed and turned to the Lord (Acts 11:21). Did you notice this passage didn't say "They did a great job...They preached good sermons...Their outlines were impeccable." No, the hand of the Lord was with them. Sure, it was their mouths that did the speaking, their feet that did the walking, their hands that did the touching, but it was God who quickened the hearers' hearts to believe.

Jesus clearly tells us to ask. "Ask and it will be given to you" (Matthew 7:7). "You may ask me for anything in my name, and I will do it" (John 14:14). "If you remain in me and my words remain in you, ask whatever you wish, and it will be given you" (John 15:7). "You do not have, because you do not ask God" (James 4:2).

So what are your dreams? Are you willing to let go of your smaller dreams and dream God-sized dreams? Dreams that only He can accomplish in His power? He is looking for ordinary people to accomplish extraordinary feats. He's just waiting for you to ask.

Remember, we should never look for "typical" dreams. God does not have cookie-cutter dreams for His children. Just as you are uniquely formed and fashion by God, His plans are uniquely formed and fashioned for you. What He does and how He does it in one person's life may be completely different than what He does and how He does it in your life. "We are God's workmanship, created in Christ Jesus to do good works, which God prepared in advance for us to do" (Ephesians 2:10). Have no doubt. He has a plan.

"You did not choose me," Jesus said, "but I chose you and appointed you to go and bear fruit—fruit that will last. Then the Father will give you whatever you ask in my name" (John 15:16). God wants us to ask. "Nothing pleases God more than when we ask for what He wants to give. When we spend time with Him and allow His priorities, passions, and purposes to motivate us, we will ask for things that are closest to His heart."[5]

M—Move When He Says Move

Once God has placed a dream in your heart and invited you to participate with Him in His work, you will have the opportunity to accept or reject the invitation. For most of us, rejection does not come in the form of actually rounding our lips and forming the word "no" but comes in the form of ignoring the call. We're good at pretending the nudge isn't there and letting our fears and doubts talk us out of moving forward.

"I would love to be involved in evangelistic ministry.
I would love organizing large crusades or conferences, then
possibly helping with the ministry part of those as well.
It seems like a big dream and it's easy for me to doubt I
could ever be involved in something like this." Geneva

At some point, God will call us to a God-sized assignment. Henry Blackaby notes, "When God invites you to join Him in His work, He has assigned a God-sized assignment for you. You will realize that you cannot do it on your own. If God doesn't help you, you will fail. This is the crisis point where many decide not to follow what they sense God is leading them to do. Then they wonder why they do not experience God's presence and activity the way other Christians do."[6] "When God gives you a seemingly impossible task, the only thing preventing it from coming to pass is your disobedience."[7]

We will face the same crossroads men and women in the Bible faced. Will we accept the invitation to join God in His work or reject it? Will we believe God can accomplish what He has purposed through us, or will we falsely believe we must accomplish the assignment in our own power and with our own resources? Will we say, "I can't do that," or will we say, "I can do all things through Christ who gives me strength"?

"I'm excited about what lies around the corner. Taking
our dreams and transforming them into realities—
that's the adventure of life in Him." Christie

In the Bible we see that God's power *follows* man's obedience. The Israelites took the first steps of faith and placed their feet in the water. *Then* God parted the Jordan River for them to cross, even though it was at flood stage (Joshua 3:15). On the seventh day of marching around Jericho, the Israelites marched around the city seven times, blew trumpets, and gave a shout. *Then* God made the walls come tumbling down (Joshua 6:1-20). At the Lord's instruction, Commander Naaman dipped his diseased body in the Jordan seven times. *Then* the Lord healed him of leprosy (2 Kings 5:14). First they moved, and then God performed the miracle! God's power follows our obedience.

God is not going to force you to obey Him or accept His invitation to abundant life, but oh, the blessings we forfeit when we forgo the walk of faith. The first generation of Israelites who were freed from Egyptian slavery wandered in the desert for 40 years. They were never allowed to enter the Promised Land. They were saved from slavery, but they never experienced the abundant life God had intended. Why? Their disobedience and lack of faith kept them circling in the sand. Did you know the same thing can happen to us? We can be saved but spend the rest of our lives circling in the sand because of our disobedience and lack of faith. That is not where I want to be. Do you? Let's dare to dream again and head for our own personal Promised Land!

When God reveals His dreams for our lives, what we do next will determine what He does next. If we obey step one, He will most likely tell us step two. However, if we do not obey step one, He will most likely not tell us step two. If your spiritual life seems at a standstill, go back and make sure you have done all that God has told you to do up to this point. It could be that He is waiting for you to complete what He has already called you to before He reveals more.

I just love the account of Peter and John's first Spirit-filled, power-packed sermon after Pentecost. When the people heard their teaching and witnessed their courage, they were amazed. Here's what Luke wrote about the scene. "When they saw the courage of Peter and John and realized that they were unschooled, ordinary men, they were astonished and they took note that these men had been with Jesus" (Acts 4:13). Oh, friend, I can think of no better compliment than that.

The summer I first caught a glimpse of what God had for my next phase of life, I spent many hours in prayer asking for clear direction. During that time, my husband and I went to Bermuda for a romantic getaway. On one particular evening, Steve and I went on a dining adventure to a five-star restaurant filled with men and women dressed in their very finest evening wear. In one corner of the dining area, a four-man orchestra filled the room with the fluid sounds of music from the '40s and '50s. At one point Steve urged, "Come on, Sharon. Let's go take a spin on the dance floor and see if we can remember the fox-trot."

"No way," I replied. "Nobody else is out there. I'm not going to be the only one on the floor with everyone staring at me. And suppose we mess up? I'd be embarrassed. It's been a long time since we've danced, and I don't remember all the steps. Let's wait until there are some other people dancing so we can hide in the crowd. Then I'll go."

Finally the first couple approached the floor. They looked like professional dancers, moving as one and never missing a beat. This did not encourage me at all but only strengthened my resolve that this was no place for my feet to tread. Then a second couple, whose steps weren't quite as perfect, joined the first. Reluctantly I agreed to go to a spot on the floor where few could see us.

After a few minutes, I noticed a fourth couple approach. There was something very special about this couple, and they took my breath away. The husband was in a wheelchair. He was about our age, slightly balding, with a neatly trimmed beard. On his left hand he wore a white glove, I guessed to cover a skin disease. As the band played a peppy beat, his wife held her beloved's healthy right hand and danced with him. He spun her around as she stooped to conform to her husband's seated position. Lovingly, she danced around his chair, and their laughter became the fifth instrument in the band. Then the musicians slowed to a lazy romantic melody. She pulled a chair up beside her husband's, facing in the opposite direction, and held him in a dancer's embrace.

My heart was so moved by this love story unfolding before my eyes that I had to turn my head and bury my face on Steve's shoulder so no one would see the tears streaming down my cheeks. As I did, I saw every person in this formal dining room had tears trickling down *their* cheeks. Then I turned to look at the band and saw tears.

"When I was a little girl, I dreamed of being a preacher. I am from a small farm town, and I used to preach to the corn. I shook their leafy hands just like a preacher." Joyce

---

After watching this incredible display of love and courage, I realized that my inhibitions of not wanting others to watch me because my steps were not perfect were gone. The Lord spoke to my heart in a powerful way.

Sharon I want you to notice, who moved this crowd to tears? Was it couple number one, with their perfect steps? Or, was it the last couple that not only did not have perfect steps, but had no steps at all? No, My child, it was the display of love, not perfection that had an effect on the people watching.

The Lord doesn't expect our steps to be perfect. He just expects us to be obedient, to take the first step, and to let Him do the rest. The man in the wheelchair never even moved his feet; his wife did the moves for him. And we need to remember that the Lord will do the same for us. We also need to remember that it is not perfect steps that the world is so desperately longing to see. The world isn't moved by seemingly perfect people who live in perfect houses with perfect children. They are moved by love—genuine, God-inspired love. That's what moves a crowd.

That night in Bermuda, God sent a lame man to teach me how to dance. No, my steps are not perfect, just obedient. And guess what? God does the dancing for me.

Sometimes I think about what my life would have been like had I said no to God. How many blessings I would have missed, how many opportunities I would have forfeited, how many dreams gone unfulfilled? A life filled with saying yes to Him is the most exciting life imaginable!

S—Stay Connected to the Vine

Jesus' last days with His disciples began as He rode into Jerusalem on a donkey's colt, just five days before Passover. Children sang "Hosanna to the King," women waved palm branches in praise, and the Pharisees continued to sweat at Jesus' unwelcome popularity. Yes, everything was going as the disciples had hoped. The kingdom of God was at hand.

But then the disciple's dreams began to crumble. In the upper room, where they shared their last Passover together, Jesus began to talk about His imminent death and about the "prince of this world" coming...and He wasn't talking about Himself. They were confused as He removed His outer garment, assumed the posture of a servant, and stooped to wash their mud-caked feet. Can you imagine what was going through their heads? *What do You mean You are going away? Why are You stooping and acting like a servant when You are the King? What do You mean "the prince of this world" is coming? I thought You were in charge.*

As the group of men left the upper room and made their way to the Garden of Gethsemane, Jesus began to tell them the family secret of success. It was not a secret in the sense that only a few could know it, but it was a secret in the sense of being the key to having their dreams come true.

> I am the true vine, and my Father is the gardener. He cuts off every branch in me that bears no fruit, while every branch that does bear fruit he prunes so that it will be even more fruitful...Remain in me, and I will remain in you. No branch can bear fruit by itself; it must remain in the vine. Neither can you bear fruit unless you remain in me. I am the vine; you are the branches. If a man remains in me and I in him, he will bear much fruit; apart from me you can do nothing...If you remain in me and my

words remain in you, ask whatever you wish, and it will be given you. This is to my Father's glory, that you bear much fruit, showing yourselves to be my disciples (John 15:1-2,4-5,7-8).

This is the place where dreams come true—in Christ, connected to the vine. How do we discover God's dreams for our lives? Abide or remain in Him. Learn to hear His voice. How do we accomplish God's dreams for our lives? Stay connected to the vine and draw strength from Him. Why does God want us to accomplish His dreams for our lives? To bring Him glory. There you have it.

Jesus has a purpose. He is the vine that provides support, nourishment, strength, and energy to the branches that sprout from its trunk.

God has a purpose. He is the gardener or vinedresser who does whatever is necessary to bring about the greatest yield of fruit from the branches.

We have a purpose. We are the branches who must stay connected to the vine, submit to the pruning of the vinedresser, and bear fruit to glorify God.

What does it mean to remain? The New American Standard Bible translates the same Greek word, *meno,* as "abide." It is a constant, conscious, communion with God, not based on emotion or feelings but is a decision to think on God, to acknowledge His presence with you, His power in you, and His workings through you. John uses the word "abide" 40 times in his Gospel and five of those times in John 15:1-6. Jesus said, "If you continue in My word, then you are truly disciples of Mine; and you will know the truth, and the truth will make you free (John 8:31-32).

Jesus tells us to abide because He knows it doesn't come naturally. You don't have to tell a child to be selfish or to eat candy. That comes naturally. A parent instructs a child to share or eat their vegetables because that *doesn't* come naturally. Abiding is an act of the will. It is a choice. When we abide in Jesus, He tells us His secrets and we begin to detect His still, small voice. "Call to me and I will answer you and tell you great and unsearchable things you do not know," God said to the prophet Jeremiah (Jeremiah 33:3). And if that's not enough to get you excited, listen to this: "The LORD *confides* in those who fear him" (Psalm 25:14, emphasis added). He tells us His secrets!

What is this fruit Jesus talked about in John 15? Fruit is accomplishing God's dreams for our lives and bringing glory to Him in our everyday lives. In Galatians 5:22-23, Paul writes of the fruit of the Spirit as being "love, joy, peace, patience, kindness, goodness, faithfulness, gentleness and self-control." This is "inner fruit." But then Paul also writes of another type of fruit I call "outer fruit." Outer fruit is produced when we allow God to work through us and in us to accomplish His dreams—His purposes in our lives. It could be leading a neighbor to Christ, becoming a missionary in India, taking a meal to a friend, writing a book to encourage others, teaching a Sunday school class for four-year-olds, or learning to fly a plane. There is no list. There is no limit.

Don't Miss It!

When I was born, my mother was under general anesthetic and woke up to the news that her baby girl was resting peacefully in the nursery. My son's delivery was quite a different story. When Steven was born, I refused to push (after 23 and a half hours of labor) until they adjusted the mirror so I could see his grand entrance into the world. I didn't want to miss it! And I don't want you to miss God birthing the dreams in your life either. Here are some points I've learned about God's dreams for our lives:

- God has dreams for you right now, right where you are today.

- His dreams for you at one stage of your life will be different than His dreams for you at another stage of life.

- God has dreams for your life regardless or in spite of the mistakes of your past. Often those very mistakes are the springboard for your ministry, and your messes become your message.

- God has dreams for your life regardless of your spiritual

maturity. However, the task will always match your character.

- God's dreams for your life will be unique and specifically designed for you. We are not to compare His dreams for our lives to what He is doing in someone else's life.

- Accomplishing God's dreams are directly related to the depth of our relationship to Him, how in tune to His leading we have become, and how dependent we are on the Holy Spirit accomplishing what He's called us to do.

God has many dreams to birth in our lives. They will not come without pain, agony, stretching, straining, and perhaps even some nausea along the way, but oh, the joy we experience when the dream is birthed and grows before our very eyes!

Come Dream with Me

W e're coming to the end of our journey exploring our dreams together, but in reality, it is only the beginning. I believe when we realize that God fulfills our childhood dreams to have a loving daddy, to be a bride, to be a mother, to be beautiful, and to have a best friend, we will be free to discover greater dreams for our lives than we ever imagined. When we get past the basics, and I believe those five are the basics, we will be able to go beyond the ordinary and experience the extraordinary!

Your life is part of God's grand design. No matter how you came into the world, no matter what your past, God has a plan for you (Jeremiah 29:11). His greatest desire is to have a relationship with you. The first question God asked in the Bible was to Adam and Eve, who were hiding in shame. "Where are you?" He asked (Genesis 3:9). He still asks that question of us today.

God accepts us just as we are, but He loves us too much to let us stay that way. He uses the hammer and chisel of life circumstances to shape us into magnificent masterpieces. Just as Michelangelo removed chunks and bits of marble to reveal the breathtaking statue of David, so God removes anything that hinders or hides the beautiful works of art He created us to be. But like all analogies, this one about the Michelangelo sculpture has a flaw. His block of marble had no choice but to submit to the artist's tools. We do have a choice. God has invited us to join Him in the process of fulfilling His purposes for our lives. It is our choice whether to yield to His working in our lives or remain a block of stone.

As women, we all have girlish dreams. There are some who have had the dreams mentioned in this book fulfilled this side of heaven. Some do have an earthly father who loves them, a husband who cherishes them, children who adore them, physical beauty that defines them, and a best friend who is committed to them. And yet if that woman doesn't know Jesus as her Savior, she will still feel an inexplicable void. Why? Because each and every one of us is born with a God-shaped vacuum that can only be filled with God Himself. Earthly relationships may muffle the heart's cry, but without Jesus it's still there. "It is only with the heart that one can see rightly. What is most important is invisible to the eye."[1] And that is a personal and ongoing relationship with Jesus Christ.

That said, come dream a little dream with me.

A Higher Dream

I hope you've caught a glimpse of God's dreams for your life. Ours are temporary. His are eternal. The highest dream we could ever dream, the wish that, if granted, would make us happier than any other blessing, is to know God and to actually experience His presence every day. "God surpasses our dreams when we reach past our personal plans and agendas to grab the hand of Christ and walk the path He chose for us. He is obligated to keep us dissatisfied until we come to Him and His plans for complete satisfaction."[2]

"I would like to set up a foundation to offer respite vacations to caregivers of those who are suffering from Huntington's Disease." Carmen

---

Remember, God's dreams are not cookie-cutter dreams. Just as we are fearfully and wonderfully made (Psalm 139:14), so are His plans for our lives. As Oswald Chambers said, "Never make the blunder of trying to forecast the way God is going to answer your prayers." What He calls one person to do has nothing to do with what He is calling you to do. After Jesus' resurrection, He told Peter the kind of death he would suffer. Peter turned and saw John following close behind. "Well, what about him? What's going to happen to him?" Peter asked. (Oh, how I love Peter.)

Basically, Jesus told Peter it was none of his business. "If I want him to remain alive until I return, what is that to you?" He answered (John 21:22).

> "I dream that I will be able to have the financial
> security to homeschool my children." Susan

God told a man to build an ark—once (Genesis 6:5-22). He spoke through a burning bush—once (Exodus 3:1–4:17). He spoke through a donkey to a wayward prophet—once (Numbers 22:21-35). He warned a rebellious king by writing on a wall with His finger—once (Daniel 5). He sent a man on an incredible journey in the belly of a fish—once (Jonah). We can't look at how the Lord directs someone else's life and make a ten-step plan for our lives. Chances are it won't work. The way to know God's dream for your life is to know God. Jesus said, "Follow Me." That's the plan. It's not a *ten-step* program but a *daily step-by-step* pursuit following Jesus every day.

Make no mistake. God has a plan for you. He told Jeremiah, "Before I formed you in the womb I knew you, before you were born I set you apart; I appointed you as a prophet to the nations" (Jeremiah 1:5).

A Bigger Dream

C.S. Lewis said the problem with Christians is that they don't want enough.[3] That is hard to imagine in our materialistic society, but Lewis wasn't referring to cars or clothes, wealth or worldly goods. He was referring to heaven's riches. "We are half-hearted creatures, fooling about with drink and sex and ambition when infinite joy is offered us, like an ignorant child who wants to go on making mud pies in the slum because he cannot imagine what is meant by the offer of a holiday at the sea. We are far too easily pleased."[4]

I am calling us to dream again and dream God-sized dreams. To discover and do that thing He has placed in our hearts to do. We must dare to dream again—but to dream God's dreams for our lives. Dreams make us fertile, and without them we are barren. "Where there is no vision, the people perish," King Solomon observed (Proverbs 29:18 KJV).

Florence Nightingale was a woman with a big dream. She was born in Florence, Italy, on March 12, 1820, the daughter of a wealthy landowner. Her father took responsibility for her education and taught her Greek, Latin, French, German, Italian, history, philosophy, and mathematics. While Florence's mother's primary concern was finding her a suitable husband, Florence had other ideas. She felt that God had called her to some unnamed cause. When she was 25 years old, after turning down many suitors, she discovered what that cause was: to be a nurse. Six years later, her father finally gave his permission for Florence to pursue her dream.

"I know God has big plans for my life, and I intend
to dance cheek to cheek with Him to fulfill those
dreams. I refuse to sit this one out!" Christie

When she began working in hospitals, she was appalled at the unsanitary conditions. In military hospitals, only one in six actually died from battle wounds; the others died of diseases due to poor conditions. Although she faced much opposition in a day when women in the workforce were looked down upon, Florence Nightingale fought and won a war of her own—to improve hospital sanitation and improve the quality of nursing care. Many of the modern nursing systems and techniques we know today can be traced back to this incredibly brave woman.

"Live your life while you have it," Florence said. "Life is a splendid gift. There is nothing small in it, for the greatest things grow by God's Law out of the smallest. But to live your life you must discipline it. You must not fritter it away in 'fair purpose, erring act, inconstant will' but make your thoughts, your acts, all work to the same end and that end, not self but God."[5]

Have you ever heard of Agnes Bojaxhiu? Probably not. But you might know her as Nobel Prize winner Mother Teresa. Mother Teresa never drove a car, attended college, married, or raised a family, but God had a big dream for this little woman. She spent her entire adult life caring for the starving and sick of Calcutta and allowed them to face death with dignity. Her legacy lives on today as Missionaries of Charity continue to care for 500,000 hungry families and 90,000 lepers worldwide.

"I would like to be able to trust myself to love again, knowing what it is really about this time. Not the fantasy of a young child, but the kind of love that keeps people together no matter what. I still have the same dreams as an adult that I had as a little girl. I think deep down inside the same dreams linger in my heart." Carol

---

Someone asked her once if she was disappointed that she didn't see more success in her ministry. She replied, "God has not called me to a ministry of success. He has called me to a ministry of mercy." She also said, "We can do no great things; only small things with great love."[6]

A Childlike Dream

One thing I love about children is that you never have to remind them to dream. There are always wonders to discover, worlds to uncover, dragons to slay, and damsels to portray. We never have to remind a child to want more. The doors of their hearts are open wide to welcome all that life has to offer. And Jesus tells us that in order to receive the kingdom of God, we must come as a little child (Luke 18:17).

It seems that all little children are born with a certain propensity to wild abandonment. A curly-headed girl twirls around with outstretched arms in a crowded airport singing "Jesus Loves Me." She doesn't care who hears. It doesn't matter in the slightest. But somewhere along the line, she learns—we learn—to tame our wild abandon, become more "civilized," and keep our thoughts to ourselves.

My little friend Hope was eight years old when she led her Hindu neighbor through the sinner's prayer.

"Hope, what did you say to Ammon?" her mother asked.

"Mom, it was simple," she explained. "I just told him that Jesus came and died on a cross to save him from his sins. Either he prays the prayer or goes down there." (She pointed to where hell is supposed to be.) Then she added, "He prayed the prayer."

"I always dreamed of living in a log cabin in the mountains and being able to help the poor or less fortunate." Beth

---

No one had explained to Hope that salvation was much more complicated than that. She knew nothing of sanctification, justification, glorification, redemption, propitiation, etc. No one told her it is next to impossible for a Hindu to come to saving faith in Christ. Nope. She just took God at His Word and believed what He said and did it. She came as a child to the Father and invited her friend to do the same.

Just as a child's initial response to the world at large is to live and love with reckless abandonment, so their dreams are without limitation. When I ask children what they want to be when they grow up, they usually answer without a moment's hesitation. Lysa wanted to be the next president of the United States until someone told her she couldn't. Barbara wanted to be an astronaut until someone told her she wasn't smart enough. Susie wanted to discover a cure for cancer until someone told her it was impossible. Amy wanted to be an Olympic gymnast until someone told her she was too tall.

Shame on us for squashing a child's dreams. Shame on others for trying to squash ours.

Jesus tells us to become as little children. My hope is *not* that you will necessarily find the cure for cancer, be the first to live on the moon, or even write the next great American novel—although each of those things may be very well within your reach! It is not the dream itself that I long to see fulfilled in you, but the burning passion to come to God as a little child and dare to dream again.

Watch Out for the Border Bullies

God had great dreams for the children of Israel. He chose them from all the other nations to be His treasured possession. He freed them from slavery, led them out of Egypt, parted the Red Sea for them to cross, swallowed up their enemies, fed them with manna, provided water from a rock, guided them with a fire by night, and sheltered them with a cloud by day. When they neared the Promised Land, the land flowing with milk and honey He had guaranteed would be theirs, Moses sent in 12 spies to see what they were up against.

When the men returned, ten gave this report to Moses and the whole assembly:

> We went into the land to which you sent us, and it does flow with milk and honey! Here is its fruit. But the people who live there are powerful, and the cities are fortified and very large…We can't attack those people; they are stronger than we are…The land we explored devours those living in it. All the people we saw there are of great size…We seemed like grasshoppers in our own eyes, and we looked the same to them (Numbers 13:27-28,31-33).

While ten spies gave an "evil report" (Numbers 13:32 KJV), the other two spies, Caleb and Joshua, tried to silence them. "We should go up and take possession of the land, for we can certainly do it," they said. "If the LORD is pleased with us, he will lead us into that land…and give it to us. Only do not rebel against the LORD. And do not be afraid of the people of the land, because we will swallow them up. Their protection is gone, but the LORD is with us. Do not be afraid of them" (Numbers 13:30; 14:8-9).

Guess whom the people believed? They believed the ten who didn't trust God rather than the two who did. Caleb and Joshua understood that God had already given them the land. All they had to do was move forward in faith and take it. But because the assembly listened to the "evil report," they missed receiving what God had already promised to give. That entire generation spent the rest of their lives wandering in the desert and finally died there. But when the next generation rose up and believed God, Joshua and Caleb led them into the Promised Land their parents were never allowed to see.

"I would love to go back to college and get my
English degree so I could teach." Rachel

As you begin to move forward to accomplish your God-given dreams, don't be surprised if you encounter a few border bullies of your own. There will be those who don't understand your call or your faith. The border bullies may be those who know you best. Perhaps they are well acquainted with your strengths and all too familiar with your weaknesses. But do not fear. Let me ask you, dear friend. Whose report are you going to believe?

Here are some common objections from the border bullies you might encounter in your own life:

- It's never been done.
- It's never been done that way before.
- You don't have the talent.
- You don't have the money.
- You aren't smart enough.
- You aren't trained in that area.
- So-and-so tried that and failed.
- That will never work.
- You don't know the right people.

- You don't have the right credentials.
- You don't have the right training.
- That's too risky.
- But we've always done it this way.

Some of us have forgotten our dreams because someone whose opinion we valued told us we'd never make it. Paul's answer to the nay-sayers in our lives is this: "I can do everything through him who gives me strength" (Philippians 4:13). As we've seen, God doesn't necessarily call the qualified, but He always qualifies the called. If He's given you the vision, He will give you the provision and the power to accomplish it.

The dream may, or I should say *will*, require sacrifices on our part. "For reasons known only to Him, God has chosen to work through men and women who are willing to make sacrifices for the sake of the 'thing' He has placed in their hearts to do."[7] Sarah had to sacrifice her comfortable home to move to an unknown land. Ruth had to sacrifice her Moabite family to go with Naomi to Bethlehem. Esther had to risk her very life to go before the king. Rahab had to risk being arrested to protect the Hebrew spies. Mary had to sacrifice her reputation to carry the Son of God. Each of these women faced giant challenges in their lives with a giant faith of their own.

"I would like to be an actress in the theater doing clean scripts—possibly a children's theater." Kristie

---

Here's a poem to fight the border bullies in your life:

It Couldn't Be Done

Somebody said that it couldn't be done,
But he with a chuckle replied,
That "maybe it couldn't," but he would be one
Who wouldn't say so till he'd tried.

So he buckled right in with the trace of a grin
On his face. If he worried he hid it.
He started to sing as he tackled the thing
That couldn't be done, and he did it.

Somebody scoffed: "Oh, you'll never do that;
At least, no one ever has done it."
But he took off his coat and He took off his hat,
And the first thing we knew he'd begun it.
With a lift of his chin and a bit of a grin,
Without any doubting or quiddit,
He started to sing as he tackled the thing
That couldn't be done, and he did it.

There are thousands to tell you it cannot be done
There are thousands to prophesy failure;
There are thousands to point out to you, one by one
The dangers that wait to assail you.
But just buckle in with a bit of a grin,
Just take off your coat and go to it;
Just start to sing as you tackle the thing
That "cannot be done," and you'll do it![8]

EDGAR A. GUEST

Choose God's Best over the World's Good

One of the dangers of being a "busy Christian" is saying yes to man's good instead of waiting for God's best. As we begin to obey God, we must be certain that we are listening to the right voice and taking on responsibilities and challenges that *God* has called us to and not what *others* want us to do. I always tell women, "The need is not the call." In other words, just because there is a need does not mean that you are the one to meet it.

Jesus gave us a good example in Mark 1. Early in His ministry, while in Galilee, He invited several men to follow Him and become His 12 closest friends. With Simon, Andrew, James, and John, Jesus traveled to Capernaum. While there Jesus taught in the synagogue, cast out demons, and healed many people. It was a very busy day!

The next morning, instead of sleeping in, Jesus rose while it was still dark and went to a place all by Himself and prayed. Sometime later, Simon and his companions interrupted Jesus' time with God and exclaimed, "Everyone is looking for you!" (Mark 1:36-37).

"I would like to be able to afford a
home, At least a trailer." Linda

They wanted Jesus to go back to Capernaum and continue ministering to the people. Would that have been a good thing to do? Yes, it would have been good, but it would not have been God's best. Jesus replied, "Let us go somewhere else—to the nearby villages—so I can preach there also. That is why I have come" (verse 38).

How did Jesus know to pick the best over the good? I believe when He spent time alone with His Father, Jesus received His marching orders for the day. Likewise, when we spend time with God each morning, we will be able to say yes and no with confidence and choose God's best over man's good. Satan knows that he may not be able to get you off course by tempting you with something blatantly evil, but he can easily get you distracted by making you busy—so busy the clatter drowns out the voice of God.

Get Ready

God will supply what we need, but that doesn't mean we don't prepare ourselves. Abraham Lincoln once said, "I will study and prepare myself and then someday my chance will come."[9] When his chance came to run for public office, he was ready for the challenge. Oswald Chambers said, "Be ready for the sudden surprise visits of God. A ready person never needs to get ready. Think of the time we waste trying to get ready when God has called."[10]

Let me give you an example. For many years I had a desire to write a book to encourage and equip mothers. This was one of my dreams. In the meantime, I prepared material and spoke to moms' groups and at women's conferences on how to be a great mom and raise great kids. Throughout the years, I added to my research, wrote down personal examples, clipped relevant magazine articles, and listened to others talk about what they felt their mothers did well and where they fell short. I collected poems that would encourage and challenge mothers and stories that would spur them on to be the best mother possible. I even read about famous people in history and discovered what their mothers did to encourage them.

"I dream about writing a book about
what God has taught me." Karen

In my research, I noticed seven key ingredients that kept coming up time and time again. To help women remember those key ingredients, I ordered them to fit the acrostic BLESSED. A great mom is a Beacon, Listener, Encourager, Self-esteem Builder, Seed-Sower, Example-Setter, and Diligent. Then, through the years, as God revealed Scripture and situations that illustrated those seven essentials, I placed them in a folder.

In the fall of 1999, I received a call from Moody Publishers. They had seen an article that my ministry partner and I had written in a magazine, knew of our radio program, and wanted to know if we had any book projects we'd like to write in the future. You guessed it. I didn't have to scramble to get ready. I was ready. Within weeks I was sitting in an office at Moody Bible Institute sharing my book proposal. *Being a Great Mom Raising Great Kids* was released in 2000.

My dream came true. It wasn't by the wave of a wand—I had to prepare. Oswald Chambers also wrote, "Dreaming about a thing in order to do it properly is right; but dreaming about it when we should be doing it is wrong."[11] But my preparation wasn't all it took. God prompted the publisher to call. I could prepare, but I could not make it happen. That is in God's hands.

Make Each Moment Count

When I was newly married, I attended a social club meeting of women whose husbands shared the same profession. There was absolutely nothing wrong with this gathering, but I left feeling empty and as though I had wasted a morning of my life.

The next month I opted not to attend. Instead, I went to a nursery to pick out some flowers to plant in my garden. While there, I spotted a woman whose husband had the same profession as mine. She and her two little girls were also purchasing flowers. Carol had cancer. She had been given only a few months to live. Suddenly, God whispered in my ear. *Sharon, if you knew you only had a few months to live, would you be at that social club meeting or buying flowers with your children?* It was a poignant moment. I want to always live as if this might be the last day of my life…because it might be.

Jonathan Edwards once said, "I resolve to live with all my might while I do live. I resolve never to lose one moment of time and to improve my use of time in the most profitable way I possibly can. I resolve never to do anything I wouldn't do if it were the last hour of my life."[12]

Do you have dreams you have put off? Consider this. If you knew you had one more year to live, would you live your life differently? The truth is, we never know how much or how little time we have on this earth. The time to accomplish what God has called us to do is now.

I do have one word of caution for those who are raising a family. I know many mothers of young children who have great aspirations of accomplishing wonderful tasks for God. However, I believe your family is your greatest mission field, and God has given you children as an investment opportunity greater than any other. As a mother, you have the responsibility and privilege of raising the next generation for Christ! What a grand dream! Theodore Roosevelt once said, "No other success in life—not being President, or being wealthy, or going to college, or writing a book, or anything else—comes up to the success of the man or woman who can feel that they have done their duty and that their children and grandchildren rise up and call them blessed."[13] So invest the short amount of time you have to raising godly children. That in itself is a God-sized dream!

Don't Give Up

Some of us have given up on our dreams because certain circumstances have seemingly placed them out of reach. Perhaps we have had an interruption. Perhaps we have put a period where God put a comma and quit too soon. William James said, "Most people never run far enough on their first wind to find out they've got a second. Give your dreams all you've got and you'll be amazed at the energy that comes out of you."[14]

Paul wrote, "I press on, that I may lay hold of that for which Christ Jesus has also laid hold of me" (Philippians 3:12 NKJV). William Barclay said this about Paul's fervor. "He was trying to grasp that for which he had been grasped by Christ...Paul felt that when Christ stopped him on the Damascus Road, He had a vision and a purpose for Paul, and Paul felt that all his life he was bound to press on, lest he fail Jesus and frustrate His dream...Every [person] is grasped by Christ for some purpose; and therefore every [person] should all his [or her] life press on so that he [or she] may grasp that purpose for which Christ grasped him."[15]

"I would like to get out of debt." Callie

Many years ago, before I had my first book published, someone told me that the difference between a published author and an unpublished author is that the published author didn't give up on her dream. I've come to see much wisdom in that word of encouragement.

Paul encouraged the Philippians, "Brothers, I do not consider myself yet to have taken hold of it. But one thing I do: Forgetting what is behind and straining toward what is ahead, *I press* on toward the goal to win the prize for which God has called me heavenward in Christ Jesus" (Philippians 3:13-14, emphasis added). The NASB says, "reaching forward to what lies ahead." Paul compared his Christian life to a race, and in this verse he tells us to keep our eye on the goal. Press on! Don't give up!

Calvin Coolidge said: "Nothing in this world can take the place of persistence. Talent will not; nothing is more common than unsuccessful people with talent. Genius will not; unrewarded genius is almost a proverb. Education will not; the world is full of educated derelicts. Persistence and determination alone are omnipotent. The slogan 'press on' has solved and always will solve the problems of the human race."[16]

While this is a wonderful quote, I'd like to add to Mr. Coolidge's words of encouragement. God is the only One who is omnipotent, but persistence and determination while relying on His power is a holy combination that's hard to beat!

Here are some fun facts to remember when we feel like quitting:

- After Fred Astaire's first screen test in 1933, the director noted, "Can't act! Slightly bald. Can dance a little."

- Louisa May Alcott, author of *Little Women*, was encouraged to find work as a servant or a seamstress.

- Beethoven's violin teacher once told him he was a "hopeless composer."

- Walt Disney was fired by a newspaper editor for lack of ideas.

- Thomas Edison's teacher said he was too stupid to learn anything.

- Albert Einstein didn't speak until he was four years old and didn't read until he was seven. His teachers described him as mentally slow.

- Isaac Newton did poorly in grade school.

- Henry Ford failed and went bankrupt five times before he finally succeeded.

- Babe Ruth, when he retired from baseball, set the home run record (714), but he also held the record for the most strikeouts (1330).

- Winston Churchill failed sixth grade.[17]

- One basketball player missed 9000 shots in his career. He

lost more than 300 games. Twenty-six times he was trusted to take the game's winning shot and missed. His name is Michael Jordan. He said, "I've failed over and over again in my life. And that's why I succeed."[18]

There have been many days when I've wanted to quit. Lugging suitcases through an airport by myself, carting boxes of books from place to place, sleeping in strange beds, eating strange food, missing my husband, fighting spiritual battles for the souls of the ones I'm speaking to, traveling across the country *alone*, spending endless hours at the computer *alone*…you get the idea. Being in ministry is an honor, but it is not glamorous! Many days I wonder, *Is all this doing anyone any good?* That's when God reminds me of the piano story.

Once there was a little nine-year-old boy who desperately wanted to stop taking piano lessons. In hopes of encouraging her son to continue, his mother took him to hear the great concert pianist Ignacy Jan Paderewski. Before the concert began, the boy slipped away from his mother and made his way to the grand Steinway positioned on the stage under the spotlight. He sat down on the piano bench, placed his chubby hands on the keys, and began to bang out the most annoying song known to man—"Chopsticks." The indignant crowd began to yell for someone to get the boy off the stage. Behind the curtain, Paderewski heard the commotion. He grabbed his coat, ran out on stage, and reached his arms around the boy to play a beautiful melody to enhance the boy's "Chopsticks." All the while he whispered in the boy's ear, "Don't quit. Keep on playing. Don't stop. Don't quit."[19]

"I would like to encourage other people
who have MS, like myself." Bunny

There are many days when my life seems just about as melodious as "Chopsticks." It is on those days when I imagine my heavenly Father placing His loving arms around me and playing a beautiful melody around my simple efforts. All the while He whispers, *Don't quit, don't stop, never give up.* It is the music of my dreams.

Once someone asked Michelangelo, "When is a painting finished?" He replied "When it fulfills the intent of the artist."[20] When is our part of fulfilling God's dream complete? When He tells us it is time to move on and our work is done.

Jump In

I was sitting on the balcony of a condominium at the beach with my computer in my lap. It was time to write the conclusion for this book, and I wasn't sure how to end. In the background I listened to the excited squeals and splashes as children played in the swimming pool below.

One particular little girl caught my attention. She appeared to be about six years old and wore bright yellow water wings wrapped around her arms like blood pressure cuffs. As she stood on the side of the pool nervously flapping her arms, her daddy was poised in waist-deep water with his arms outstretched.

"I would like to learn how to drive a car." Christin

"Come on, honey, you can do it," he coached. "Go ahead and jump. I'm right here."

"But I'm scared," she said, whining and flapping. "You might not catch me."

"Don't be afraid. I'm right here."

"But you might move!"

"I'm not going to move. I'm not going to let anything happen to you," he assured her.

This bantering went on for at least fifteen minutes. I was amazed at the father's patience and persistence. But finally, she jumped! Applause went up all around the pool! By the end of the morning, the little girl was swimming like a minnow and making her way across the once seemingly treacherous waters.

Then God began to speak to my heart. *Sharon, sometimes you're that little girl.* And suddenly I began to see myself standing on the edge of the ocean of God's dreams for my life.

Come on, honey, you can do it, my heavenly Father coaches. *Go ahead and jump. I'm right here.*

"But I'm scared," I whine. "You might not catch me."

Don't be afraid. I'm right here.

"But You might move!"

I'm not going to move. I'm not going to let anything happen to you, He assures me.

So I've learned to jump in with both feet, but I never let go of His hand.

"I would like to write historical novels." Janet

As women, we all have girlish dreams hidden in our hearts and God, our heavenly Father, longs to fulfill them. "No matter how many promises God has made, they are 'Yes' in Christ. And so through him the 'Amen' is spoken by us to the glory of God" (2 Corinthians 1:20). Jesus fulfills all our dreams when we place our hand in His hand, our hopes in His keeping, and our dreams in His tender care.

Who needs a fairy godmother when our Father is a heavenly God? Who needs a yellow brick road when our final journey will take us down streets of gold? Who needs a knight in shining armor when we can walk hand in hand with Jesus Christ, the Prince of Peace? Is the God who fulfills our dreams a fairy tale? I think not. This, my friend, is a dream come true! "Things which the eye has not seen and the ear has not heard, and which have not entered the heart of man, all that God has prepared for those who love Him" (1 Corinthians 2:9 NASB).

Dreams I Dream for You

You taste the tears
You're lost in sorrow
You see your yesterdays
I see tomorrow

You see the darkness
I see the light
You know your failures
But I know your heart

The dreams I dream for you
Are deeper than the ones you're clinging to
More precious than the finest thing you knew
And truer than the treasures you pursue
Let the old dreams die
Like stars that fade from view
Then take the cup I offer
And drink deeply of
The dreams I dream for you

You see your shame
But I see your glory
You've read one page
I know the story

I hold a vision
That you'll become
As you grow into the truth
As you learn to walk in love

Let the old dreams die
Like stars that fade from view
Then take the cup I offer
And drink deeply of
The dreams I dream for you[21]

Bible Study Guide

Introduction

I Dreamed a Dream

These first questions are for those meeting in a group setting who are having an introductory meeting. No preparation is required. These questions will serve as discussion starters and will prepare hearts and minds for the material ahead. If your group has already read the "I Dreamed a Dream" and chapter 1, you can incorporate the introductory questions along with Lesson 1.

1. As a little girl, what did you dream about becoming when you grew up? (You don't have to limit yourself to only one dream.)

2. What did you see yourself doing one day?

3. What did each of those dreams look like in your imagination?

4. How have those dreams come true?

5. How have those dreams *not* come true?

6. How is your life different from the life you imagined?

7. What would you like to be different in your life than it is today?

8. What dreams do you have for your future?

9. If you could be assured of success and money were no object, what would you like to accomplish in your life?

Lesson 1

A Daddy Who Loves Me

In chapter 1 we looked at the tender dream of every woman—to have a daddy who loves me. In this lesson, let's take a look at how God wants to fulfill that dream in each of our lives.

1. What is God's promise to you in 2 Corinthians 6:18?

2. Look up the following verses and note what you learn about the Fatherhood of God.

    a. 1 Corinthians 8:6

    b. Ephesians 1:3-5

    c. Galatians 4:6-7

    d. James 1:17

3. Look up the following verses and note what you learn about the love of the Father.

    a. Psalm 63:3

    b. 1 John 4:9-10,16

    c. Psalm 89:2

    d. Numbers 14:18

    e. John 3:16 (How has He given His love to us? How much?)

4. How can we know what God is like? John 14:9; Hebrews 1:3

5. How did Jesus exemplify God's love during His 33 years of ministry? Give several examples.

6. Read the following and note what believers in Christ are called.

   a. John 1:12

   b. Philippians 2:15

   c. 1 John 3:1

   d. 2 Corinthians 6:18

7. What do the following verses teach us about how our Father disciplines us, His children?

   a. Proverbs 3:11-12

   b. Hebrews 12:7-11

   c. Deuteronomy 8:5

8. Is the discipline of a loving Father positive or negative?

9. How does our Father use His words in the Bible to discipline or train us? 2 Timothy 3:16

10. If you are a mother, how would you describe the love you have for your child or children? How does it make you feel that God feels similarly about you?

11. How does knowing that God is your Father affect your everyday life?

12. Make a list of every characteristic you can think of for the perfect father. Now put a check by the ones you have experienced in God as His child.

13. End today's lesson thanking God for making you His dearly loved child.

Lesson 2

Here Comes the Bridegroom

In chapter 2, "To Be a Bride," we learned that in biblical times the bride-to-be had several months to prepare for her wedding day. Today, let's look at ways we can get ready to be united with our heavenly Groom.

1. First, let's look at the extravagant bride price that Jesus paid for His bride. Read the following and note what you learn about the price He paid for you.

   a. Acts 20:28

   b. Ephesians 5:1-2

   c. Galatians 2:20

   d. 1 Timothy 2:5-6

   e. Titus 2:11-14

2. Read Revelation 19:6-8 and write out the imagery of this scene. What has the bride done before the Groom's arrival?

3. Read Matthew 25:1-13. What happened to the five virgins who were not prepared? Where were they when the groom arrived?

4. Let's look at some ways we can get ready for our Groom.

   a. Read Ephesians 4:25–5:21 and list everything Paul tells us about purifying our character.

b. Look up Colossians 3:1-17and 4:1-6 and, again, list everything Paul tells us about purifying our character.

Between those two lists, I think we have plenty to work on until Jesus returns!

5. One of the most important things we can do as we wait for our Groom is to come to a deeper understanding of Jesus' love for us, His bride. What did Paul pray the Ephesians would understand about Jesus' love for His bride? Ephesians 3:18-19

6. Paul gives earthly husbands an example of how they should love their wives. What is their example and what are they to emulate? Ephesians 5:25-27

7. How does Paul describe what Jesus did for His bride in Philippians 2:6-8?

8. Describe the day when our Groom will come to get His bride. 1 Thessalonians 4:16-17; 5:1-2

9. Describe our heavenly home where Jesus is now preparing our room. Revelation 21

10. I don't know about you, but I can't even begin to imagine the beauty of heaven. I suspect that is why John kept using the word "like" as he tried to explain his vision of heaven in the book of Revelation. There were not words to accurately describe the beauty that awaits the bride. End today's lesson thanking God for choosing you to be the bride for His only Son.

Lesson 3

From Barren to Bountiful

Today we are going to be looking at one particular woman and how God fulfilled her dream to be a mother. And I want us to look at this on a much deeper level. This is a woman who had a shattered dream, a restored dream, and many emotions in between. Let's see what we can learn from Hannah.

Read 1 Samuel 1 and answer the following questions.

1. Why was Hannah barren?

2. What is Peninnah called in verse 6? What did she do and why?

3. How long had Peninnah been provoking Hannah? The King James Version says Hannah was provoked "sore." Have you been provoked sore? Has someone else's fulfilled dream ever rubbed salt in the wound of your emptiness?

4. What signs of depression do you see in Hannah? What emotions are listed in chapter 1? Do you see a progression?

5. Would you say Hannah's husband did or did not understand his wife's pain? What does he say to make you answer as you did?

6. Verse 16 says that Hannah was grieved. What do we usually associate with the word grief?

7. Where did Hannah take her grief?

8. Describe the depth of her prayer.

9. When Eli accused her of being drunk, did she become angry? Did she respond in pride or humility?

10. How did her countenance change after Eli promised her a child?

11. What was the result of his prediction?

12. Hannah kept Samuel until he was weaned (until he was two to three years old), and then she gave him to God's service in the temple. She gave him back to the Lord. Suppose she had clung to her child and reneged on her promise. How would that have changed history?

13. What had Hannah learned about God during this trial in her life? 1 Samuel 2:1-10

14. Hannah had her dreamed fulfilled, but she then turned around and gave that dream right back to God. Have you ever had a dream fulfilled and then realized that the ultimate fulfillment was a relationship with God Himself, and not what you had originally longed for? Explain.

15. After Hannah gave her dream back to God, how did He continue to bless her? 1 Samuel 2:18-21

16. Even though a woman may never have children born of her womb, what does the imagery of Psalm 113:9 suggest?

17. In biblical times, a woman's identity was wrapped up in being a wife and a mother. What did a woman in the crowd call out to Jesus? What was Jesus' response to her? Luke 11:27-28

As with all our dreams, the ultimate cause for rejoicing in all of our lives is that our names are written in the Lamb's Book of Life! Every other dream pales in comparison.

End today's lesson by thanking God for your relationship with Him.

Lesson 4

A Radiant Reflection

I don't know of any woman who doesn't long to be beautiful. Today, let's take a look at what it means to be spiritually beautiful—a beauty that begins on the inside and shines for all the world to see.

1. According to Isaiah 43:7, why were we created?

2. We were created for God's glory and to reflect God's glory. How do we do that?

3. The glory of created things, including man, is when they are what God intended them to be in their purest form. Can man, apart from Christ, reflect God's glory? Why or why not? Romans 3:23

4. What happens when we accept Christ, according to Galatians 2:20 and 3:26?

5. What does 2 Corinthians 3:18 say about our continual transformation?

6. Read Exodus 34:28-35 and answer the following questions.

   a. Where had Moses been for 40 days and 40 nights?

   b. What effect did this extended time in God's presence have on his face?

   c. What happened over time as he left God's presence? 2 Corinthians 3:7-8

      d. How can that scenario relate to our time spent in God's presence?

      e. Have you ever felt as though you had a "holy glow" after spending time with God? If so, when?

      f. Have you ever felt that glow begin to fade because of not spending time in His presence? How did that make you feel?

      g. How can we get the glow back? James 4:8

7. Read the following verses and note the secrets to being a beautifully radiant woman.

      a. Psalm 19:8

      b. Psalm 34:5

      c. Isaiah 52:7

8. Read Job 23:10. List several characteristics of highly polished silver or gold.

9. What does God say about how trials polish us? What is His ultimate goal in our trials? Isaiah 48:10; 2 Corinthians 4:16-18

10. Can you think of a time when a specific trial brought you closer to God, removed dross from your life, or made you more spiritually beautiful in the end?

11. In summary, what is the best beauty treatment available? Describe a *spiritual* beauty regimen as if you were a salesperson. Ecclesiastes 8:1

Lesson 5

Friends for Life

I haven't met a woman yet who doesn't long to have a best friend. Let's delve into God's Word together and see how Jesus is the best friend a girl could ever have.

1. Read John 15:13-15.

   a. What did Jesus call His disciples?

   b. What did He say was the ultimate act of friendship?

   c. What is the difference between a servant and a friend?

2. Read the following aspects of friendship and note how Jesus personified each one.

   a. Galatians 6:2 and Matthew 11:29-30

   b. Roman 12:15 and John 11:35

   c. Romans 12:10 and John 13:3-5

   d. Romans 15:7 and Mark 2:15-17 (Whom did He accept?)

   e. Hebrews 3:13 and Matthew 14:28-29

   f. Hebrews 10:24 and Mark 6:37

   g. Ephesians 4:32 and John 21:15-17 (This was after Peter had denied knowing Jesus three times.)

   h. 1 Thessalonians 5:11 and John 14:12

3. If you have ever felt betrayed by a friend, Jesus knows how you feel.

   a. How is this confirmed in Hebrews 4:14-16?

   b. What did the disciples do after Jesus' arrest? Matthew 26:56

   c. What did Peter do when a servant girl questioned if he was one of Jesus' disciples? Matthew 26:69-75

   d. Did Jesus continue to love Peter even though he had betrayed Him? John 21:15

   e. What does Jesus tell us about forgiving those who hurt us? Luke 17:4; Matthew 18:21-22

   f. Did the apostles think this was going to be difficult? Luke 17:5

   g. Is it enough just to say the words? Matthew 18:35

   h. What happens in our hearts when we refuse to forgive?

   i. Is there a friend you need to forgive today? Go back and reread Ephesians 4:32.

4. Read and record Jesus' promise to us found in Hebrews 13:5.

5. How did Jesus give us an example of how to be a friend in John 13:1-17? Note how that is emphasized in the following verses.

   a. 1 Peter 4:10

   b. Galatians 5:13

   c. Philippians 2:3

6. One of the best acts of friendship is to pray earnestly for someone. In closing, read Jesus' prayer for His disciples and for you found in John 17:6-24. Make a list of the specifics He prayed for you.

Lesson 6

Who's in Control?

The first woman to interfere with God's dream was the first woman. That's a bit frightening to think about, isn't it? Let's look at the book of Genesis and see how Eve took control of her own life and the devastating results that followed.

1. Read Genesis 2–3 and answer the following questions.

   a. What was the one restriction placed on Adam and Eve by God?

   b. What did the serpent say to cause Eve to question God?

   c. What did the serpent say that implied God was not telling the truth?

   d. What did the serpent say that implied God was holding out on Eve?

   e. What do you think appealed to Eve the most—the food or the ability to be like God and be in control?

   f. What was the result of her disobedience? Genesis 3:16

   g. What has been the result of Adam and Eve's disobedience on all the generations that followed? Romans 5:12

   h. Give an example of how one act of disobedience or sin can affect many generations to come.

2. One reason we tend to interfere with God's plans is because we get tired of waiting for Him to act. Read Exodus 24 and answer the following questions.

    a. When Moses went up to Mount Sinai to meet with God, how long did he wait before God appeared? Exodus 24:16

    b. What do you think Moses did while he waited?

    c. What would you have thought or done when God did not show up on days 1 and 2?

    d. How long did Moses stay with God on the mountain? Exodus 24:18

3. Now let's skip over to Exodus 32 and let's see what the people who were waiting on Moses to return were up to.

    a. What did they say to Aaron in Exodus 32:1?

    b. What did they do? Exodus 32:2-6

    c. The calf was most likely similar to the Egyptian bull-god, Apis. What are some modern day idols that people fabricate to take the place of a relationship with God?

    d. What was God's reaction to their lack of patience and obedience? Exodus 32:10

    e. I can't leave this section without pointing out the ridiculousness of Aaron's reply to Moses. How did Aaron say the calf came about? Exodus 32:21-24

    f. Have you ever been in a situation where you interrupted God's plan by running ahead of Him and then tried to gloss over what you did when it turned out badly? (You don't have to answer this question out loud. Just think about it.) What would have been the better response from Aaron? Psalm 51:4

    g. What was the end result of the people not waiting on God but turning to an idol instead?

h. What can we learn from this incident of how the children of Israel grew tired of waiting on God and ran ahead with a foolish plan of their own?

4. What do the following verses teach us about waiting on God and His timing?

   a. Psalm 5:3

   b. Psalm 37:7

   c. Proverbs 20:22

   d. Isaiah 30:18

   e. Isaiah 40:27-31

   f. Isaiah 64:4 (This is one of my favorite verses!)

5. What do we learn about God's time frame in 2 Peter 3:8-9?

6. What promises do we have that God will accomplish what He says He will do? Psalm 33:10-11; Psalm 138:8

7. What does Psalm 127:1 tell us about trying to fulfill our own plans in our own ways?

8. If you are waiting on God to fulfill His plans for your life, just remember: He does not need our interference. He simply requires our obedience. Take time today to commit to wait on God's leading, direction, wisdom, and provision for your life.

Lesson 7

Remembering to Remember

Today, let's look at two women in the Old Testament who forgot their dreams and see how God restored them.

1. Read 1 Kings 17 and answer the following questions.

    a. Who cared for Elijah during the drought?

    b. Why did God send Elijah to Zarephath?

    c. Note the similar words in 17:5 and 17:10.
        So he_____. So he
        _____.

    d. What was the widow doing when Elijah arrived?

    e. Would you say she was hopeful or hopeless?

    f. What was Elijah's promise to her and what was the outcome?

    g. Suppose she had not trusted God and cooked her last meal for her and her son as she had planned. What do you think the outcome would have been?

    h. Did God need the widow's help to take care of Elijah?

    i. Why do you think God sent Elijah to her?

    j. The widow was blessed because of her obedience. As a result, who else was blessed?

2. Sometimes, the best way to get beyond a seemingly desperate situation is to help someone else. Have you ever experienced that in your own life?

3. What does Jesus teach about this principle of giving and receiving? Luke 6:38

4. Now let's look at another prophet and another woman who was just about to forget her dream. Read 2 Kings 4:1-8 and answer the following questions.

   a. Describe the widow's circumstances.

   b. What did Elisha ask her to do?

   c. How many jars did he tell her to collect and what did he tell her to do with the jars?

   d. How many jars do you think God would have filled?

   e. The woman told Elisha she had nothing…except a little oil. How much does God need to restore a dream?

5. Interestingly, both of the women were widows—women who had lost their hopes and dreams for the future. How does this support Deuteronomy 10:18 and Psalm 68:5?

6. What similarities do you see between these two women and Naomi, whom we studied in chapter 7?

7. Sometimes, when we have a broken dream, it is easy to feel God has forgotten all about us. How do these three women and their stories show that God never forgets us?

8. Read and record Hebrews 13:5.

Lesson 8

Saying Yes to God

In chapter eight, we looked at Esther, the little orphan girl who courageously fulfilled God's plan for her life. In this lesson, let's flip over to the New Testament and visit with three Marys to see how each one of them fulfilled God's very unique and specific plans for their lives.

1. Read Luke 1:26–2:52 and answer the following questions.

    a. What do we learn about Mary in the opening verses?

    b. What about the verses let us know that she was an ordinary girl?

    c. What plan did Gabriel reveal to Mary?

    d. Luke tells us that she was afraid, and yet what was her response to God's call on her life?

    e. What did Elizabeth reveal about Mary's heart?

    f. For a woman to be pregnant and not married in those days, she risked her parents disowning her, her fiancé putting her away, and/or the religious community stoning her. Explain why you think Mary moved forward with such confidence and assurance.

    g. What was the outcome of her obedience?

2. Now let's visit with Mary of Bethany. Read Luke 10:38-42 and answer the following questions:

a. Where did Jesus go to dinner? In whose home?

b. The fact that one particular sister's name was mentioned as the hostess implies that she was the elder of the two.

c. What did Mary do?

d. In those days women were not allowed to sit in a room full of men while the men ate. Also, a woman was not allowed to sit under a rabbi's teaching. Even in the temple, the women were kept separate from the men by a partition or a flight of steps leading to a separate level for the men only. With that information, explain the amount of courage it took for Mary to enter this room and sit at Jesus' feet with the men.

e. What did Jesus' say about Mary's bold move to become a student in Jesus' classroom?

f. This wasn't the last time Mary of Bethany showed great courage. Read John 12:1-7 and note Mary's bold move. What did she do and why did she do it? Again, remember that women were not permitted at such a gathering. How does this add to the picture of courage?

3. Let's take a look at one more Mary—Mary Magdalene.

a. What do we learn about Mary Magdalene from the following verses? Luke 8:1-3; Luke 24:1-12; John 19:25

b. Read John 20:10-18 and answer the following questions:

> To whom did Jesus first appear after His resurrection?

> Who had previously visited the empty tomb that Jesus did not appear to?

> In a time in history when women were not allowed to testify in court because they were viewed as un-reliable, what did Jesus tell Mary Magdalene to do?

    c. What can you surmise is Jesus' opinion of women? Of you? (I hope this gets you excited!)

4. God had specific and unique plans for each one of these Marys, and He has specific and unique plans for you. If you are willing to do whatever God has planned for you, go back to Luke 1:45 and fill in the blank with your name.

> "Blessed is _____ who has believed that what the Lord has said to her will be accomplished!"

Lesson 9

Picking up the Pieces

Sometimes it is easy to feel God has forgotten us when our dreams are shattered. But the Bible assures us that God sees, God hears, and God understands.

1. Read the following verses and note what you learn about our God who sees.

    a. 2 Chronicles 16:9

    b. Proverbs 15:3

    c. Psalm 34:15

    d. Psalm 121:3

2. Hagar was a woman who felt that God had forgotten her. But after the angel of the Lord appeared to her, He assured her He had not. What did Hagar say about God and what name did she give Him? Genesis 16:13

3. Read the following verses and note what you learn about our God who hears.

    a. Genesis 21:17

    b. Exodus 2:24

    c. Psalm 55:17

    d. Psalm 145:19

4. Read the following verses and note what you learn about our God who cares.

   a. Hosea 11:8

   b. Isaiah 63:9

   c. 2 Kings 13:23

   d. Nehemiah 9:27

5. Like Father, like Son. Read the following and note how Jesus had compassion on those with shattered dreams.

   a. Matthew 14:14

   b. Matthew 15:29-32

   c. Matthew 20:34

   d. Mark 1:41

   e. Luke 7:12-15

6. Let's take one final look at a man with a shattered dream and what He learned about God. Read Psalm 73:21-26 and answer the following questions.

   a. How did Asaph describe himself during this difficult time?

   b. What characteristics of God did he cling to?

   c. What was his praise to God?

7. Turn back to lesson 7. How does what you learned in this lesson support what you learned about how God cared for the widow in 1 Kings 17, the widow in 2 Kings 4, and Naomi?

8. If you are dealing with a shattered or unfulfilled dream today, how does what you learned in this chapter give you comfort and hope?

Lesson 10

Creating the Mosaic

I love watching the sun shine through a stained glass window in a church—perhaps because I see that as a picture of my own life. God takes the broken pieces of our lives, makes a beautiful mosaic, and then shines the light of Christ through the panes to create a spectacular masterpiece. Let's take a look and see how He did that throughout Scripture.

1. Job was a man who lost just about everything except a nagging wife and a few critical friends. Read Job 1–2:10 and note everything that Job lost.

2. What did Job's wife suggest he do? Job 2:9

3. What was Job's response to her? Job 2:10

4. There was a lot of suffering between Job 1 and Job 42, but let's move ahead to the end of the story to see how he fared in the end. Read Job 42 and answer the following questions.

   a. At the end of his struggle, what had Job learned about God? Job 42:1-5

   b. How did God restore Job's dreams? Job 42:10-17

   c. Did Job praise God before or after He restored his dreams?

   d. What lesson can we learn from Job?

5. What are the promises found in Psalm 34:15-19?

6. Read the following and note how God restored each person's dream.

   a. Hagar: Genesis 21:18

   b. Joseph: Genesis 41:39-40

   c. Naomi: Ruth 4:13-15

   d. Bathsheba: 2 Samuel 12:15-25

7. Let's turn our attention to the New Testament. Read the following and note how Jesus restored each woman's dreams. Also note in which case the woman's faith was mentioned and in which case it was not.

   a. Matthew 9:20-22

   b. Matthew 15:21-28

   c. Luke 7:11-16

   d. Luke 13:10-13

   e. John 8:1-11

It is always important that we do not put God in a box. He does what He pleases. As you see here, some of these women had great faith. On the other hand, the woman with the dead son didn't ask for Jesus' help at all. She probably didn't even know He was present, and there was no mention of her faith. Sometimes He blesses us in ways we would never even think to ask!

8. As you are thinking about your shattered or unfulfilled dreams, read and record the following verses:

   a. Jeremiah 32:17

   b. Mark 9:23

   c. Luke 1:37

9. End today's lesson by praising God that there is nothing He cannot do!

Lesson 11

Taking an Intermission

As we turn our attention to interrupted dreams, let's look at Miriam, Moses' older sister.

1. How did God use Miriam as part of His dream to free the Israelites from slavery? Exodus 2:1-10

2. What was Miriam's role in the exodus from Egypt? Exodus 15:20-21

3. Read Numbers 12:1-15 and answer the following?

   a. What did Miriam and Aaron begin to do?

   b. How did they attempt to exalt themselves?

   c. What did God say to Miriam and Aaron?

   d. What was Miriam's punishment?

   e. Who prayed for Miriam to be healed?

   f. What did the Israelites do while she was in a time-out?

   g. Sometimes, when God interrupts our dreams to teach us a lesson or bring us to repentance, others suffer as well. When Moses was 40 years old and took control of God's plan, the entire Israelite nation had to wait 40 more years for deliverance. Can you think of a time in your own life when you were experiencing an interrupted dream and others were affected?

4. Sometimes we have an intermission or an interrupted dream because God is developing our character to fit our calling. Read the following verses and note the passage of time between each person's calling and when the calling actually came to fruition.

  a. Abraham: Genesis 12:1-4 and Genesis 21:1-5

  b. Joseph: Genesis 37:2-11 and Genesis 41:41; 50:18-21

  c. David: 1 Samuel 16:6-13 and 2 Samuel 2:2-4

5. What do these three examples teach you about how God develops a person's character to fit their particular assignment?

6. What do the following verses teach us about how trials develop and mature our character?

  a. Romans 5:3-5

  b. James 1:2-4

  c. 1 Peter 1:6-8

7. Pride in self is a surefire way of experiencing an interrupted dream or a shattered dream. What do the following verses teach us about pride and humility?

  a. 2 Chronicles 7:14

  b. Proverbs 11:2

  c. Proverbs 16:18

  d. Proverbs 29:23

8. The book of Daniel contains a dramatic story of a shattered dream, an interrupted dream, and a restored dream. Read Daniel 4:28-37 and describe each one. (For a clearer picture, begin at verse 1.)

9. Peter was a man who had a brief interrupted dream.

  a. What did Jesus warn him was about to happen? Luke 22:31-34

b. Pay close attention to the words, "And when you have turned back, strengthen your brothers" (verse 32). What do those words mean to you?

c. After Jesus' resurrection, what do we see Peter doing? John 21:1-3

d. Who showed up the next morning and what did He ask the fishermen to do? John 21:4-14

e. Jesus had a private conversation with Peter. Explain the scene in John 21:15-17.

f. After an interrupted dream, which we may feel is a shattered dream, it is very easy just to fall back into a regular rhythm of doing what we have always done. Certainly that's what we see Peter doing. But Jesus had other plans for Peter. He was calling him to get back in the game! Intermission over, my friend. Now it's time to take care of these sheep. Remember, what Jesus told Peter he would do after he had "turned back"?

10. Have you fallen back into just doing what you have always done, or is Jesus calling you back to a forgotten dream?

Lesson 12

Discovering God's Dreams

Nehemiah was a man who dreamed a God-sized dream. Let's look at how the fulfillment of that dream follows the D-R-E-A-M-S model in chapter 12, "Discovering God's Dreams."

1. What news did Nehemiah receive about his homeland? Nehemiah 1:1-3

2. I'd like for us to read straight through the progression of the dream-come-true, but first flip over to Nehemiah 2:5 and record Nehemiah's God-sized *dream*.

3. Now let's look at how Nehemiah *remembered* who God is. Read Nehemiah 1:4-11 and list his words of remembrance.

4. What evidence in Nehemiah's prayer do we have that he had *examined* the Scripture? Nehemiah 1:4-11

5. What did he *ask* of God? Nehemiah 1:11; 2:4

6. What did he ask of the king? Nehemiah 2:5-8. How does this show that Nehemiah was a man who prayed and also a man who prepared? What a winning combination!

7. To what did Nehemiah attribute his success? Nehemiah 2:8

8. Next, Nehemiah *moved* into action. How did he motivate others to move with him? Nehemiah 2:17-18

9. The walls had been broken down for approximately 150 years, and yet how long did it take this man who prayed and prepared to fulfill this God-sized dream? Nehemiah 6:15

10. All the while, Nehemiah ***stayed connected to the Vine.*** Read and note how he and the Israelites stayed connected. Nehemiah 1:4-11; 4:4,9; 6:9; 8:1-3; 8:6; 9:6; 13:30

11. What did the enemies surmise after the completion of Nehemiah's God-sized dream? (6:16)

12. Wow! What is our ultimate goal in the completion of any God-sized dream?

13. What insights did you glean from learning about how Nehemiah accomplished God's plan?

14. How can you apply these truths to your own life?

Daring to Dream Again

If you have forgotten your dreams, are you ready to dream again? If you have been dreaming too small, are you ready to dream God-sized dreams? Let's spend our last lesson together considering the resources God has given us and looking ahead to the future.

1. As you begin to dream God-sized dreams for your life, remember the resources that are at the fingertips of your hands folded in prayer.

   a. Colossians 2:2

   b. Philippians 4:19

   c. Ephesians 1:18-21

2. While you may not feel qualified to do what God has called you to do, remember, He doesn't need much, and yet He wants it all.

   a. What did Jesus use to feed the 5000? How much of his lunch did the boy give? Mark 6:30-44

   b. What did Jesus use to make wine? How full did the servants fill the pots? (John 2:7)

   c. What did God use to bless the widow in 2 Kings 4:2?

   d. How much education did the disciples who changed the world possess? Acts 4:13

e. Acts 4:13 is key. Write out the last part of that verse: "They took note_____."

3. What did Jesus say about reaching His goal? Luke 14:32. From memory, recall as many people as you can who tried to stop Him.

4. What do the following verses say about God's plans?

a. Isaiah 14:24

b. Isaiah 41:2-7

c. Isaiah 46:11

5. God has given us many gifts (1 Corinthians 12), much power (Acts 1:8), and magnificent treasures of wisdom and knowledge (Colossians 2:2-3). Let's turn our attention to Jesus' parable of the landowner who gave talents to his servants and think about what we will do with all God has entrusted to us. Read Matthew 25:14-30 and answer the following questions.

a. Why was the landowner pleased with the servants to whom he gave five talents and two talents?

b. Why was he angry with the servant to whom he gave one talent?

c. Why did the servant with one talent hide his talent instead of invest it?

d. Have you ever considered your past life experiences and spiritual gifts as "talents" that God wants you to invest into the lives of others? How could you invest what God has entrusted to you?

6. Read 1 Corinthians 1:3-5 and record the verse in your own words.

(I wish I were there with you, so I'm going to take this opportunity to share my answer to this question. God doesn't comfort us to make us comfortable. He comforts us to make us comfort-able...able to comfort others. That's investing in other people in a way that will bring great dividends!)

7. Let's step into the future for a moment. Suppose you were going to write your own eulogy. What would you like for it to say? In writing it, answer these five questions.

   a. Who were you?

   b. What did you accomplish on earth?

   c. What did you leave behind?

   d. Whose life did you impact?

   e. What lasting impact will your life have on generations yet to come?

8. In closing, go back to the introductory lesson and review your answers. Are there any you would answer differently today?

9. What are you going to do differently as a result of this study?

Notes

Introduction—I Dreamed a Dream

1. "I Dreamed a Dream" from the musical *Les Misérables* by Alain Boublil and Claude-Michel Schonberg, music by Claude-Michel Schonberg, lyrics by Alain Boublil, Herbert Kretzmer, and Jean-Marc Natel. © Alain Boublil Music Ltd. (ASCAP) Used by permission.

2. Beth Moore, *Breaking Free: Making Liberty in Christ a Reality in Life* (Nashville, TN: Lifeway, 1999), 194.

Chapter 1—To Have a Daddy Who Loves Me

1. Adapted from a sermon by Gayle Montgomery. Used by permission.

2. Bob Carlisle, *Butterfly Kisses: Tender Thoughts Shared Between Fathers and Daughters* (Nashville, TN: Countryman Books, 1997), iii.

3. J.I. Packer, *Knowing God* (Downers Grove, IL: InterVarsity Press, 1973), 182.

4. John MacArthur, *The MacArthur New Testament Commentary: Romans 1-8* (Chicago, IL: Moody Press, 1991), 436-37.

5. J.I. Packer, *Knowing God*, 195.

6. Mary A. Kassian, *In My Father's House: Women Relating to God as Father* (Nashville, TN: Lifeway, 1993), 13.

7. J.I. Packer, *Knowing God*, 187-88.

8. Anabel Gillham, *The Confident Woman: Knowing Who You Are in Christ* (Eugene, OR: Harvest House Publishers, 1993), 27.

9. Ibid, 29.

10. Beth Moore, *Breaking Free*, 160.

11. W.E. Vine, Merrill F. Unger, William White Jr., *Vine's Complete Expository Dictionary of Old and New Testament Words* (Nashville, TN: Thomas Nelson Publishers, 1985), 143.

Chapter Two—To Be a Bride

1. Dee Brestin and Kathy Troccoli, *Falling in Love with Jesus* (Nashville, TN: W Publishing Group, 2000), 27.

2. Brent Curtis and John Eldredge, *The Sacred Romance: Drawing Closer to the Heart of God* (Nashville, TN: Thomas Nelson Publishers, 1997), 109.

3. Lyrics by Judie Lawson, copyright © 1995, Pyewacket Frog (ASCAP). Used by permission.

Chapter Three—To Be a Mommy

1. "Trust His Heart," Eddie Carswell/Babbie Mason, © 1989 Causing Change Music (Admin. by

Dayspring Music, LLC), Dayspring Music, LLC, May Sun Music (Admin. By Word Music, LLC), Word Music, LLC. All rights reserved. Used by permission.

2. <http://www.cdc.gov/nchs/fastats/fertile.htm>.

3. <http://www.allaboutlifechallenges.org/miscarriage-statistics.htm>.

4. Joyce Brothers, "When a Dream Doesn't Come True," *Parade,* March 24, 2002, 6.

5. Pamela Reeve, *Parables of the Forest* (Sisters, OR: Multnomah Publishers, 1989).

6. Ken Gire, *The Reflective Life* (Colorado Springs, CO: Chariot Victor Publishing, 1998), 137-38.

7. Emily Pearl Kingley, "Letting Go of Disappointments" from an October 1992 "Dear Abby" column appearing in the *Oregonian.*

Chapter Four—To Be Beautiful

1. Sharon Jaynes, *Becoming Spiritually Beautiful* (Eugene, OR: Harvest House Publishers, 2003/2007), 13.

2. <http://www.facebook.com/topic.php?uid=21435141328&topic=9559#!>.

3. John Eldredge, *Wild at Heart* (Nashville, TN: Thomas Nelson Publishers, 2001), 16-17.

4. Bruce Marchiano, *Jesus, the Man Who Loved Women* (New York, NY: Howard Books, 2008), 51.

5. <http://www.imow.org/dynamic/pdfs/curricula_blocks_pdf_48.pdf>.

6. Laura Pulfer, "What Really Sent Barbie to the Body Shop," *The Cincinnati Enquirer,* November 23, 1997. <http://www.enquirer.com/columns/pulfer/1997/11/112397_lp.html>.

7. <http://www.ywca.org/atf/cf/%7B3B450FA5-108B-4D2E-B3D0-C31487243E6A%7D/Beauty%20at%20Any%20Cost.pdf>.

8. Ibid.

9. Nancy Leigh DeMoss, *Biblical Womanhood in the Home* (Wheaton, IL: Crossway Books, 2002), 33.

10. Mimi Avins, *The Press Democrat,* Santa Rosa, CA, July 3, 2001, D1.

11. DeMoss, *Biblical Womanhood in the Home,* 34. (From "Reshaping the World" sidebar summary by Mac Maragolis, Paige Bierma, Mahion Meyer, Hideo Takayama, and Shehnaz Sutervaloia, in *Newsweek International* (Atlantic Edition), August 16, 1999, 38.)

12. Nancy Stafford, *Beauty by the Book* (Sisters, OR: Multnomah Publishers, 2002), 31.

13. Willard Harley, *His Needs, Her Needs* (Grand Rapids, MI: Fleming H. Revell, 1986), 100.

14. Thomas Watson, *Gleanings from Thomas Watson* (Morgan, PA: Soli Deo Gloria Publications, 1995), 49.

15. Nancy Stafford, *Beauty by the Book,* 118.

16. Dee Brestin and Kathy Troccoli, *Falling in Love with Jesus,* 11.

17. Jan Meyers, *The Allure of Hope* (Colorado Springs, CO: Navpress, 2001), 64.

Chapter Five—To Have a Best Friend

1. L.M. Montgomery, *Anne of Green Gables* (Pleasantville, NY: The Reader's Digest Association, Inc., 1992), 48-50. Used by permission.

2. Janet Lever, "Sex Differences in the Games Children Play," *Social Problems,* 23, 1976, 478-87.

3. Elliot Engel, "Of Male Bondage," *Newsweek,* June 21, 1982, 13.

4. Lori Andrews, "How Women Think," *Parents*, April 1986, 74.

5. Pam Kruger, "Can You Be Too Close to a Friend?" *Good Housekeeping*, September 1997, 76.

6. Ibid.

7. S.E. Taylor, L.C. Klein, B.P. Lewis, T.L. Gruenewald, R.A.R. Gurung, and J.A. Updegraff, "Female Responses to Stress: Tend-and-Befriend, Not Fight-or-Flight," *Psychological Review*, 2000, 107 (3), 411-29.

8. Dee Brestin, *The Friendships of Women* (Wheaton, IL: Victor Books, 1988), 37.

9. Beth Moore, *Jesus, the One and Only* (Nashville, TN: Lifeway Press, 2000), 137.

10. L.M. Montgomery, *Anne of Green Gables*, 73.

Chapter Six—Sarah—A Woman Who Interfered with God's Dreams

1. Kathy Collard Miller, *Women of the Bible* (Lancaster, PA: Starburst, 1999), 37.

2. Billy Graham, *How to Be Born Again* (Waco, TX: Word, 1977), 129-30.

Chapter Seven—Naomi—A Woman Who Forgot Her Dreams

1. Jill Briscoe, as quoted by Kathy Collard Miller, *Women of the Bible*, 195.

2. Bruce Wilkerson, *Secrets of the Vine* (Sisters, OR: Multnomah Publishers, Inc., 2002), 33.

3. Ibid., 73.

4. Ibid., 74-75.

5. Kathy Collard Miller, *Women of the Bible*, 149.

Chapter Eight—Esther—A Woman Who Fulfilled God's Dreams

1. William M. Taylor, "Ruth the Gleaner" and "Esther the Queen," *Bible Biographies*, as quoted in Kathy Collard Miller, *Women of the Bible*, 137.

2. Judith Couchman, *Esther—Becoming a Woman God Can Use* (Grand Rapids, MI: Zondervan Publishing House, 1999), 43.

3. Gustav Niebuhr and Laurie Goldstein, "Who Will Take Graham's Place on the World Stage?" *The Charlotte Observer*, Saturday, January 2, 1999, 15A.

4. Robert J. Morgan, *Nelson's Complete Books of Stories, Illustrations, and Quotes* (Nashville, TN: Thomas Nelson, 2000), 151.

Chapter Nine—Shattered Dreams

1. Sharon Jaynes, *Being a Great Mom Raising Great Kids* (Chicago, IL: Moody Publishing, 2000), 11.

2. Neil Anderson, *The Bondage Breaker* (Eugene, OR: Harvest House Publishers, 1990), 23.

3. Larry Crabb, *Shattered Dreams* (Colorado Springs, CO: WaterBrook Press, 2001), 35.

4. Florence Littauer, *Dare to Dream* (Dallas, TX: Word Publishing, 1991), 260.

5. Beth Moore, *Breaking Free*, 136.

Chapter Ten—Restored Dreams

1. Oswald Chambers, *My Utmost for His Highest* (Grand Rapids, MI: Discovery House, 1992), August 5.

2. Kenneth L. Barker and John R. Kohlenberger III, *Zondervan NIV Bible Commentary* (Grand Rapids, MI: Zondervan Publishing House, 1994), 93.

3. Beth Moore, *Breaking Free*, 132.

Chapter Eleven—Interrupted Dreams

1. Charles Ryrie, *Ryrie Study Bible* (Chicago, IL: The Moody Bible Institute, 1976) footnote for Exodus 2:10, 94.

2. John MacArthur, *The MacArthur Bible Commentary* (Nashville, TN: Thomas Nelson, 2005), 84.

3. Anabel Gillham, *The Confident Woman*, 117.

4. Spiros Zodhiates, et al., eds., *The Complete Word Study Dictionary: New Testament* (Chattanooga, TN: AMG Publishers, 1992), 229.

5. Beth Moore, *Breaking Free*, 120.

Chapter Twelve—Discovering God's Dreams

1. Henry T. Blackaby and Richard Blackaby, *Experiencing God Day by Day* (Nashville, TN: Broadman & Holman Publishers, 1997), 3.

2. Ibid., 344.

3. William Backus and Marie Chapian, *Telling Yourself the Truth* (Minneapolis, MN: Bethany House Publishers, 2000), 31.

4. Bruce Wilkerson, *The Prayer of Jabez* (Sisters, OR: Multnomah Publishers, 2000), 24.

5. Bruce Wilkerson, *Secrets of the Vine*, 115.

6. Henry T. Blackaby and Claude V. King, *Experiencing God: Knowing and Doing the Will of God* (Nashville, TN: Lifeway, 1990), 109.

7. Henry Blackaby and Richard Blackaby, *Experiencing God Day by Day*, 137.

Chapter Thirteen—Come Dream with Me

1. Antoine de Saint-Exupery, *The Little Prince,* translated by Katherine Woods (San Diego, CA: Harcourt Brace Jovanovich, 1993), 87.

2. Beth Moore, *Breaking Free,* 132.

3. Jan Meyers, *The Allure of Hope* (Colorado Springs, CO: NavPress, 2001), 84.

4. C.S. Lewis, *The Weight of Glory and Other Addresses* (New York, NY: Touchstone, 1975), 27.

5. <www.livinglifefully.com/character.html>.

6. Bruce Wilkerson, *The Prayer of Jabez Devotional* (Sisters, OR: Multnomah Publishers, 2001), 23.

7. Andy Stanley, as quoted by Bruce Wilkerson in *The Prayer of Jabez Devotional*, 36.

8. Quoted by Florence Littauer in *Dare to Dream* (Dallas, TX: Word Publishing, 1991), 261.

9. Ibid., 70.

10. Ibid., 111.

11. Ibid., 242.

12. Bruce Wilkerson, *The Prayer of Jabez Devotional*, 83.

13. Linda Webber, *Mom, You're Incredible* (Colorado Springs, CO: Focus on the Family, 1994), 101.

14. Bruce Wilkerson, *The Prayer of Jabez Devotional*, 39.

15. William Barclay, *The Letter to the Philippians, Colossians, and Thessalonians*, rev. ed. (Philadelphia, PA: Westminster Press, 1975), 66.

16. Rob Gilbert, ed., *Bits and Pieces*, Vol. N/4, 1, Fairfield, CT.: Economic Press.

17. Jack Canfield and Mark Hansen, eds., *Chicken Soup for the Soul* (Deerfield Beach, FL: Health Communications, 1993), 228-30.

18. <www.brainyquote.com>.

19. Alice Gray, ed., *Stories from the Heart* (Sisters, OR: Multnomah Publishers, 1996), 41.

20. Nell W. Mohney, *From Eve to Esther* (Nashville, TN: Dimensions for Living, 2001), 43.

21. Copyright © 1997 Sparrow Song (BMI) And the Beat Goes on Music (BMI) River Oaks Music Company (BMI) (adm. at EMICMGPublishing.com). All rights reserved. Used by permission.

About the Author

Sharon Jaynes is an international inspirational speaker and Bible teacher for women's conferences and events. She is the author of many books, including *Becoming the Woman of His Dreams*, *The Power of a Woman's Words*, *Your Scars Are Beautiful to God*, *Becoming Spiritually Beautiful*, *"I'm Not Good Enough"... and Other Lies Women Tell Themselves*, and *Becoming a Woman Who Listens to God*. Her books have been translated into several foreign languages and impact women around the globe. Her passion is to encourage, equip, and empower women to walk in courage and confidence as they grasp their true identity as a child of God and a co-heir with Christ.

Sharon is a cofounder of Girlfriends in God, a conference and online ministry that crosses denominational, racial, and generational boundaries to unify the body of Christ. To learn more visit www.girlfriendsinGod.com.

Sharon and her husband, Steve, have one grown son, Steven. They call North Carolina home.

Sharon is always honored to hear from her readers. You can contact her directly at Sharon@sharonjaynes.com or at her mailing address:

Sharon Jaynes
PO Box 725
Matthews, NC 28106

To learn more about Sharon's books and speaking ministry or to inquire about having her speak at your next event, visit www.sharonjaynes.com.

Other Books
by Sharon Jaynes

YOUR SCARS ARE BEAUTIFUL TO GOD
Sharon shares with women how emotional scars can lead to healing and restoration. Encouraging chapters and inspirational stories reveal how you can give your past pains over to the One who turns hurts into hope and heartache into happiness.

BUILDING AN EFFECTIVE WOMEN'S MINISTRY
This unique yet practical how-to manual offers a wide-range of help to women, from those just starting out to those who have a thriving ministry but could use a fresh idea or two. For groups large and small, this is a treasure trove of detailed information on how to serve and care for women.

BECOMING THE WOMAN OF HIS DREAMS
Sharon provides a thoughtful look at the wonderful, unique, and God-ordained role a woman has in her husband's life. If you would like a little "wow!" back in your relationship with the man you married, let seven simple secrets, biblical wisdom, and tender stories of both men and women inspire you to truly be the wife your husband longs for.

BECOMING A WOMAN WHO LISTENS TO GOD
"When I pore over the pages of Scripture," says Sharon, "I discover that some of God's most memorable messages were not delivered while men and women were away on a spiritual retreat, but right in the middle of the hustle and bustle of everyday life. He spoke to Moses while he was tending sheep, to Gideon while he was threshing wheat, to the woman at the well while she was drawing water for her housework. It is not a matter of does He speak, but will we listen." Discover with Sharon what it means to become a woman who listens to God.

**"I'M NOT GOOD ENOUGH"...
AND OTHER LIES WOMEN TELL THEMSELVES**
Sharon looks at the common lies women tell themselves and shows them how they can replace those lies with truth. This book is a handy reference tool that will help you renew your mind and think God's thoughts rather than be swayed by the enemy's deceptions.

HARVEST HOUSE
PUBLISHERS

To learn more about books by Sharon Jaynes or
to read sample chapters, log on to our website:

www.harvesthousepublishers.com

HARVEST HOUSE PUBLISHERS
EUGENE, OREGON